Bibliotheca Indo-Buddhica Series No. - 42

# THE HISTORY OF BUDDHISM IN INDIA AND TIBET

## The Jewelry of Scripture

By
BU STON

Translated from Tibetan by
E. OBERMILLER

With an Introduction by
Prof. TH. STCHERBATSKY

**Sri Satguru Publications**
*A Division of*
**Indian Books Centre**
Delhi - India

*Published by :*
Sri Satguru Publications
*A Division of*
Indian Books Centre
Indological and Oriental Publishers
24/4 Shakti Nagar,
Delhi-110007
(INDIA)

ISBN 81-7030-026-6

First Edition : 1931
Second Edition : Delhi, 1987, 1998, 2026

# Contents and Systems.

# Book II.

# Introduction.

To European readers Tibetan historiography is known from Tārānātha's History of Buddhism in India, translated simultaneously by two members of the St. Petersburg Academy of Science, W. P. Wassilieff into Russian and A. Schiefner into German.[1]) But this is not the only work of this kind which the Tibetan litterature contains. There are many others. Among them „The History of Buddhism in India and Tibet"[2]) by the great scholar *Bu-ston Rin-chen-grub-pa* (pronouce Budon Rinchenḍub), also called Budon Rinpoche, is held in great esteem by Tibetan and Mongolian learned lamas. It is distinguished from the work of Tārānātha by the plan of its composition. It consists of three parts. The history proper is preceded by a systematical review of the whole of Buddhist litterature so far as preserved in Tibet, and it is followed by a systematical catalogue of works, authors and translators of all the litterature contained in the Kanjur and Tanjur collections. The first part is of an overwhelming scientifical value. It represents a synthesis of everything which directly or remotely bears the stamp of Buddhism, that synthesis which is also the ultimate aim of the European investigation of that religion. The whole of its litterature, sacred and profane, is here reviewed as divided in periods, schools and subject-matter. No one was better qualified for such a task than Budon, for he was one of the redactors of the Kanjur and Tanjur great collections in their final form. As a matter of fact his "History" is but an introduction and a systematical table of contents to the Narthaṅ editions of the Kanjur and Tanjur.

His work has not failed to attract the attention of European scholarship. Wassilieff quotes it in the first volume of his Buddhism, Sarat Candra Das has translated some excerpts out of it. I myself have published a translation in French, in the Muséon 1905 ("Notes de littérature bouddhique. La littérature Yogācāra d'après Bouston"), of the part devoted to the litterature of the Yogācāra school, and, in English, of the part dealing with the Abhidharma litterature of the Sarvāstivādins, included in Prof. Takakusu's work on the Abhidharma litterature of the Sarvāstivādins. In the years 1927 and 1928 I have interpreted the work to my pupil E. E. Obermiller making it the subject of our seminary study. He then has made an English translation which was revised by me and is now published, thanks to the kind attention accorded to it by the Heidelberg Society for the Investigation of Buddhist Lore and by its president Professor M. Walleser.

The translation of the first part, now published, was not an easy task, since it consists predominantly of quotations, many of them having the form of mnemonic verse (kārikā's). They had to be identified and their commentaries consulted. With very few exceptions all has been found out by E. E. Obermiller in the Tanjur works. The high merit of this self-denying, absorbing and difficult work will, I have no doubt, be fully appreciated by fellow scholars who have a personal experience of that kind of work.

***Budon Rinpoche*** was a native of Central Tibet. He lived in the years 1290—1364. He consequently belongs to the old school of Tibetan learning, the school which preceded the now dominant Gelugpa sect (the yellow-caps) founded by ***Tsoṅkhapa***. Besides the History he has written many other works. A full block-print edition of all his works in 15 volumes has recently appeared in Lhasa. No copy of it has as yet reached Leningrad. Among his works there is one on logic, Tshad-ma-rnam-ṅes-pai-bsdus-don = Pramāṇa-viniççaya-piṇḍārtha, with his own commentary. A block-print containing his biography (rnam-thar) is in my possession. It will be analyzed by E. E. Obermiller in the Introduction also dealing with the sources of Tibetan historiography, which will be attached to the translation of the whole work. The Translation is made from the text of the old block-print edition, a copy of which is found in the Asiatic Museum of the Academy of Sciences of the U. S. S. R.

Th. Stcherbatsky,

Member of the Academy of Sciences of the U. S. S. R.

[Salutation to Buddha 1. 1—2 a. 4.]

Saluted be the blessed Buddha, the Lion of the Çākya clan.

1. (a) [Victorious be the Buddha], the Sun,[1]) who, nourished by the nectar of His Creative Effort[2]) and of His virtuous deeds,[3]) has appeared, shining with the beautiful lustre of unthinkable forbearance,

(b) and has attained the limits of His Three Bodies,[4]) a precious jewel of immeasurable value, swiftly moving by the force of His previous vows, and who, being (the Absolute), free from the attire of differentiation into subject and object,[5])

(c) is a leader in those vast skies,[6]) where the clouds[7]) of both the Obscurations[8]) are dispersed, whose nature it is to move from East to West in pursuit of the welfare of others in its various forms,[9])

(d) He, who by His immaculate word, — a light with millions of rays, producing heat, which he expands from region to region,

2. (a) Darkens the lustre of Brahma,[10]) Vishṇu,[11]) Manmatha, Çiva,[12]) Ganeça,[13]) Skanda[14]), Indra,[15]) Bṛhaspati[16]) and the other (gods), —

(b) a multitude of planets, that shine with great pride, claiming to be the guides[17]) in these three worlds,[18]) [2 a]

(c—d) and blinds[19]) that swarm of owls — the sages Kapila, Akṣapāda,[20]) Bādarāyaṇa,[21]) the Digambaras,[22]) Cārvākas, Vyāsa, Dantavaktra, Valmīki and the rest, stopping their course;

3. (a) at whose appearance, (like) bees, full of desire to behold (the flower), to enjoy its fragrant odour, and that exquisite honey, which gives delight to the senses, humming and infatuated with pride,

(b) the Çrāvakas, Pratyekabuddhas and Bodhisattvas, those worthy receptacles of heavenly bliss, assemble,[23])

(c) As that celestial flower — the Nirvāṇa[24],) — unfolds its leaves and expands its odour through the ten quarters of the sky.

(d) Victorious be He, this Buddha, the gem of Heaven, who has attained the double aim (of all human activity) and created the nectar of Omniscience!

[Salutation to the Compilers of Scripture and to the great Teachers of Buddhism 2 a. 4—b. 2.]

4. (a) [I bow before the Compilers of the Doctrine][25] who, for the sake of vanquishing the evil teachings of an Eternal Soul and of Nihilism,[26] — though (themselves) they were free from all confusion, —
(b) to reject the contempt of the Gods of Light[27], — though the eight egoistic qualities of praise,[28] censure and the rest had been abandoned (by them) before, —
(c) and, out of compassion for living beings, to secure a long existence for the Teaching (of Buddha), — though they had renounced all wordly attachments, —
(d) have collected the Doctrine from the mass of (Buddha's) Speeches and written it down.[29]

5. (a) I salute the Assembly of the Saints,[30] the Teachers free from error, whose greatness the highest of Buddhas had foretold, the Propagators of the Doctrine, who, thoroughly apprehending the stainless work (of Buddha) [2 b.],
(b) in full possession of all the great Lord's Highest Truth, have duly expounded the systems of the Three Vehicles,[31]
(c) and made the Teacher's Word perfectly clear; them, who, endowed with great wisdom and a powerful mind,
(d) have mercifully composed elucidating works.[32]

[Salutation to the Translators of Scripture, the Sages of Tibet and the Author's own Teachers. 2 b. 2—4]

6. (a) The perfect Translators of the mighty streams of Words, that descend from the snowy mountain of Buddha's Omniscience,
(b) and those of the holy Compilers of the Doctrine,[33]
(c) and of that Lake, adorned by the lotuses of explanatory works[34]
(d) — the noble Lotsavas and Paṇḍitas, I honour with a reverential bow.

7. (a) [The Elephants], who, covered by the golden net of the Three Disciplines,[35]
(b) the four methods of Propaganda[36] being their powerful well-grown tusks,
(c) have vanquished in contest their adversaries by speech, controversy and works, —
(d) the great Sages of Tibet,[37] I worship.

8. (a) [Those swords], which, obtained from the precious element of the Doctrine,
(b) hardened in the fire[38] of Perfect Analysis,

(c) and endowed with the vigour of fine words,[39])
(d) rent asunder the net of my mind's doubts, —

9. (a) The Assembly of Lamas,
(b) the twelve, who are weighty by the burden of their virtue,
(c) and, foremostly, the six Teachers full of benevolence,
(d) I look to for protection with a devoted mind.

[Introduction. 2 b. 5—3 a.$_3$.]

10. (a) Cherished by teachers, affectionate as a mother,
(b) in that Garden of Lotuses, — the Man-Lion's perfect Word,
(c) like a bee, full of delight, clinging to its flowers,
(d) the mind grows wide in the boundless Doctrine.

11. (a) Therefore, the ocean of Çākya's Word,
(b) the immeasurable, infinite, I wish to cross,
(c) and, though unable of penetrating into its depth,
(d) why should I not secure the precious jewel of its marvellous meaning?

12. (a) But though I have obtained it, it will be, like a jewel in a beggar's hands,
(b) my composition, pure and stainless (by itself),
(c) but defiled by the spirit of rivalry, hatred, and envy (of others).
(d) Who, therefore, will accept it, as an object of appreciation[40]) and belief? [3 a.]

13. (a) Nevertheless, though disregarded (by enemies), why should not this nectar of the Highest Doctrine,[41])
(b) remove my own mental agony,
(c) and if, moreover, it would be accepted by some (friendly critics),
(d) would it not appease the fever of their painful doubts?

14. (a) Therefore, to relieve the poverty of my own mind,
(b) and, amongst those that strive for religion,
(c) to magnify the triumph of the greatest of doctrines, —
(d) I open the doors to the Jewelry of Scripture.

15. (a) From it, of the various Vehicles, the great and the small,
(b) the diverse jewels of their meaning shall come forth,
(c) which I present to you without restraint.
(d) May you, full of delight, partake of them as you desire!

# Book I.

## [A Review of Buddhist Teachings.]

3 a. 3.

Our Teacher, the Foremost of the Çākyas, endowed with the four miraculous powers,[42] as with a four-membered army, has vanquished in battle the Evil One,[43] whereupon, having united the converts (to His Faith) within the sphere of His Church[44] by the four methods of propaganda,[45] He has revealed (His) Doctrine in all its (three) forms.[46]

The most holy regents of Buddha's religious realm[47] have duly preserved this teaching of virtue, which, being the foundation of happiness and welfare for all living beings, including the gods, must be zealously maintained. No other means exists for this, but only preaching the Doctrine and acting according to it, and, as action requires previous study (of the Doctrine) and preaching (of it to others), one must be aware of the methods for practising both.

There are four (such methods): —

I. Recognition of the merit, gained by studying and preaching the Highest Doctrine,

II. Knowledge of the true character of this teaching, which is to be studied and preached,

III. Consideration and fulfillment of the rules prescribed for study and teaching, [3 b. and]

IV. (Knowledge) of the way in which the Doctrine took its origin (— the History of Buddhism).

### I. The Merit of Studying and Preaching the Doctrine.

(It is necessary to distinguish) two (principal topics): —

A. The merit of study and of preaching with regard to the Highest Doctrine in general.

B. The special merit of studying and teaching the Doctrine of Mahāyāna.

*The merit of Studying and Teaching the Doctrine in general.*

A. Three kinds of merit (are to be regarded here): —
- a) of Study,
- b) of Teaching,
- c) of both together.

*The merit of Study.*

Aa. The ***Bodhisattvapiṭaka*** says:[48]) —

(1) He, that studies, comes to know the Doctrine,
(2) He, that studies, will abstain from sinful deeds,
(3) He, that studies, will reject all that is vain,
(4) He, that studies, attains Nirvāṇa.

According to the *Vyākhyāyukti*,[49]) the four lines of this verse respectively mean: —

(1.) Knowledge of the doctrines to be accepted or rejected through an investigation of orthodox and heretical philosophical systems.

(2.) Subjection to Moral Discipline[50]) and rejection of immoral conduct.

(3.) Subjection to Mental Discipline[51]) and abandonment of vain desires.

(4.) Subjection to training in Highest Wisdom,[52]) and through it — destruction of passions with Nirvāṇa as the result.

Otherwise: —

(1.) Acquirement of the right philosophical point of view,
(2.) Liberation from defilement,[53]) such as the influence of former deeds,[54])
(3.) passions,[55]) and
(4.) the remaining elements of phenomenal existence.[56])

And in third way: —

(1.) Devotion to the Doctrine and religious discipline,
(2.) Monastic life,
(3.) Suppression of the senses;[57]) this leads to liberation from passions, that arise from vain desires, and thus to rejection of all that is harmful.
(4.) Knowledge of the (Four) Truths (of the Saint) conducive to Nirvāṇa.

It is said in the *Vyākhyāyukti*:[58]) — Five kinds of merit, (obtained) through studying the Doctrine, have been mentioned by the Lord: —

(1.) Study of matters unknown before,
(2.) Reconsideration of the parts studied,[59])
(3.) Solution of doubt,
(4.) Establishment of a correct view, [4 a.] and
(5.) Knowledge of the words and the deepest sense of the Climax of Wisdom.[60])

The meaning of this is, taken respectively: —

(1.) Extensive study,[61])
(2.) Elucidation and perfect clearness (of the object studied),
(3.) Acquirement of certainty,
(4.) Consideration (of objects) from the correct point of view,
(5.) Knowledge of the (Four) truths (of the Saint).[62])

It is said (with regard to this passage), that the first two points convey complete clearness of the wisdom obtained by study,[63]) the next two — of that arising from investigation,[64]) and the last — of that, which is the result of deepest meditation.[65])

It is said further on:[66]) —

In studying the Highest Doctrine, there is merit[67]) of five kinds: —

(1.) Things, unknown before, are apprehended,
(2.) False points of view abandoned,
(3.) Matters doubtful — made certain,
(4.) The ascertained truth is internally realized, and
(5.) The Saint's pure vision of the Absolute truth attained.[68])

Again:[69]) —

Water renders service of five kinds: — it moistens rice-grains etc., cleanses body, clothes, and vessels, withdraws the suffering of the body in the hot season, appeases thirst and heat, and, giving rise to grass, corn, and woods, causes them to thrive.

In like way, faith in the word of Buddha having arisen, hardened hearts are made soft, the stains of immorality purged, the burning heat of passions appeased, thirst for repeated births in the Saṁsāra quenched, and roots, seeds, and woods of virtue, harmonizing with Enlightenment[70]) are produced and caused to thrive. These five kinds of service may otherwise mean — acquirement of faith and achievement of the three Disciplines with action corresponding to them. [4 a.]

Therefore, if there be a desire to obtain such help, the word of Buddha must be studied with devotion.

Fire does four kinds of work:[71]) — it consumes, cooks, singes, and illuminates. Similar is the fire of Buddha's Word, destroying all that is sinful in the converted,[72]) bringing to maturity the roots of virtue in those on the path to conversion, causing pain to those, that take delight in the Saṁsāra by creating disgust (to it) and giving light, — by showing the right way and the wrong to the sorrowful, the doubting, and to those, that have gone astray. For this reason, the Doctrine is to be zealously studied.

A pleasant sandy-beach[73]) is frequented for five (different motives, namely, to wash, to obtain refreshment, to appease thirst, to enjoy mirthful sport (in the water)[74]), and to cross from this shore to the opposite. Accordingly, the pleasant soil of Buddha's Word, (that resembles such a sandy-beach) is repaired to for the sake of removing the stains of immorality, appeasing the heat of passions and the thirst for repeated births,[75]) enjoying the pleasure of possessing the special virtues of mystic absorption,[76]) the (six) supernatural faculties,[77]) the (four) limitless feelings,[78]) the (eight) degrees of liberation (from materiality)[79]) etc., and, finally, for passing from this shore of real individuality[80]) to the opposite of (impersonal) Nirvāṇa. Consequently, those desirous of betaking themselves to the pleasant sandy-beach, must devotedly study the Word of Buddha. —

*The Merit of Preaching.*

I Ab. (This merit is of four kinds):

$a_1$. (The propagation of the Doctrine) is the highest means of worshipping Buddha the Teacher.

$b_1$. (It) is superior to material gifts and more serviceable,

$c_1$. Secures a good memory[81]) and intellectual power,

$d_1$. Augments virtue and leads to Enlightenment.

*Worship of Buddha by Preaching the Doctrine.*

I $Aba_1$. (The Teacher says): —

Wherever, for helping (living beings),
My Doctrine be duly preached, I shall be worshipped (through this),

But as to the offerings of flowers, ointments, and lamps, —
Such are no real means for honouring a Buddha. —

*Superiority to material gifts.*

I $Abb_1$. The *Maitreya-siṁhanāda-sūtra*[82]) says: —
If one completely fills (all) the worlds of the Buddhas[83])
Which are (numberless) as the sands of the Ganges
With the seven kinds of treasures,
Thus joyfully sacrificing to the Lord;
And if another one delivers a verse (of Scripture)
To a single living being,
The great offering of precious jewels
Is unable to match, even by its number, even partly,
This gift of a verse that is granted out of mercy.
The merit of two or three (such verses) is, therefore, beyond evaluation. —
And[84])
If one, who sacrifices gold and jewels,
Immeasurable as the sands of the Ganges,
Be compared to another who in bad times,
Pronounces a single verse (of Scripture),
The help that the latter affords, shall not be found with the former. —

*Good Memory as a result of expounding Scripture.*

I $Abc_1$. It is said in the *Siṁha-paripṛcchā*:[85]) —
He that grants the gift of Scripture, comes to remember his previous births. —

And in the *Sāgara-nāgarāja-paripṛcchā*:[86]) —

By the gift of Scripture the supernatural faculty of destroying passions is intensified. —

And the *Ratnāvalī*:[87]) —
Recollecting the ultimate aim of the Doctrine,
And, likewise, the meaning of the sacred texts, [5 b.]
And granting the pure gift of Scripture (to others), —
— All this secures remembrance of previous states of existence.

*Augmentation of virtue through preaching the Doctrine.*

I $Abd_1$. It is to be read in the *Adhyāçaya-saṁcodana-sūtra*:[88])
(Buddha said): — O, Maitreya, the merit of that immaterial gift of him, who, free from the desire of gain and renown,

bestows the Teaching (upon others), is twentyfold, as follows:
He is possessed of a good memory (1)
and intellect (2),[89]
of discrimination (3),[90]
faith (4),
and philosophical insight (5);
he penetrates (the sphere of) the Highest Wisdom of a Saint (6),[91]
becomes devoid of passions (7),
of enmity (8),
and of ignorance (9), and
offers no opportunity[92] to the Evil One (for harming him) (10).
He is, furtheron, respected by the Buddhas (11),
protected by spirits (12),[93] and
endowed with corporeal beauty and strength,[94]
bestowed upon him by the gods (13).
He presents no vulnerable points to his enemies (14),
and is never deserted by his friends (15).
Moreover, (he becomes one), whose words are trustworthy (16),
secures (the four kinds of) moral intrepidity (17),[95]
is full of mental satisfaction (18), and
praised by the Wise (19).
And, finally, his gift of Scripture will be remembered in times to come (20).
Such, o Maitreya, is this twentyfold merit!
And the *Çikṣā-samuccaya*[96] says: —
The immaterial gift of Scripture
Is the cause for virtue to be augmented.

*The merit of study and preaching taken together.*

I Ac. (Three kinds of merit are to be distinguished):

$a_1$. Increase of that element (of virtue, through which a human being from nature belongs to the family of one) of the three Vehicles;[97]

$b_1$. General esteem, through becoming learned.

$c_1$. Attainment of Enlightenment through observation (of the precepts) of the Doctrine.

*Increase of the element of virtue.*

I $Aca_1$. The *Vyākhyāyukti* says:[98] —

The seed of virtue, (that leads to) heavenly bliss,

And that of Highest Wisdom, through which Nirvāṇa is attained, [6 a]
Are caused to thrive by him, who studies (the Doctrine) full of faith.

And a Commentary adds: — The Wisdom, that is obtained by study, gives increase to the element of attention.
(Here the following objection may be met with): All that has just been said, concerns only the merit of study, but is not correct as regards preaching, for study and preaching are not the same thing. (Such an objection) ist not founded, for, says the *Abhidharma-samuccaya*:[99]) — Apprehension, recitation, and preaching, [100])are to be regarded as having (all of them) one origin, which is study.

*Honour through becoming learned.*

I Acb. The *Āgamavibhanga* says:[101]) —

He that has extensively studied, reaps merit of five kinds: —
1) Proficiency in (the theory of) the (5) groups of elements,[102])
2) „ „ „ „ „ the (18) component elements of an individual,[103])
3) „ „ „ „ „ the (12) bases of cognition,[104])
4) „ „ „ „ „ causality,[105])
5) One's instructions and precepts will not depend on others.

It is said in the *Jātakas*:[106]) —

1.[107]) Knowledge is a light, that disperses the gloom of ignorance
the greatest of treasures, which thieves etc. cannot rob,
a weapon, vanquishing the all-deluding enemy,[108])
and the best adviser, that guides one by instructions, morals, and means.
2. It is the great treasury of fame and glory,[109])
the special cause[110]) for receiving presents from persons of high rank,
for giving delight to the learned in (their) assemblies,
and for blinding one's adversaries, like the light of the sun.
3.[111]) (Moreover, it is the cause) of refined and brilliant flash of ideas, —
a sudden enclosure of great fame, — and
of good style.

Its full splendour knowledge attains in clear perception of reality[112]) through deep meditation.[113])

4)[114]) Having acquired learning, one stands firmly and free from contradiction,
on the path of the three aims[115]) (of man in life),
internally realizes them according to one's learning,
[6 b.] and is easily delivered from the dungeon of births.

*Attainment of Enlightenment through observation of the precepts of the Doctrine.*

I Acc. Preaching and Study (both of them) lead to observation of the religious precepts, as says the *Abhidharmakoça*:[116]) — Observation (of the precepts) consists exclusively in preaching and acting according to them.

All the merit of keeping the Doctrine is beyond the reach of human intellect.

The *Tathāgata-guhya-nirdeça*[117]) says: —

All the virtues (attained through) keeping the Highest Doctrine, have been ardently proclaimed by all the Buddhas during millions of aeons, but still (up to this time), their number is not exhausted.

The *Sāgaramati-paripṛcchā*[118]) says: —

1.[119]) He that keeps the Highest Doctrine of the Buddhas
is favoured by them, as well as
by gods, Nāgas and Kiṁnaras,
favoured on account of his virtue and wisdom.

2.[120]) He, that keeps the Highest Doctrine of the Buddhas
becomes endowed with a good memory, discernment and intellectual power,
with great wisdom and divine knowledge, —
a sage that rejects all that is sinful and
the inclination (towards passions).

3.[121]) He, that keeps the Highest Doctrine of the Buddhas
protects the world as Indra or Brahma,
becomes a universal sovereign, a chieftain of men,
and, full of mental delight, attains Enlightenment.

Such and many other kinds of merit have been mentioned.

I B. The merit of studying and preaching the Doctrine of Mahāyāna (is of three kinds): —

a. Superiority with regard to the merits of the Small

Vehicle and augmentation of the Mahāyānistic family — from the initial time of taking the vow of a Bodhisattva.[122])

b. Removal of all the obscurations and, through this, superiority to every other kind of virtue — when abiding on the (Mahāyānistic) Path.[123])

c. Certainty of attaining omniscience — at the time of final Illumination.[124]) [7 a.]

*Predominance over Hīnayānistic virtues.*

I Ba. It is to be read in the *Prajñāpāramitā*:[125]) —

(Buddha asked): O Ānanda, if the living beings in all the millions of worlds, were to become, all of them, Saints of the Small Vehicle (Arhats), what thinkest thou would be the virtues of such saints, that have their origin in charity, pure morals, and deep meditation?[126]) Would not the aggregate of these virtues be abundant? — O Lord, o Blissful, great and abundant would it be, — was the answer. The Lord said: — However, o Ānanda, if a Bodhisattva recites, to whomsoever it may be, even for a single day, the Doctrine, that contains the Climax of Wisdom, the aggregate of his virtues will be greater.

And further on:[127])— This gift of Scripture, o Ānanda, that is granted by the Bodhisattva, prevails over all the roots of virtue that exist in all living beings adhering to the Small Vehicle.[128]) —

*Superiority to every other kind of virtue, when abiding on the Path.*

I Bb. It is said in the *Uttaratantra*:[129]) —

1. One, that strives for Enlightenment,
daily[130]) presents to the Buddhas their immeasurable worlds, filled with gold and jewels;
Another, if he hears a single word (of Mahāyānistic Scripture) and through this comes to faith,
will attain merit, greater than that of an offering.

2. One, wise and desirous to attain Supreme Enlightenment, through many aeons,
preserves, without difficulty, body, speech and mind in stainless chastity; [7 b.]
Another, if he hears a single word (of Mahāyānistic Scripture) and through this comes to faith,
attains merit greater, than that of pure morality.

3. One, suppressing the fire of passion in the three spheres of existence,[131])
abides in mystic absorbtion, which transfers him to the abode of the gods and that of Brahma[132])
and is a sure means of attaining final Enlightenment;
Another, if he hears a single word (of Mahāyānistic Scripture) and through this comes to faith,
attains merit greater than that of deepest meditation.

4. As charity brings about (wordly) enjoyment,
pure morals — (the attainment of) heavenly bliss,
deep meditation — the rejection of passions,
and Highest Wisdom — removal of all the obscurations, —
the (latter) is the greatest of virtues — and its source is study.

### *Attainment of Omniscience.*

I Bc. It is said in the *Sūtrālaṁkāra*:[133]) —

1.[134]) He, that makes an effort to retain two verses (of Scripture whether merely their words or their meaning ), —
is the wisest of living beings, that comes to reap tenfold merit:

2.[135]) Full increase of the elements of virtue,[136]) (1)
highest delight at the hour of death, (2)
rebirth, according to one's desire, (3)
remembrance of all previous births, (4)

3.[137]) Encounter with Buddhas,[138]) (5)
study of the High Vehicle obtained from them, (6)
faith connected with knowledge, (7)
the two media for Enlightenment,[139]) (8—9)
and attainment of the latter at an early date. (10)

In other works a great deal more is mentioned (with regard to the merit of Study and Preaching), but, for fear of too much detail, we do not enlarge upon it.

These parts omitted are of a similar subject matter as the (following verse of the) *Vyākhyāyukti*[140]) —

If[141]) the essential part of the Doctrine, the meaning
of the Sūtras, comes to be studied,
He that makes (the pupils) devoted to study and observation (of the Teaching),
Must first of all mention its aim.

## II. General Review of the Scripture of Buddhism, the Doctrine to be studied and preached.

(The Sanscrit term for the Doctrine of Buddhism is *dharma*. As this word has many different meanings, it is necessary to know): —

A. The various objects that bear the appelation of *dharma*.
B. The etymology of the word.
C. Definition and [8 a.]
D. The various kinds of *dharma* (when the word appears in the sense of the Doctrine or of what is taught by it).

### *The different meanings of dharma.*

II A. The word *dharma* has ten different meanings, as says the *Vyākhyāyukti*:[142]) —

*Dharma* means:

1) an element of existence (in general),
2) the Path,
3) Nirvāṇa,[143a])
4) a non-sensuous element,[143b])
5) virtue,
6) life,
7) the Doctrine,
8) (the quality of) constant becoming,
9) religious vow, and
10) worldly law.

Accordingly[144]) 1) (in the sentence) — "the *dharmas*, of which some belong to the phenomenal world[145]) and some are eternal,"[146]) *dharma* means an element of existence (in general).[147])

2) (It has been said): — "The true philosophical insight[148]) is *dharma*"; — here the word signifies the Path.

3) In "I seek refuge in the *dharma*" — the meaning applied to the word is — Nirvāṇa.

4) In the term "the *dharma* — base of cognition *(dharma-āyatana)*" — *dharma* is used in the sense of (a non-sensuous element), corresponding to the receptive faculty of the intellect.[149])

5) It is said: "The noble ladies in the queen's attendance and the young princes behave, with regard to each other,

according to *dharma*;" — in such a context the word *dharma* is synonymous with „virtue."

6) "Worldlings are attached to the present, the worldly *dharma*;" — the meaning of *dharma* is here — life.

7) (Buddha said): "The *dharma* is, as follows — the Sūtras etc." In this place the term *dharma* is equivalent to "the Doctrine".

8) (It is said): "This body is endowed with the *dharma* of decrepitude;" — in this sentence *dharma* stands for (the quality of) constant becoming (change).[150])

9) In "the four *dharmas* of a monk"[151]) — *dharma* is used in the sense of "religious vow".

10) "The *dharma* of a country, the *dharma* of a tribe (or caste)." — The meaning of the word is here "worldly law (or custom)".

These are the principal (objects, designated by the appelation of *dharma*). There are, however (still others), not included in their number, for in the verse: —

An object is recognised by (its) *dharma*,
but not by that, which is not *dharma*,

the word has the sense of a quality, which, in logic, forms the object of inference, in the affirmative *(dharma)* or negative (not-*dharma*) sense.

*Etymology of »dharma«.*

B. The word *dharma* is a derivate of the verbal root *dhṛ*, which signifies "to hold" (to bear, maintain, support, withhold, etc.) Accordingly 1) The elements of existence (in general, are *dharmas*, being the bearers (holders) of the twofold essence, — the Particular,[152]) to begin with that of matter, which is impenetrability,[153]) and up to that of Omniscience — direct perception of all elements of existence (in a single moment), [8 b] and of the Universal, as — impermanence, (the Universal Essence) of all (active) elements of the phenomenal world, phenomenal reality — that of all elements influenced by defiling agencies, nonsubstantiality — of all (separate) elements in general, and Quiescence — of every kind of Nirvāṇa.

2) (Mental phenomena), corresponding to the intellectual faculty are *dharmas*, being the bearers of their Particular Essence on one side, and being perceived (held) by the intellect, — on the other.

3) Life is *dharma*, as it sustains bodily existence and the uniformity of species.
4) The Doctrine — "of the Sūtras etc." as says the *Vyākhyāyukti*,[154]) "(is *dharma*), as it is a bearer of true and incontrovertible meaning".
5) (The quality of) constant becoming is *dharma* by being a support of perpetual origination.
6) (A religious vow) — by being held by a person, that performs acts of religious observance.
7) Worldly law (or custom) — by maintaining the habits of a country or race

The Path, Nirvāṇa, and virtue are all of them *dharmas*, as they withhold from (moral) fall. (One must distinguish): 1) preservation from fall into evil births and 2) that from falling into the Saṁsāra.

1) The *Udānavarga*[155]) says: —

In this world and beyond it
those that have practised *dharma* sleep in peace.

Here the word means practice of the ten virtues,[156]) or of (the four stages of) mystic absorbtion *(dhyāna)* and of the (four kinds of) meditation which transfer into the immaterial sphere,[157]) — by him, that has obtained faith in the Law of Retribution and adheres to the correct point of view with regard to this world. Such practice is *dharma* as it withholds from fall into evil births. This (kind of *dharma*) is likewise to be found in some of the heterodox systems.

2) That which preserves from fall into transmigratory existence is Nirvāṇa "the highest ideal of those, that have taken refuge in the Teaching of Buddha and become dispassionate,"[158]) and the Path, by which it is attained, with its preliminary stages.[159]) [9 a.]

The Mahāyānistic Nirvāṇa, Path, and Doctrine (are *dharmas*, withholding from fall into the Small Vehicle. The high knowledge of Relativity,[160]) Love, and Great Commiseration[161]) etc. taken together, prevent from falling into the Saṁsāra and the (egoistic, Hīnayānistic) Nirvāṇa.[162])

The special Etymology of the (Sanscrit) term *saddharma* — the Highest Doctrine — applied to Buddhism.

The word *sat* = High, may be taken to mean "the Supreme Buddha"; the Doctrine *(dharma)*, being taught by Him, is *saddharma* — the Doctrine of the High One. (the compound *sad-dharma* is in this case of the *tatpuruṣa, ṣaṣṭhīsamāsa* type: *sato = saṁbuddhasya dharma iti saddharmaḥ*).

Otherwise — *sat* may have the sense of "that which is the highest"; the Doctrine, through being such, is *saddharma* — the Highest Doctrine. Here the compound is (a *karmadhāraya* — *sañç ca dharmaç ce' ti saddharmaḥ*), in which the two members are in apposition.[163])

In a third way (*sat* may signify a virtuous person) and, the Doctrine, as its precepts are to be observed by such a person, — as, for instance, the four great vows of a monk, — is *saddharma* — the Doctrine for a high, virtuous being *(sataḥ satpuruṣasya caritavyo dharma iti saddharmaḥ)*.

*Definition of dharma in the sense of the Doctrine.*

II C. (First of all) it is necessary to make the following ascertainment: — the Highest Doctrine is, — viewed from the point of its principal subject-matter, — virtue, the Path, and Nirvāṇa, and, — from the point of view of its expression in speech, — Scripture.

It is defined as "that, which being relied upon, is a means for human beings to remove (moral) defilement, as it is said: —

The Highest Doctrine is that, which puts an end to all phenomenal existence,
And to every kind of defilement.

Here it is necessary to distinguish, — the Doctrine as the practice,[164]) and the Doctrine as the theory, the word of Scripture.[165]) The *Abhidharmakoça* says:

The Teacher's Doctrine is of two kinds, —
Scripture and (its) subject-matter (— the positive part).

The Doctrine, viewed as (the positive part of) the subject-matter is defined as "deliverance from passions and that, by means of which such is attained".

The *Uttaratantra*[166]) says: —

The Doctrine has its essence in the two (last) truths (of the Saint),
that which represents liberation from passions,

and that which leads to it, —
the Truth of Extinction[167]) and that of the Path,
in both of which deliverance from passions is contained.
Accordingly "that which represents liberation from passions" corresponds to the Truth of Extinction (of phenomenal existence = Nirvāṇa), and that by means of which it is realized, is the Path. Of these two, the Truth of Extinction [9 b.] is to be defined, according to the *Abhidharmasamuccaya*,[168]) as "the Extinction of all active elements of life, being merged in the Absolute". It represents, therefore, the rejection of all defilement[169]) and even of the saintly individuality,[170]) the final Nirvāṇa after death,[171]) and the Cosmical Body of Buddha according to Mahāyānistic conception.
The definition of the Path is: — undefiled transcendental knowledge, which, in connection with preliminary stages, is a means of realizing Nirvāṇa. The *Abidharmakoça* speaks of it as "the undefiled Truth of the Path", and the *Uttaratantra*[172]) — as "the pure and brillant antidote (of passion). The Path is therefore, that of Illumination,[173]) Meditation,[174]) and of the Ultimate Result,[175]) or, as the *Uttaratantra* views the Mahāyānistic Path — the first two, — the Path of Illumination and that of Meditation. The Path of Accumulating Merit[176]) and that of Subsequent Training[177]) are to be regarded as preliminary stages.[178])
The Doctrine viewed as Scripture, is defined as "the Word that introduces into the (sphere of) the Doctrine, viewed as the practice. It is necessary to distinguish that kind of verbal expression which agrees with the habit[179]) of viewing a pluralistic universe[180]) and such, which is the natural outflow of (the conception of) a (monistic) Absolute.[181]) The first, as for instance talk about horses, oxen etc, is of (exclusively) worldly nature, whereas Scripture, in its twelve parts,[182]) is, as stated before (— the natural outflow of the Absolute), as it is the natural outflow of the (intention of) teaching the true transcendental Essence of the Universe,[183]) or the natural outflow of the knowledge of the (monistic) Absolute. The Madhyāntavibhanga[184]) says (of the Absolute): It is the highest aim of its natural outflow[185]), and the *Sphuṭārtha* says: It (the Word) is the natural outflow of the Absolute. The Paṇḍit *Sunayaçrī*[186]) says: The whole of the Doctrine is

based upon the knowledge of Relativity. The three kinds of Enlightenment,[187]) that resemble small, middle-sized, and large birds soaring in the skies, [10 a] are secured by means of the knowledge of the two kinds of non-substantiality, — that of the individual and that of all the (separate) elements of existence.[188]) (Consequently, the Word of Scripture), as it harmonises with the conception of Nirvāṇa, is of transcendental nature.

It is said in the *Nirvāṇa-sūtra*:[189]) The four great streams, that fall into the ocean, flow descending toward it. In a like way all the Doctrine, that has its goal in Nirvāṇa, has consequently its course directed toward it.

### *The various aspects of the Doctrine.*

II D. The Doctrine has already been viewed as the subject-matter, and the Word of Scripture. (We may otherwise)[190]) discriminate between a) the Doctrine viewed from the aspect of ultimate result, b) the Doctrine (as that which leads to) realization (of this result), and c) Scripture.

### *The Doctrine from the point of view of result.*

II Da. This is Nirvāṇa, which is defined as the Quiescence of all phenomenal existence, as well as of the cause that produces it. This Quiescence is of seven kinds,[191]) namely that of

1) birth,
2) decrepitude,
3) death,
4) meeting the disagreeable,
5) forsaking the agreeable,
6) unfulfillment of desires,
7) corporeal suffering.

Otherwise, it is the state opposed to the four kinds of impermanence, (which is characterized as follows): —

Accumulated (wealth) is to get finally exhausted,
the body will finally be subjected to decay,
the end of every union is separation, and
that of every life is death.

### *The Doctrine as the means of realizing Nirvāṇa.*

II Db. This is the Path, the complement of all the attributes conducive to the ultimate result (Nirvāṇa). These attributes are four in number, namely: 1) (the Path is) straight,[192]) as it conveys to the city of Nirvāṇa, but not to that of Saṁsāra.

2) It is uninterrupted, being closely connected with (its aim) — Nirvāṇa and free from hindrance and vicissitude.

3) It is free from danger, as it not exposed to the rapine by robbers, such as passions etc.

4) It is endowed with the perfection of enjoyment, by being connected with partaking of the food of the delightful Doctrine [10 b.].

*The Doctrine as the Word of Scripture.*

II Dc. The Doctrine, viewed as the Word of Scripture, is the perfect elucidation of the facts constituting the Path. Its functions, are four in number, —

namely 1) Declaration, as — "this is the Path".

2) Ascertainment — "only this is the Path, but not anything else".

3) Elucidation of the means of attainment — "the (four) methods of intense mindfulness[193]) etc. are the cause of the Path."

4) Demonstration of (the various kinds of) defilement, as — "the defilement of passion, that of former deeds, and that of (the remaining elements of phenomenal) existence,[194]) are the impediments on the Path." — So is it to be read in the *Pratītya-samutpāda-ādi-vibhanga-nirdeça-ṭīkā.*

This Doctrine of Scripture has two main divisions:

$a_1$) The Word (of Buddha) and

$b_1$) The theoretical treatises (Çāstra)

It is said: —

The whole of the Doctrine is contained in the Word
of Buddha and the learned treatises, —
the perfect Word and the works that explain its meaning;
By means of the (two), the Teaching of Çākya is to abide
for long in the lands of this world.

*The Word of Buddha.*

II Dca$_1$. With regard to the first (of these two divisions) — the Word of Buddha, we must know: —

$a_2$) — its definition,

$b_2$) — the etymology (of the word *subhāṣita*, which is its appelation in Sanscrit).

$c_2$) its varieties.

*Definition of the Word of Buddha.*

II $Dca_1a_2$. A certain (lama of) the Chim-pa tribe defines it as "the Introductions, the Sermons, and (the words of) approval (from the part of the adherents) — such is the Word of Buddha fully accomplished, as regards words and meaning."

(The correct definition is): — "the Word, which, being in close connection with the Doctrine, that forms its subject-matter, speaks of the work to be done, namely, — the rejection of all defilement in the three spheres of existence[195]) and of the result, which is the bliss of Quiescence (Nirvāṇa); it is produced by the agency of Buddha, who is its principal determining cause.[196])

The *Uttaratantra*[197]) says:

That, which, in close connection with the Doctrine — its subject-matter,

speaks of the rejection of all defilement in the three spheres of existence,

and shows the bliss of Quiescence, — [41 a]

is the Word of the great Anchorite; all that disagrees with it, is of other origin.

*Etymology of the word Subhāṣita.*

II $Dca_1b_2$. (One of the appelations for the Word of Buddha) in the Sanscrit language is "*Subhāṣita*". The particle "*su*", which is used in ten different senses, — (in this case) signifies "well", and "*bhāṣita*" has the meaning of "spoken". The Word of Buddha is, consequently, "that, which is well spoken". (Here the following question may arise): — Why is (the Word of Buddha) called "the well-spoken"? (To this we may answer): — It is the "well-spoken" from ten different points of view. It is said in the *Vyākhyāyukti*:[198]) — How comes (the Word of Buddha) to be called "the well-spoken"? — It is such from ten different points of view, namely: its

1) final accomplishment,[199])
2) regard (for all living beings)[200])
3) perserverance,
4) completeness,[201])

5) manifoldness,
6) foundation,
7) way of making itself intelligible,
8) (character of) teaching
9) time, and
10) exclusive qualities.

The meaning of this is as follows: —

(The Word of Buddha) is called the "well-spoken", as it has been spoken: —

1) after the attainment of Final Enlightenment (by Buddha),
2) with regard for all living beings,
3) not merely occasionally, at intervals, but repeatedly and uninterruptedly,
4) fully, without any omissions made,[202] as it is the case with teachers, that conceal their books.
5) in accordance with the intellectual faculty of the various human beings,
6) by means of the voice, endowed with the five perfections[203]
7) making itself intelligible, — though having been spoken in one way, — in all the innumerable lands of the world, and reaching all its adherents, whosoever they might be,[204]
8) indicating the Path, that leads to rejection of the two extremities[205] [11 b]
9) to converts, that have attained complete maturity, and
10) endowed with the sixty distinctive features of perfect speech.

Now, of what kind are these sixty distinctive features? (The answer will be as follows):[206]

(The Word of Buddha is) —

Soft, — as it supports the roots of virtue in the character of a human being, (1)[207]

Mild, — as the contact with it even in worldly life causes delight, (2)[208]

Pleasing, — by its good meaning, (3)[209]

Agreeable, — by its exquisite sound, (4)[210]

Pure, — because it has been obtained after the highest transcendental contemplation, (5)[211]

Immaculate, — as it is free from the influence of the impression left by passions, (6)[212]

Brilliant, — through the perfect clearness of its words and sounds, (7)[213]

Charming, — because it possesses the force and merit of vanquishing all the teachings of heretics and of the evil-minded, (8)[214])

Worthy of being studied, — because, — through realization of it, — Nirvāṇa is attained, (9)[215])

Without defect, — for it cannot be damaged by its antagonists, (10)[216])

Sweet, — as it gives pleasure to all, (11)[217])

Cultured, — since it is averse to passion, (12) [218])

Not harsh,—being an easy means of teaching discipline,(13)[219])

Not unkind, — because in the case of transgression, it shows a means of salvation (through confession), (14)[220])

Highly cultured, — as it teaches the Discipline of the Three Vehicles, (15)[221])

Agreeable to hear, — because it keeps off distraction, (16)[222])

Producing bodily ease, — being conducive to trance, (17)[223])

Causing mental satisfaction, — since its result is the supreme delight of transcendental knowledge, (18)[224])

Gladdening the heart, — as it clears all doubt, (19)[225])

Bringing about satisfaction and happiness [12a], — by removing all that is wrong or uncertain, (20)[226])

Never causing pain, — since there can be no regret if (its precepts are) realized; (21)[227])

It must be known thoroughly, — for it is the foundation of the complement of knowledge, that is attained by study; (22)[228])

It must be known in detail, — being (likewise), the foundation of the complement of knowledge, which is the result of investigation; (23)[229])

It is perfectly clear, — because it shows the Doctrine as it is, and not subjected to mutilation by some teacher, (24)[230])

It is to be welcomed, — as it is favourable to those, that have attained their personal aim, (the Arhats) (25)[231]) and met with rejoicing, — because it is craved for by those that have not yet attained their aim, (26)[232])

It gives thorough knowledge, — as it teaches, from a correct point of view, matters that belong to the Transcendental Sphere, (27)[233])

And gives knowledge in detail, — for the same reason, (28)[234])

It is correct, — because it is not contrary to logic, (29)[235])

Duly connected (with its subject-matter), — because it teaches its adherents in the right way, (30)[236])

Free from the defect of tautology, — as it never speaks without a special aim, (31)[237])

Powerful, like the lion's roar, — as it terrifies all the heretics, (32)[238])

Sounding like the cry of an elephant, — by its high, dignified tone; (33)[239])

(It is like) the roll of thunder, — by its deepness, (34)[240])

The voice of the Nāga-king, — because it is worthy of being heard, (35)[241])

The concert of Gandharvas, — by its sweetness, (36)[242])

The song of the Kalavinka, — as it is clear and melodious, (37)[243])

The sound of Brahma's voice, — as it reaches far (38)[244]) and

The tune of the Chakora-bird, — as it is a lucky omen, that preceeds every kind of success. (39)[245])

In all these cases (in the original text) the words *svara*,[246]) *ruta*,[247]) and *ravita*[248]) are used (in the sense of "voice", "sound" etc.). *Svara* has the meaning of — "indicating such and such word", [12. b.] *ruta* — "showing, that the word is full of meaning", and *ravita* — "communicating the conventional meaning of such and such sounds".

Moreover, (the Word of Buddha is): —

Delightful, like the voice of Indra, — since it cannot be surpassed by anything else, (40)[249])

Sounding like a drum, — as it preceeds victory over all the demons and antagonists, (41)[250])

Free from arrogance, — as it is not spoiled by flattery (42)[251])

Free from humiliation, — as it is not defiled by censure (43)[252])

Fit for all (the various forms of) verbal expression, — because it accomodates itself to the forms and character of every kind of grammar, (44)[253])

Free from corrupt ungrammatical language, — since such never appears through want of memory, (45)[254])

Not incomplete, — because it assists at all times the converts in their acts, (46)[255])

Independent, — as it is not influenced by profit and honours, (47)[256])

Not timid, — being free from fear ,(48)[257])
Joyful, — as it is completely devoid of sorrow, (49)[258])
Comprehensive, — because it shows proficiency in every branch of science, (50)[259])
Perfect, — since it brings about fulfillment of all the aims of living beings, (51)[260])
Fluent, — because it is not interrupted, (52)[261])
Handsome, — as it appears in a variety of forms, (53)[262])
Accomplishing the aim of all (the diverse) sounds, — because through the pronunciation of one word, many words in different languages are communicated. (54) [263])
Giving satisfaction to all the faculties, — by connoting many ideas in one, (55)[264])
Irreproachable, — since it accomplishes what it has promised, (56)[265])
Reliable, — as it refers to future results, (57)[266])
Not rash, — as it does not speak inconsiderately, (58)[267])
Reaching all its adherents, — because it is equally heard from far and near, (59)[268])
Possessed of the best of forms, — as it uses all the worldly objects as parables. (60)[269])

Such are the words of the Saint Asanga, — says the *Pañcaviṁçatisāhasrikā-ālokā.*[270]) In other translations the word *akhila* ("perfect") is rendered by "accomplished" *(chub-pa)* and *lalita* ("handsome") by "beautiful" *(ḥbel-ba).*

The passage concerning the sixty distinctive features appears exactly in the same form in the five volumes of the *Yogacaryābhūmi,*[271]) the *Çatasāhasrikā-bṛhat-ṭikā,*[272]) the Commentary on the *Sūtrālaṁkāra* and in the *Vyākhyāyukti.* Now, the *Tathāgata-acintya-guhya-nirdeça* mentions sixty-four distinctive features, namely after "reaching all its adherents (59)", the following are added: —

Calming passion, (60)
Pacifying anger, (61)
Withdrawing ignorance, (62) and
Putting an end to the plots of Māra (63).

Maitreya,[273]) however says: "the Word, endowed with sixty distinctive features and of transcendental nature." Moreover, Āryāsanga, Vimuktasena, Vasubandhu and other authorities (profoundly versed) in Scripture say that that very Sūtra (the *Tathāgata-guhya*) mentions sixty distinctive features.[274]) It is therefore necessary to consider, whether (the passage just mentioned) is an interpolation or not.

*Varieties of the Word of Buddha.*

II $Dca_1c_2$. The Word of Buddha, with regard to its various parts, may be viewed from six aspects, namely: —

$a_3$ time,
$b_3$ subject-matter,
$c_3$ style,
$d_3$ that, against which it is directed,
$e_3$ (the various kinds of) converts, and
$f_3$ chief determining cause.

*Varieties of the Word with regard to time. The three "Wheels of the Doctrine".*

II $Dca_1c_2a_3$. (We must distinguish): —

1) The Teaching[275]) of the four Truths of the Saint[276]) preached at the earliest period.
2) The Teaching of Non-substantiality,[277]) preached in the intermediate period.
3) The Teaching, founding the conception of Absolute Reality,[278]) — preached last of all. These three (subdivisions) are mentioned in the *Saṁdhinirmocana-sūtra.*[279])

*Varieties of the Word with regard to the Subject-matter. The discourses of conventional and direct meaning.*

II $Dca_1c_2b_3$. It is said: —

The Buddhas have preached the Doctrine, [13 b.]
basing upon the twofold Reality.

Accordingly, the discourses, referring to the Empirical Reality[280]) and not founded upon arguments, are of conventional meaning, and those, that treat of the Absolute Truth[281]) and are vindicated by arguments — of the direct meaning.

The *Akṣayamati-nirdeça*[282]) says: — the (discourses) which demonstrate Empirical Reality are of conventional, and those, that refer to the Absolute, — of the direct meaning.

As to the opinion, that all the Sūtras are, with regard to Buddha, of conventional meaning, and, with regard to the converts, — of the direct, — it is to be held as completely erroneous.

*Varieties with regard to form. The twelve classes (Anga) of sacred texts.*

II $Dca_1c_2c_3$. (The texts of) Scripture (with regard to form) belong to twelve classes.[283] The commentary on the *Aṣṭasāhasrikā-prajñāpāramitā*-called *Sārottamā*[284] says: —

The *Sūtras,*[285] *Geya,*[286] *Vyākaraṇa,*[287]
*Gāthā,*[288] *Udāna,*[289] *Nidāna,*[290]
*Avadāna,*[291] *Itivṛttaka,*[292]
*Jātaka,*[293] *Vaipulya,*[294]
*Adbhutadharma*[295] and *Upadeça*[296]
these are the twelve classes of Sacred Texts.

The Class of Sūtras (proper) contains (such sayings), in which the subject-matter is expressed briefly, in the form of aphorisms.[297] Now, (may it be asked), why have not the topics been entered upon in detail? The *Abhidharma-samuccaya*[298] (gives the following answer): — The Lord has preached the Doctrine in the form of aphorisms, considering ten kinds of advantage (of teaching in such a manner), namely,

It is easy to establish (such and such a thesis). (1)
to preach, (2) and
to retain in memory; (3)
He, that is devoted to the Doctrine, will, at an early date, achieve the accumulation of merit, (4) and
apprehend the true transcendental essence of the Universe (5)[299]
obtain faith in Buddha (6),
in the Doctrine and the Church, after having come to know (their essential character), (7) experience the highest bliss[300] during this worldly life, (8) give mental satisfaction to the wise, by bringing about decision (of religious questions) through controversy,[301] (9) and come to be reckoned among the wise, (since everybody will point to him saying), "this is a wise man"! (10)

The Geya (sing-song) Class is called so, because (the texts that belong to it), in the middle or at the end of the Sūtras, render the contents of such in verse, [14 a] or because they communicate, (in sing-song, the chief points of) the Sūtras of conventional meaning.[302]

The Vyākaraṇa Class (prophecies or revelations) bears this appelation, because it contains the prophecies concerning the death or birth of (diverse) Çrāvakas, as for instance, (the prophecy in) the *Saddharma-puṇḍarika,*[303]) or otherwhere, because it explains the Sūtras of direct meaning and reveals their sense.

The Gāthā Class (verses) consists of (the sayings) in verse. These verses may be of two quarters[304]) as: —

O Brethren, this is the Teacher,
he has attained Quiescence and is free from passion,

Of three quarters: —

Here, (viewed from the aspect of Absolute Reality) there is neither an Ego, nor a living being,
and life is likewise unreal, (for)
all these things are relative.[305])

Of four quarters, as: —

All elements of existence have a cause,
(this cause has been explained by Buddha
and the Great Ascetic has likewise taught
About their annihilation).[306])
And of five and of six quarters: —
All this is an illusion,
as that which is perceived in a dream.
If one awakens from the sleep of ignorance,
all the phenomenal world will appear unreal.
Therefore, if, with regard to whatsoever it may be,
the thought (of its being a separate Reality) does not appear,
one becomes a Buddha.[307])

The Udāna Class (solemn utterance) is, as says the *Vyākhyāyukti*[308]) "that, which is spoken, not with regard to (separate) individuals, but only in the interest of maintaining the Doctrine". Such are the utterances of joy and praise. For instance, if a Buddha brings about (moral) purification of the world and the living beings, all the Buddhas (grant their approval) saying: — Conversion is praiseworthy, Quiescence is praiseworthy!

The Nidāna Class contains that which is spoken for the sake of special individuals; it is the teaching of religious discipline, connected with a tale (of instructive character). Such are, for instance, the precepts given to Dhanika,[309]) forbidding him to steal. [14 b.]

The Avadāna Class is that, which is related in the

form of parables, in order to elucidate the meaning of the Sūtras.

The Itivṛttaka Class contains legends of former times, as the stories about Gautama.

The Jātaka Class is that, which tells of the deeds of (Buddha during his existence as a) Bodhisattva in his previous births as, for instance, the story of Viçvaṁtara.[310]

The Vaipulya Class ("that of great extension") contains Mahāyānistic Scripture.[311] It is called so, because it is the foundation of welfare and bliss for all living beings and because it demonstrates the Doctrine in an extensive, grand and profound form. It is called "completely crushing",[312] as it suppresses all defilement, "the matchless"[313] as it cannot be compared to anything else, and "the great Vehicle", for being endowed with the seven kinds of greatness.[314]

The Adbhuta-dharma Class has for its subject-matter the miraculous faculties of the Çrāvakas, Bodhisattvas and Buddhas.

The Upadeça Class is that which demonstrates the essence of all elements of existence in its true form. The meaning of the Sūtras etc. is thus rendered clear by it.[315]

***Varieties of the Word with regard to that against which it is directed. The three Codes. (Piṭaka.)***

II $Dca_1c_2d_3$. (From this point of view) — the Word of Buddha is to be regarded as consisting of the three Codes[316] (of sacred texts). It is necessary to know: —

$a_4$) The classification of the twelve varieties (just mentioned) as contained in the three Codes.

$b_4$) The etymology of the word *piṭaka* (which is the common appelation of the Codes in Sanscrit).

$c_4$) The motives for founding three Codes (of Scripture).

$d_4$) The etymology of each of their appelations (*Sūtra, Abhidharma* and *Vinaya*).

***The twelve Classes of texts contained in the three Codes.***

II $Dca_1c_2d_3a_4$. The first five classes, namely, the *Sūtra* (proper), *Geya, Vyākaraṇa, Gāthā,* and *Udāna* are contained in the Çrāvaka Code (of Sūtras)[317] The *Nidāna* Class, teaching discipline in connection with some (instructive) tale, forms the principal part of the Vinaya Code[318] and the three following

Classes, — *Avadāna, Itivṛttaka*, and *Jātaka* are of a similar character;[319] all the four therefore belong to the Vinaya. [15 a.]

The *Vaipulya* and *Adbhuta-dharma* Classes form the Mahāyānistic Code of Sūtras. The exclusive faculties of the Buddhas and Bodhisattvas are of transcendental nature and full of grandeur; the Adbhuta-dharma Class, which treats of these (miraculous powers), is therefore to be regarded as a part of the Mahāyānistic Sūtra-Code.

The *Upadeça* Class (as a whole) forms the Abhidharma Code,[320] both Hīnayānistic and Mahāyānistic.

This classification is given by the *Abhidharma-samuccaya*;[321] in other works it is different.

*Etymology of the word piṭaka.*

II $Dca_1c_2d_3b_4$. In the Sanscrit language (a Code of sacred texts) is called *piṭaka*. This word may, in one way, be regarded as a synonym of *piṇḍa*, which has the sense of "heap" or "collection". (A Code of sacred texts) is a *piṭaka*, because it is a collection of many topics or of all the objects of study which are its subject-matter.[322]

Otherwise, the word *piṭaka* may be taken as the appelation, given in Central India to a large *droṇa* measure, which contains a great number of small *droṇas*. Accordingly, (a Code of Scripture) is a *piṭaka*, because many topics and disciplines are contained in it.

*The motives for founding three (separate) Codes.*

II $Dca_1c_2d_3c_4$. The three Codes have been founded for nine causes,[323] namely: —

$a_5$ — with regard to (the three points) that are to be rejected (with their help),

$b_5$ — with regard to the (three) Disciplines,

$c_5$ — with regard to (the three kinds of) objects to be known.

*The three Codes with regard to the points to be rejected.*

II $Dca_1c_2d_3c_4a_5$, The Code of Sūtras has been founded as an antidote against the defiling element of doubt,[324] because the Sūtras (proper) etc. (which are contained in it) have been preached for the sake of putting an end to all the doubts of the converts as regards the (Three) Jewels and the Absolute Truth.

The Vinaya Code is directed against the defilement of the two extremities (in life). Being averse to the accumulation of riches out of greediness, it condemns such even in its slightest form and thus brings about rejection of the extremity of licence;[325]) on the other hand, as it permits (the possession of) houses with 100 storeys, food of 100 different tastes and clothes worth 100,000 Karṣapaṇas, if such are obtained without covetousness and by a person of pure morals, — it causes the extremity of self-torture to be abandoned.[326])

The Abhidharma Code acts against the defilement, which consists in maintaining the theory of an existing personality[327]), for it shows in detail the true character of all elements of existence.

*The three Codes with regard to the three disciplines.*

I $Dca_1c_2d_3c_4b_5$. The Code of Sūtras is destined to teach (all) the three Disciplines; it enlarges upon them, giving clear knowledge of them to the converts.[328])

The Vinaya Code is conducive to moral and mental training, for, through subjection to monastic discipline, the complete purification of morals and, as a consequence, there being no regret (as to this having taken place), — the concentration of mind is gradually brought about.[329])

The Abhidharma Code leads to realization of the training in Highest Wisdom, since it largely enters upon the means of a thorough and deep analysis (of existence) into its elements.[330])

*The three Codes with regard to the subject studied.*

II $Dca_1c_2d_3c_4c_5$. The Code of Sūtras is intended to communicate the Doctrine and its meaning; it gives full knowledge of words and sense.[331])

The Vinaya is destined to form a foundation for the realization of the (ultimate) aim of the Doctrine. Accordingly, this Code conduces to (moral and mental) training; as a consequence, in the process of investigation and through pure morality, the concentration (of one's mind) is produced. In such a way all defiling elements are annihilated and the aim of the Doctrine realized.[332])

On the basis of the Abhidharma, controversies are conducted and the true meaning ascertained.[333] The complete enjoyment of this kind of knowledge produces a condition of felicitous feeling, as the true character of existence (divided into) particular, universal etc. becomes clear.

Through study of these three Codes (the Doctrine) is suggested (to the mind);[334] by means of investigation, the meaning (of the Codes) comes to be known[335] [16 a], subsequently, by profound meditation, concentration of mind is brought about,[336] which removes moral defilement. Finally, supreme transcendental knowledge enables one to apprehend the Absolute Truth[337] and to become delivered from the roots of sin. Having this in mind, (the author of) the *Sūtrālaṁkāra*[338] says: —

Three or two[339] Codes, being (each) a collection (of sacred texts),
are taken in consideration for nine causes.
through suggestion, clear understanding, pacification and transcendental knowledge,
they conduce to final salvation.

*Etymology of „Sūtra", "Abidharma", and "Vinaya".*

II Dca$_1$c$_2$d$_3$d$_4$. The *Sūtrālaṁkāra*[340] says:
"Sūtra", "Abhidhharma", and "Vinaya",
are, in short, considered to have (each of them) four meanings.
The Sage, that comes to know (these three Codes)
will attain the state of Omniscience.

Here the word "meaning" *(artha)* has the sense of "etymology", and it would be a mistake, if we took it to mean "definition". The Sage, that is a Bodhisattva, through the thorough knowledge of the three Codes, is able to attain Omniscience.[341] A Çrāvaka, having come to know the meaning of a single verse (of the Codes) may attain arhatship,[342] as Çāriputra or Kṣudrapanthaka.[343]

Now, in Sanscrit, the word *sūtra* means aphorism, brief indication.[344] Accordingly (a Sūtra) indicates place,[345] as "in Rājagṛha",[346] the essence (of an element of existence), as "solidity is the essence of the solid element", the Word of the Doctrine and its meaning.[347] Such aphorisms, combined together, form a class or section. The *Sūtrālaṁkāra*[348] says: —

The Sūtra (is called so) as it is an indication
as to place, essence, the Doctrine and its meaning.

In "*Abhidharma*" — "*abhi*" may, in one way, be taken to mean "*ābhimukhya*", that is "made manifest". The Abhidharma is in this case called so, because it is a teaching *(dharma)* of the Absolute Reality, which is made manifest by it.[349]) "*Abhi*" appears here in the direct meaning of the word.[350])

Otherwise, "*abhi*" may be regarded, as (an abbreviation) of "*abhīkṣṇa*", which means "repeatedly". In this context, Abhidharma has this appelation, because it is the Doctrine (dharma) which demonstrates repeatedly, and in various aspects the (5) groups of elements,[351]) the (18) component elements of an individual,[352]) the (12) bases of cognition,[353]) the objects existing in reality[354]) and such, that are mere logical constructions.[355]) [16 b.] Such (is the etymology), met with in books.[356])

Moreover, "*abhi*", may have the sense of "*abhibhū*" — "to predominate, surpass". Accordingly, thorough knowledge of the Particular and the Universal Essence of all elements of existence enables one to show one's predominance over adversaries, in deciding (religious questions) by means of controversy, or otherwise in silencing all bad orators.[357])

And, finally, "*abhi*" may" be *abhisamaya*" — "full comprehension". The Abhidharma, from this point of view, is called so, because it gives full knowledge of all objects, whatsoever they may be, of such that are existing in reality and of mere logical constructions.[358]) (Consequently, as says the *Sūtrālaṁkāra*:[359]) —

The Abhidharma (is called so), because it makes manifest,
(teaches) repeatedly, (is a cause of) predominance, and gives
full comprehension.

As concerns "Vinaya", two groups (of ideas, each containing) four are expressed by it,[360]) namely: —

1. *vipatti*[361]) — "(moral) fall", — it is *vinaya*, because it demonstrates this fall and makes it sure.

(2. *utthāna* — "the cause of this fall"),[362])

(3. *vyutthāna* — "recovering from it"),

(4. *niḥsaraṇa* — "means of salvation");

or: —

1. *viniçcaya* — "decision"; — it is *vinaya*, because it brings about *(nayati)* decision, —
(2. *pudgala* — "the Individual", to whom discipline is taught"),[363])
(3. *prajñapti* — "the teaching by itself"),
(4. *pravibhāga* — "the different forms of teaching").
(Accordingly, as says the *Sūtrālaṁkāra*:[364]) —

The Vinaya is to be viewed from the point of (moral) fall,
its cause, improvement, and (means of) salvation,
the Individual, the teaching, (its) different forms and decision.

*Varieties of the Word with regard to the converts.*

II $Dca_1c_2e_3$. It is said in the *Sūtrālaṁkāra*:[365]) "Three or two Codes (of sacred texts)." (The "two Codes" are those of Hīnayānistic and Mahāyānistic Scripture).[366]) The Çrāvaka Code (Hīnayāna) is preached for converts that adhere to Low Church,[367]) and the Mahāyāna Code, — for those who are devoted to High Church. The Great Vehicle differs from the Small, by being possessed of the seven kinds of greatness, or, as says the *Mahāyāna-saṁgraha*:[368])

By the subjects studied, (their) essence, by (the converts), that adhere to it,
by its cause, effect and varieties,
by the three disciplines, their result, and that, which is rejected through them,
as well as by Divine knowledge, — the Vehicle, which (is called) the Great One — predominates.

Consequently, from the Hīnayānist point of view, "the Code of great extension" *(vaipulya)*, has this appelation, because the Sūtras (belonging to this Code) contain a great number of chapters and are very diffused. The Mahāyānists, in their turn, regard *vaipulya* otherwise [17 a], etymologically; (they say), it is called so because it is a large, spacious Vehicle (toward Salvation)[369]) It is: —

1.) great, with regard to the Doctrine (expounded by it), since it contains (the teaching of the Climax of Wisdom) of 100 000 verses,[370])
2) great, if viewed from the point of the creative Effort (of the Bodhisattvas that adhere to it), because such is directed

toward Supreme Enlightenment, in pursuit of the welfare of all living beings,

3) great as concerns faith, since (its adherents) found their belief in a Doctrine profound and magnificent,

4) great, by the thoughts, (acquired through it), — as it leads to equal treatment of oneself and of other living beings,[371])

5) great, as regards the accumulation of merit, because (the Bodhisattva), after having entered upon the Path of a Saint, amasses every moment virtue and wisdom immeasurable.

6) great, viewed from the aspect of time, — since the energy of the Bodhisattvas manifests itself during innumerable aeons, and

7) great, by its result, because (by means of it), the state of a Buddha, incomparable to anything else, is attained.

In the *Sūtrālaṁkāra,*[372]) the characteristic of) the seven kinds of greatness, slightly differs from that (just mentioned). Moreover, (with regard to the different converts) we have to distinguish: —

1) The "Vehicle of the Cause", — that of Philosophy,[373]) — for a person of feeble intellect, craving for the Cause (of Salvation);[374]) it is conducive to the realization (of this cause).

2) The "Vehicle of the Effect", — that of Mysticism,[375]) for a convert possessed of acute faculties, who strives for miraculous, instant production of both Cause and Effect. This Vehicle is to convey such an (immediate) result.

It is said in the *Rājāvavādaka?*[376]) — Mañjuçrī asked: —

O Lord, if Thou hast with certainty taught,
of the three Vehicles, conducive (to Salvation),
why hast Thou not mentioned that sure Vehicle,
which miraculously produces the Cause and the Effect,
and where no other help for becoming a Buddha is needed.

(The Lord answered): —

The Teaching of that, which is the Cause,
having been duly preached for those, that are devoted to this Cause,
the Vehicle of Magic,[377]) which is a shorter way,
will in future times appear.

As to the difference between the Vehicle of Mysticism and

that of Philosophy, we read in the *Naya-traya-pradipa*, the work of the teacher *Tripiṭakamāla*[378]) [17 b], as follows:

Infallible, in regard of the unique aim[379]) (of Buddhism),
affording means numerous and easy, and
accessible to (a convert) of acute faculties, —
the Vehicle of Mysticism[380]) is superior (to other doctrines).

Accordingly, neglecting all external means (the Vehicle of Mysticism brings about the realization of the six transcendental virtues through internal contemplation,[381]) and thus proves infallible as regards means. Further on, it possesses a great number of expedients, as it teaches about the mystic contemplation of the Mind, the Word and the Body (of the Buddhas) which is a concentration of mind upon the Most Subtle — the thought and its manifestations, the Subtle, — the (symbolic) letters and sounds, and the Gross, — the images (of the Buddha) and the attributes of mystic ritual; likewise, it demonstrates the Absolute Truth. Moreover, it is not something wearisome, as it accomodates itself to the wishes of the converts and shows them easy means of fulfilling (these wishes), such as mystic gestures[382]) etc. It is to be realized by one possessed of exclusive faculties, who will remain undefiled by deeds, that would conduce others, if they committed them, to evil births. In these four ways the Vehicle of Mysticism shows itself superior (to that of Philosophy). It is considered by Āryadeva as a fourth, separate Code of sacred texts — that of Esoteric Science.[383]) The teacher Ratnākaraçānti says, that it forms a part of the Sūtra Code, because it communicates topics of profound meaning in an abridged form. The teacher Abhayākaragupta regards it as belonging to all the three Codes, as it contains the teaching of the three Disciplines.

*Varieties of the Word of Buddha with regard to the chief determining cause.*

II $Dca_1c_2f_3$. From the point of view of the chief determining cause, the Word of Buddha is of three kinds, namely: —

$a_4$. that, delivered (by Buddha) personally,

$b_4$. that, which is the result of Buddha's blessing[384]) (and is communicated by a Çrāvaka or Bodhisattva),

$c_4$. the passages, containing the expression of Buddhas will[385]) (as to the compilation of Scripture etc.).

*The Word delivered personally.*

II $Dca_1c_2f_3a_4$. To this class belongs, for instance, the *Āryasaṁcaya.*[386])

*The Word which is the result of blessing.*

II $Dca_1c_2f_3b_4$. In the Commentary on the *Aṣṭasāhasrikā-prajñā-pāramitā* three kinds of blessings are mentioned:

1) Corporeal (as laying hands on the head of the disciple etc.),
1) Verbal, and
3) Mental.

The Word, derived from the first kind of blessings, may be illustrated by the *Daçabhūmaka-sūtra*, that, which is the result of the second kind, — by the *Ajātaçatru-kaukṛtya-vinodana*,[387]) and that issuing from the third, by the *Samantabhadra-caryā-nirdeça.*[388]) Some authorities distinguish three kinds of mental blessings, [18 a] namely, that of the contemplative mind, that of the mind full of Great Commiseration, and that of the mind endowed with the power of Truth. The first may be illustrated by the *Prajñāhṛdaya*,[389]) the second — by the magic formulas uttered by the Yakṣas etc. through Buddha's blessing, and the third — by the words of the Doctrine, issuing from musical sounds, from the rays of light and from the skies, — likewise a result of the blessing of Buddha.

*The passages containing the expression of Buddha's will.*

II $Dca_1c_2f_3c_4$. Such are: The introduction (to a discourse),[390]) the conjunctive parts (of it) and the words of approval.[391]) For instance, we have in the *Dharmasaṁgīti-sūtra*[392]) — "O brethren, compile the Doctrine, saying — thus have I heard," and "It is necessary to teach in due connection and order." Such utterances express the will (of Buddha).

*The Division of the Exegetical Treatises (Çāstra).*

II $Dcb_1$. (In analysing the division of the) Exegetical Treatises, we take in consideration three points: —

$a_2$) Definition (of an Exegetical Treatise on Buddhist Scripture),
$b_2$) Etymology (of the word çāstra, — its appelation in Sanscrit),
$c_2$) Varieties (of Exegetical Treatises).

*Defintion of an Exegetical Treatise.*

II $Dcb_1a_2$. (An Exegetical Treatise on Buddhist Scripture) is an interpretation of the meaning of Buddha's Word, which is composed by a trustworthy author and harmonizes with the Path toward Salvation. It is said in the *Uttaratantra*[393]): —

That, which, referring exclusively to the Teaching of Buddha,[394])
is an explanation of it by a trustworthy (teacher),
in harmony with the Path, that leads to Salvation —
is to be revered, as if it were the Word of the Great Anchorite (Himself).

*Etymology of "çāstra".*

II $Dcb_1b_2$) In Sanscrit, an Exegetical Treatise is called *çāstra.* (*çās* has the sense of) *çāsana* — "ruling". Indeed, an Exegetical Treatise (in Buddhism) rules over the cause of moral defilement, the three sources of evil [95]) and the deeds, that result from them, — by teaching the three Disciplines.

*(tra)* is *trāyi* or *tāraṇa*[396]) — "saving" (An Exegetical Treatise on the Word of Buddha) saves from phenomenal existence, from evil births and transmigration (in general) — the consequence (of former deeds). Such an etymology is met with in Scripture.[397]) The *Vyākhyāyukti*[398]) says: [18 b] The Word of Buddha is in harmony with the true essence of a Çāstra. As to the etymology, — *çāstra,* — an Exegetical Treatise, — bears this appelation since it rules *(çāsti)* and saves *(trāyate* or *tārayati).*

That, which rules over our enemies, the passions, (whatsoever they may be),
and saves us from evil births and transmigratory existence (in general), —
is a Çāstra by these its virtues of ruling and saving,
which cannot be met with in any other doctrine (except Buddhism).[399])

Therefore, the Word of Buddha, being, by its qualities of ruling and saving, *the Çāstra,*[400]) one must be keen upon its study.

*The various kinds of Exegetical treatises.*

II $Dcb_1c_2$. (The Exegetical Treatises) are to be discriminated from the point of view of —

$a_3$) (quality) — superior or inferior,

$b_3$) aim,
$c_3$) subject-matter,
$d_3$) interpretation,
$e_3$) various classes.

*Varieties of treatises as regards quality.*

II $Dcb_1c_2a_3$. In the *Yogacaryābhūmi*[401]) nine kinds of treatises are mentioned: —

| | 1. | 2. | 3. |
|---|---|---|---|
| | senseless, | propagandistic, | formalistic, |
| | erroneous, | unscrupulous, | polemical, |
| | correct | conducive to the extinction of phenomenal existence. | conducive to practical results. |

Of these nine kinds, the latter (of each triad) are superior in quality, whereas the other two (are to be regarded as) inferior. Some class the formalistic and polemical treatises among the superior, (thus admitting) five (kinds of treatises of this order). This is not correct, for in the *Nirṇayasaṁgraha*[402]) the two kinds of treatises just mentioned are regarded as hetorodox. Therefore, only the latter (of each triad) are to be regarded as superior (in quality), since they are mentioned in the Word of Buddha.[403])

*The aim of the different treatises.*

II $Dcb_1c_2b_3$. (From this point of view, we distinguish three kinds of treatises, namely): —
1) Condensing excessively large (portions of) Scripture,
2) Giving an analysis of (its) profound meaning,
3) Arranging in a regular system that, which (in Scripture) is in disorder. [19 a.]

(The treatises of) the first kind are those, like the *Vinaya-sūtra*,[404]) of the second — like the *Abhisamayālaṁkāra*, and of the third — like the *Sūtrālaṁkāra* or the *Çikṣā-samuccaya*.

*The various treatises with regard to subject-matter.*

II $Dcb_1e_2c_3$. (As regards the subject-matter), — there are three kinds of works to be distinguished: —
$a_4$) treating on Empirical Reality,[405])
$b_4$) demonstrating the Absolute Truth,[406])
$c_4$) conducive to Salvation and Omniscience.

*Works on Empirical Reality.*

II $Dcb_1c_2c_3d_4$. (The treatises of this kind )may be

1) on general topics, and
2) on special (branches of science).

The works of the first kind are those on worldly policy[407] (or ethics), as the 18 Examinations, the *Prajñā-çataka*,[408] the *Jana-poṣaṇa-bindu*,[409] the *Āryākoça*,[410] etc. These works are conducive to worldly happiness, as says the *Prajñā-çataka*:

(The form of existence, which is) the foundation of Nirvāṇa may be attained (in the following manner):
If worldly laws and customs are duly observed, —
it will not be far to go to reach the abode of the gods.
In ascending the stairs of godly and human existence,
one draws near to final Salvation.

Of a similar nature are the *Sāmudrika*,[411] works on horses, elephants etc.

Of the second category are the treatises on the principal branches of science. It is said in the *Sūtrālaṁkāra*:[412] —

The highest of Saints, if he were not zealous in the five branches of science,
would never attain the state of an omniscient being.
Therefore, to vanquish and to hep others,
as well as to obtain thorough knowledge himself, he is earnestly applied to study.

Accordingly, the sciences of Logic[413] and of Grammar (and Literature)[414] (are studied) in order to vanquish one's adversaries (in controversy); the sciences of Medicine[415] and of Art,[416] — for administering help to others, and that of Metaphysics,[417] — to acquire thorough knowledge for oneself.

The works on Logic contain an analysis of direct sense-perception,[418] inference,[419] syllogism,[420] the relative meaning of words,[421] examples, and futile answers (or logical fallacies).[422] A summary exposition of these six points is given by the *Pramāṇa-samuccaya*,[423] the seven treatises (of Dharmakīrti) commenting on it, the 7 Examinations,[424] the 8 Proofs,[425] the 7 secondary works etc. The seven treatises (of Dharmakīrti) consist of three main works, which may be compared to a body, and four supplementary, which act as its members. The first are the *Nyāyabindu*, *Pramāṇa-viniçcaya*,[426] and *Pramāṇa-vārtika*[427] which demonstrate a means of easily apprehending the modes of correct knowledge[428]) for (scholars of acute, mediocre, and weak intellectual faculty. "The *Pramāṇa-viniçcaya*", says the Kashmirian Paṇḍit Jñānaçrī,[429]) "is not to be regarded as a commentary on the *Pramāṇa-samuccaya*; nevertheless, I shall elucidate its theory". The teacher Dharmottara,[430]) on the contrary says that it is a commentary on the work in question, and this opinion is to be regarded as correct.

The four supplementary works do not enlarge upon the chapter of sense perception. (The subject of) inference is treated in detail by two works — the *Hetubindu*[431]) which contains an investigation of the major and the minor premises,[432]) — and the *Saṁbandha-parīkṣā*,[433]) — a discussion on difficult points, such as concomitance or logical fallacies. The syllogism is enlarged upon in the *Vāda-nyāya* which describes the disputant, (his) adversary, (the process of) controversy, victory, defeat, and the reason of the latter.[436]) The *Saṁtānāntara-siddhi*[437]) shows that, from the point of view of Empirical Reality, the inference of the existence of other minds on the basis of the existence of their words and actions does not conflict with Idealism, as follows:

Having observed that one's own purposive acts are preceded by knowledge,
when observing the same fact with others,
the existence of other minds is conjectured.
This will not be in conflict with Idealism.

These and other works on Dialectics are regarded by (some) Tibetan authorities as belonging to the Abhidharma Code. This is not correct, for Dialectics are (the subject-matter of) the treatises on the Science of Logic [20 a], whereas the Abhidharma consists (exclusively) of works on Metaphysics. It is said in the *Vyākhyāyukti*:[438]) —

(A Logician is to be recognized) —
by his disposition (to argue),[439]) by analysis[440]) and discussion (of matters),
by practise, obtained in former births, by non-perception (of the Absolute Truth),[441]) and
by having no recourse to Scripture.

The merits of the logicians are considered to be of five kinds:
energy, thorough attention (as to the object investigated),

tradition, complete apprehension (of the modes of proof),[442] and perfect moral purity.[443])

(The logicians are thus characterized) as not founding (their discussions) upon the Word of Scripture. On the other hand, the *Sūtrālaṁkāra*[444]) says:

Dependent (on Scripture),[445]) uncertain, incomprehensive,[446]) empirical, wearisome, —
Logic is to be viewed as the sphere of worldlings;[447]) (the Great Vehicle is therefore not its object).

(All this) disagrees with (our view of) the Abhidharma, since the latter is (our revered) Mother.[448]) The *Pramāṇa-samuccaya* says: —

It (the *Pramāṇa-samuccaya*) has been composed in order to cause those, that adhere to heterodox views, to abstain from them, since they are false, — by discussing the modes of cognition and their (respective) objects. It does not, however, intend to convert anyone to Buddhism by these means only, for the Doctrine is not the object of dialectics. (But), if (heretical views) are rejected, the Teacher's Doctrine is studied and apprehended without difficulty, since all the numerous impediments are withdrawn.

Moreover, the same work has the following verse:

He, that leads to the Absolute Truth by the way of Dialectics,
will be very far from the Teaching of Buddha and fail.
Nevertheless, if the essence of the Lord's Teaching
will endure change, it is advisable to probe it (by Logic).

### *Grammar.*

The works on Grammar contain the analysis of three main points, namely: —

1) The crude forms (of words),
2) The various suffixes,[449]) and
3) The formation (of sentences and compounds, according to the rules of euphony etc.)

(These works are): — the fundamental grammatical aphorisms (of Pāṇini)[450]) and the supplementary (treatises on special parts of grammar). The crude forms are [20 b] the verbal roots[451]) and the nouns (and adjectives) in their uninflected form. The suffixes are primary *(kṛt)*[452]) used for the derivation of a noun from a verbal root and secondary *(tad-*

*dhita)*[453] which form nouns and adjectives from primary derivatives. The latter are divided into suffixes of generality, unlimited plurality and abstract nouns.

The inflections which are used to form a word from a verbal root and differ with regard to time are called tense-terminations *(tiṅ)*, and those forming a word from the basis of a noun and varying as to their meaning — case-terminations *(sup)*. The insertions of letters or syllables between the crude form and the suffix are called augments *(āgama)*, and the particles, which alter the meaning of a verbal root — prefixes *(upasarga)*.[454] The latter are regarded as a part of the crude form of a verbal root.

The formation (of sentences and compounds). The elision and change of letters according to the rules of euphony[455] etc. as well as the formation of compounds and the like are treated under this head.

Such are the principal topics, that form the subject-matter of grammar. Otherwise the main part of it is an exposition of euphonic rules, the nouns, the verbs, and the suffixes; the verbal roots, the prefixes and the uṇādi terminations being viewed as secondary subjects. In this order (grammar is taught) by the *Kalāpa-sūtra*[456] or the *Vacana-mukha*,[457] the latter being a summary teaching of phonetics, etymology, and syntax. All these works ought to be studied since they are conducive to the four departments of knowledge;[458] they do not however belong to any of the three Codes.

*Prosody and Lexicography.*

In close connection (with the grammatical treatises) are the works on Prosody[459] such as the *Chando-ratnākara*,[460] which demonstrate the rules for employing (metrically) long and short vowels and give a tabular representation (of such vowels in a metre).[461] The synonyms of words, the differentiation of the three genders and the homonyms are treated in the lexicographical works such as the *Amarakoça*[462] etc.

*Poetics (Alamkāraçāstra).*

The works on Poetics, the *Kāvyādarça*[463] and the works on dramatical composition that teach in accordance with it etc. demonstrate the definition of a poetical composition, the various schools of poetics, the thirty-five poetical figures [21 a], the acrostychs, and the poetical suggestions.[464]) In such a form poetics etc. are a part of the science of grammar and literature. Otherwise, they are a part of the Veda.[465]) (The *Amarakoça* says: —

The *Sāma* —, the *Ṛc* —, and the *Yajurveda*, —
These are the three Vedas.

*Medicine.*

The works on the Science of Medicine describe various diseases, their origin, the medicaments acting as an antidote against them, and the methods of treatment, or otherwise: —

The body (of a pregnant woman), the infant, (its) diseases,
the body (its interior), its upper part,
the (wounds inflicted by) weapons and bites, as well as
the remedy against infirmity, —
such are the eight (principal) spheres,
where medicinal treatment is applied.

Accordingly, pregnancy (and female diseases in general), infant-diseases,[466]) the body, — that is its internal part or the trunk, the upper part, — the head, further on, (the sphere of surgery) — the wounds inflicted by weapons and those caused by bites, and, finally, the Himalayan lizard (which affords a remedy against infirmity) are treated in the medical works, such as the *Aṣṭāṅga-hṛdaya*[467]). The works on the Science of Art are those on Alchemistry,[468]) on the dimensions of images[469]) etc.

*Metaphysics.*

The works on Metaphysics demonstrate the (5) groups of elements, the (18) component elements of an individual, the (12) bases of cognition, the difference between them, and their special characteristics, — from the standpoint of Empirical Reality. Such is the Abhidharma-literature, the *Mahāyāna-lakṣaṇa-samuccaya*,[470]) etc.

*Treatises referring to the Absolute Reality.*

II $Dcb_1c_2c_3b_4$. The works referring to Absolute Reality demonstrate the four Truths of the Saint, or non-differentiation into subject and object, and Non-substantiality, as the *Satya-dvaya-viniçcaya*,[471]) the *Triṁçaka* (of Vasubandhu) or the *Madhyamaka-alaṁkāra*.[472])

*The treatises conducive to Salvation and Omniscience.*

II $Dcb_1c_2c_3c_4$. (The treatises) that show the way to Salvation and Omniscience are those like the *Bodhisattva-bhūmi*,[473]) the *Çrāvaka-bhūmi*,[474]) the *Bodhicaryāvatāra* etc. Some authorities say, that each of these works treats on a special topic (and is to be regarded as) a treatise of the smaller type [21 b], whereas the great works, that contain the exposition (of the Doctrine) as a whole, are those like the *Abhidharma-samuccaya* or *Abhidharmakoça*.

*Varieties of interpretation.*
*The different conceptions of Buddhism.*

II $Dcb_1c_2d_3$. (We have to distinguish) the interpretation of Buddha's Word in general and that of special parts of it (relating to the different periods). With regard to the first kind it is said that the verbal part (of the Doctrine) is elucidated by the grammatical treatises, and the contents — by the works on the Science of Logic. I, however, do not share this opinion.

As to the interpretation of special divisions of Scripture (that of the early, the intermediate and the latest period), the works containing them are, (respectively), of three kinds, as follows: —

*Treatises interpreting Hīnayānistic Scripture.*

The treatises that give an interpretation of early Scripture are of two kinds, — those elucidating the theoretical part an' those referring to religious practise.

*Works on Abhidharma.*

Of the first kind are the seven (fundamental) treatises on Abhidharma, which are: —

The *Dharma-skandha*,[475]) — of Çāriputra, (1)
The *Prajñāpti-çāstra*,[476]) — of Maudgalyāyana, (2)
The *Dhātu-kāya*,[477]) — composed by Pūrṇa,[478]) (3)
The *Vijñāna-kāya*,[479]) — by Devaçarman,[480])
The *Jñāna-prasthāna*,[481]) — of Kātyāyana[482]) (5)
The *Prakaraṇa-pāda*,[483]) — of Vasumitra,[484]) (6) and
The *Saṁgīti-paryāya*,[485]) — composed by Mahākauṣṭhila,[486]) (7) so runs the tradition.[487])

The Kashmirian Vaibhāṣikas regard these seven works as belonging to the Word of Buddha. They say, that they contain sermons delivered by the teacher at various times, at different places and to diverse persons separately, the Arhats and Çrāvakas having subsequently collected them, as, for instance, it is the case in the *Udānavarga*.[488]) Otherwise, they say, the three Codes of Scripture would not be complete.

The Sautrāntikas and the other (schools) say, that the Abhidharma is included in both the Sūtras and the Vinaya, or otherwise, has been expounded at intervals, and that no mistake is made (by admitting such an order). As to the seven works, (the schools just mentioned) regard them as exegetical treatises. The contents of these works is rendered, in abridged form, by the *Mahāvibhāṣā*, which in its turn is condensed in the *Abhidharmakoça* and other treatises.

*Treatises on Vinaya.*

(The practical side of Early Scripture) is exposed in the *Vinaya-sūtra*,[489] )which first of all demonstrates the tenets of monkhood[490]) the first of the 17 subjects of Vinaya, then, having for its principal subject-matter (the contents of) the two *Vinayavibhanga* [22 a], and the (remaining) 16 subjects, — it explains (all these points), referring to passages from the *Uttara-grantha*[491]) — the chapter of questions[492]) and that of instructions,[493]) — and the divisions of the *Vinaya-kṣudraka*,[494]) when necessary. (Other works) as the *Puṣpamālā*[495]) or the *Triçata-kārikā*[496]) expound (Vinaya) on the basis of the *Vinaya-vibhanga*, with references, when needed, to the other (canonical works on Vinaya).

*Treatises on the Madhyamaka Doctrine and the Prajñāpāramitā.*

The exegetical treatises interpreting Intermediate Scripture are likewise of two kinds, — those elucidating the theoretical, and those referring to the practical part. Four "Waylayers of the Vehicle" are known, as follows: —

*The six main treatises of Nāgārjuna.*

1) The six main treatises of the Mādhyamika Doctrine (by Nāgārjuna[497]) demonstrating that, which is expressed by the Sūtras directly, or otherwise, the essential meaning (of the Doctrine). These works are, —

The *Çūnyatā-saptati*,[498]) — expounding the theory of the Relativity of all elements of existence, devoid of the extremities of causality[499]) and pluralism,[500]) and

The *Prajñā-mūla*,[501]) — denying the reality of origination from self and non-self;[502]) — these two works (are to be regarded as) the fundamental or principal. Next come:

The *Yukti-ṣaṣṭikā*,[503]) — containing a logical vindication (of the theory).

The *Vigraha-vyāvartanī*,[504]) — refuting the challenges of antagonists,

The *Vaidalya-sūtra*,[505]) — demonstrating the methods of controversy with adversaries and logicians (in general) and

The *Vyavahāra-siddhi*,[506]) showing that, from the point of view of the Absolute Truth — Non - substantiality, and from the empirial standpoint — worldly practise go along together.

### *Works on the Prajñāpāramitā.*

2) The *Abhisamayālaṁkāra*[507]) has for its principal subject-matter the meaning of that, which is taught indirectly, — namely, the knowledge of the practical way (to attain the dignity) of a Buddha. It is a summary of the following eight subjects:[508]) —

The three kinds of Divine Wisdom, which are: —

The Omniscience of the Buddha,[509])

The Knowledge of the Path, (Hīnayānistic and Mahāyānistic, — by the Bodhisattva),[510])

The Knowledge of the Empirical World, (accessible to the Hīnayānist Saint),[511])

The four Methods of Realization, which are: —

The thorough Knowledge of all the forms of the 3 kinds of Wisdom (beforesaid) and of their respective objects,[512])

The Culmination of the Process of Illumination,[513])

The Progressive Process of Illumination,[514])

The Final, Momentary Intuition,[515]) and

The Result of the Path, which is the Unity of the Cosmos, viewed as the Body of the Buddha.

3) The *Aṣṭasāhasrikā-piṇḍārtha*[516]) explains the subjects of Prajñāpāramitā in 32 paragraphs. It says:[517]) —

The Founder (of the Faith), the adherents,
the deeds (of virtue) the concentration of mind,
the varieties (of the aspects of objective Unreality), the (two) signs,
(moral) fall and the merit of virtuous life —
(these subjects) are discussed (here).

Accordingly[518]) the founder (of the Faith) — that is Buddha the Teacher, the adherents — the converts (Bodhisattvas etc.), the deeds — action according to the Climax of Wisdom. The ten forms of meditation act as an antidote against the ten kinds of mental confusion which consist in the imputation of nonsubstantiality,[519]) of reality,[520]) imagined presence[521]) and its repulsion, [522]) of unity, [523]) plurality,[524]) substance,[525]) quality,[526]) of the correspondence of objects with their names[527]) and the reverse.[528]) The varieties are those of the aspects of objective Unreality, sixteen in number, — to begin with the Unreality of the internal bases of cognition,[529]) and up to the Unreality of the essence of non-ens.[530]) The signs are those of the activity of the Evil-one and of (the Bodhisattva), who has attained the irretrievable state. The fall into evil births is a consequence of abstaining from the teaching of the Climax of Wisdom. The merit is that of practising the highest form of virtue in acting according to this teaching, — virtue, that is greater than offerings, which fill the innumerable worlds with gold and jewels. All (the contents of the Prajñāpāramitā) is comprised in these 32 points, which are entered upon repeatedly, when it is necessary.

4) The Commentary on the *Çatasāhasrikā*, (the *Pañcaviṁçati-sāhasrikā* and the *Aṣṭadaça-sāhasrikā*[531]) is an exposition of the Doctrine of the Climax of Wisdom) in the form of the three "media" and the eleven instructions. The subject is opened upon by means of an introduction. Then comes "the medium of teaching in abridged form" as "o Çāriputra, the Bodhisattvas and Mahāsattvas, who wish to attain complete Enlightenment, with regard to all the elements of existence, in all their forms, — must be keen upon (the study of) the Climax of Wisdom", — where the individual, the cause, the subject and the way (of studying) is briefly indicated. Next comes "the medium of moderate teach-

ing" — up to the close of the first chapter,[532]) and finally, "the medium of teaching in detail", — up to the end. [23 a.] The eleven instructions are: — the precepts delivered to Çāriputra, the speech of Subhūti,[533]) the two instructions delivered to Indra, the four — to Subhūti, and one — to Ānanda. It is said, that this Commentary is the work of Dāṁṣṭrasena, but it will be more correct to regard it as composed by Vasubandhu. This work, as well as the *Aṣṭasāhasrikā-piṇḍārtha* expound (Prajñāpāramitā) from the standpoint of the Yogācāra System.

(The works referring to the practical side of Intermediate Scripture are the *Çikṣā-samuccaya,*[534]) *the Sūtra-samuccaya*[535]) or the *Bodhicaryāvatāra* and the three "Degrees of Meditation",[536]) where the theoretical and the practical part (of the Doctrine) are expounded jointly.

### *Yogācāra works.*

The works elucidating Scripture of the latest period are (as in the two former cases, commentaries) on the theoretical and the practical part (of the Teaching). The treatises of the first kind are as follows:

### *The works of Maitreya.*

1) The works of the Lord Maitreya, which are: —
The *Sūtrālaṁkāra,*
,, *Madhyānta-vibhanga,*[537])
,, *Dharma-dharmatā-vibhanga,* [538]) and
,, *Uttaratantra.*

Some authorities say, that the first two of these four (treatises) belong to the Abhidharma Code, the latter two — to the Sūtra Code, and the *Abhisamayālaṁkāra* — to the Vinaya Code. I however see no reason (for such a classification).

*The Sūtrālaṁkāra* contains an exposition of all the Mahāyānistic Doctrines in abridged form: —

Like wrought gold, like an unfolded lotus flower,
like well prepared food, enjoyed by those that were starving,
like a message agreeable to hear, or like an opened chest full of jewels, —
the Doctrine, that is expounded here, is the cause of the highest delight.[539])

In such a form its contents is presented (to the reader).

The *Madhyānta-vibhanga*. *Anta* — "extremity", — means the extremities of Realism and Nihilism, or otherwise, those of Eternalism and Materialism. *Madhya* — "the middle", — is the middle way shunning both these extremities. The treatise, as it gives an analysis *(vibhanga)* of both these points, is called *Madhyānta-vibhanga*. It treats on seven subjects, as follows: —

The three aspects (of Reality),[540]) the Obscurations, the Absolute Truth,
the antidotes (against defilement), profound meditation,
its sphere and the Highest of Vehicles, through which the ultimate result is attained.

The *Dharma-dharmatā-vibhanga*. "*Dharma*" are the elements of existence, that belong to the phenomenal world and are influenced by defiling agencies. "*Dharmatā*" is the true essence of all the elements — Nirvāṇa. The work, being an investigation of these two principles, bears the name, *Dharma-dharmatā-vibhanga*. The *Uttaratantra* is called so, because it is the highest *(uttara)* of the series *(tantra)* of the Mahāyānistic teachings, — it consequently contains the Highest of Doctrines. Otherwise *uttara* may signify "latest". (The *Uttaratantra* is in this case called so) as it is an interpretation of the latest teaching of the Mahāyāna. It enlarges upon the Three Jewels, their character, the ultimate result, which is Enlightenment, the 64 qualities of the Buddha[541]) and the deeds achieved by him as follows: —

Buddha, the Doctrine, the Church, their character, Enlightenment,
the qualities of Buddha, and, finally His achievements,
these are the seven diamond subjects, —
the contents of the whole work taken in short.

### *The five divisions of the Yogacaryā-bhūmi.*

Having adjoined (to these four works) the *Abhisamayālaṁkāra* (mentioned before) we shall have all the 5 treatises of Maitreya. In harmony with these treatises are: — the great work of Āryāsanga, — the *Yogacaryā-bhūmi* in its five volumes,[542]) the two summary works (of the same author), and the eight treatises of Vasubandhu. Of these the *Yogacaryā-bhūmi* is to be regarded as the principal. It has the following five divisions: —

The *Bahubhūmika-vastu*,[543]) expounding (the Yogācāra Doctrine) comprised in 17 subjects. The summary (at the head of the work) is as follows: —

The subject of the five kinds of sensation,
that of the intellect and of the following three —
(subconscious thought) associated with a search[544]), a fixation of mind[545]) etc.,
the subject of concentration and non-concentration of mind,
that of consciousness and unconsciousness, [24 a]
the subjects of study, investigation, and meditation,
that of three Vehicles, and (of Nirvāṇa) with rest[546]) and without it.[547])

These seventeen subjects are demonstrated with reference to the person, the conduct, and the result. They are, accordingly, of three kinds, as follows: — The subject of the five kinds of consciousness and that of the intellect are the foundation of personal (progress). The subject of (subconscious thinking) associated with a search and an attempt to fix the mind, [548]) of (subconscious thought) associated with an attempt to fix the mind and without search[549]) and that of (thought) which is neither searching nor attempting to fix the mind[550]) are the modes of action of the person. Concentration of mind and the absence of such, consciousness and unconsciousness are the different states (of the person).

As regards the conduct, we have three subjects, — that of study, of investigation and of meditation. With reference to the result, — the subject of (the three Vehicles), — of the Çrāvakas, Pratyekabuddhas, and Bodhisattvas, — concerning the preliminary result, and the subject (of Nirvāṇa) with rest, — in the form of the (five) groups of elements, and that without it, — which is the final result.

The *Nirṇaya-saṁgraha*[551]) acts as a commentary on the preceeding volume. It is an investigation of the verbal part and the subject-matter of the *Bahubhūmika-vastu* by the method of quadrilemmas[552]) etc. With the exception of the subject (of the Vehicle of) the Pratyekabuddhas it contains a summary analysis (of the different subjects). These two volumes completely elucidate the meaning of Scripture (belonging to the latest period).

The *Vastu-saṁgraha*[553]) demonstrates the order in which

(the contents of the *Bahubhūmika-vastu*) should be combined in accordance with the three Codes (of Scripture). Having briefly indicated this order, it then enlarges upon the part, which is to be included in the Sūtra and the Vinaya Code only. The Abhidharma, as it comprises all the five divisions of the *Yogacaryā-bhūmi* (in general), is not mentioned separately. "The subject of study," says the *Nirṇaya-saṁgraha*, "is the Abhidharma, which is contained in the 17 subjects (of the *Bahubhūmikavastu*) and in the four compendia (*Nirṇaya-saṁgraha* etc.)."

*The Paryāya-saṁgraha*[554]) gives the synonyms of the words expressing the different subjects, and especially that of the purifying[555]) and defiling[556]) elements. [24 b]. These two works, (the *Vastu-saṁgraha* and *Paryāya-saṁgraha*) are explanatory.[557])

The *Vivaraṇa-saṁgraha*[558]) enlarges upon the methods of teaching (adopted by the preceeding works). Consequently, with regard to the meaning of Scripture, the explanations and the methods of teaching, — five divisions of the *Yogacaryā-bhūmi* are to be distinguished.

### *The summary works.*

The two summary works (of Āryāsanga) are: —

The *Abhidharma-samuccaya*, which is a general summary of the Doctrine) in common with (all) the (three) Vehicles and an exposition of five points, — the definitions of all the subjects (of the Abhidharma), investigation of the (four) Truths (of the Saint),[559]) of the Doctrine,[560]) of the ultimate result[561]) and of the methods of teaching,[562]), and the *Mahāyāna-saṁgraha*,[563]) — a summary of (the Doctrine of) the Great Vehicle. It demonstrates, in abridged form, ten points, — the varieties of the elements of existence etc. from the Mahāyānistic standpoint.

### *The treatises of Vasubandhu on Idealism.*

The eight treatises of Vasubandhu are as follows: —

The *Triṁçaka-kārikā-prakaraṇa*,[564]) teaching that all the elements of existence are but modes of one conscious principle.

The *Viṁçaka-kārikā-prakaraṇa*, [565]) — a vindication of this theory by means of Logic.

The *Pañcaskandha-prakaraṇa*,[566]) — a vindication of the theory of the five groups of elements, which is the foundation of Logic.

The *Vyākhyāyukti*, vindicating the possibility of studying and preaching (the Doctrine), — in conformity with the theory of Idealism.

The *Karma-siddhi-prakaraṇa*[567]) — vindicating the acts of the three media (from the same standpoint).

These five works are independent. Next come interpretations of other works as follows: —

The Commentary on the *Sūtrālaṁkāra*,[569]) — vindicating the practice of the six Transcendental virtues,

the Commentary on the *Pratītyasamutpāda-sūtra*,[570]) — vindicating the twelve-membered formula of the evolution of individual life, and

the Commentary on the *Madhyānta-vibhanga*,[571]) — a vindication of the three aspects of Reality. Such are these eight works according to the tradition.

Some authorities say that, since this teacher has composed many more treatises, including the commentary on the *Daçabhūmaka-sūtra*[572]) etc., the limitation of their number to eight is incorrect, and so is likewise that of twenty treatises connected with the teaching of Maitreya. Those that insist on a definite number with regard to the latter, count the five volumes of the *Yogacaryā-bhūmi*, the two summary works, the five books of Maitreya and the eight treatises (of Vasubandhu).

The treatises elucidating the practical part of the Doctrine are the *Bodhisattva-saṁvara-viṁçaka*[573]) etc.

### *The various classes of exegetical treatises.*

II $Dcb_1c_2e_3$. With regard to the various classes of exegetical treatises, we have to distinguish those, that do not base upon the Scripture of Buddhism [25 a], and their reverse. As to the treatises of the latter kind, — such may be interpretations of the Word of Buddha (proper) and independent works, dealing with its contents (in general). Of the first kind are: 1) the great Commentaries elucidating the verbal part and meaning (of the Doctrine) such as the *Pratimokṣa-sūtra-ṭikā*,[574]) consisting of fifty chapters, 2) (special) Commentaries on the verbal part, as the *Udānavarga-vivaraṇa*,[575]) 3) Commentaries on difficult points, explaining such, as the two Commentaries on the *Saṁcaya*,[576]) 4) works that give a brief account, rendering the principal part of the subject-matter (of the canonical text in question) in abridged form, — as the works of Vimalamitra and 5) Commentaries explaining the meaning of whole sentences, condensing such. Of the second kind are the treatises, which —

1) give a complete review of such and such part of Scripture,
2) demonstrate in a regular system that, which in Scripture is scattered, and
3) render the contents of many different parts of Scripture, taken together. Of the first kind are the ***Sūtrālaṁkāra*** or the ***Vinaya-sūtra***, — of the second — the ***Çramaṇera-kārikā***, and of the third, — the ***Çikṣā-samuccaya*** or the ***Suhṛllekhā***.[577])

Commentaries in general bear different names, such as ***vṛtti***,[578]) ***bhāṣya***,[579]) ***vyākhyā***,[580]) ***nibandhana***,[581]) ***piṇḍārtha***,[582]) ***pañjikā***,[583]) ***ṭīkā***,[584]) ***saṁskāra***,[585]) ***vibhanga***,[586]) and many others. Such a differentiation of exegetical treatises has been made with regard to scientific works in general, (which are to be studied) in order to increase (the sphere of) knowledge. We do not consider it to be in conflict with the definition and etymology (of exegetical treatises) mentioned above,[587]) since such concern only the special treatises (on the Scripture of Buddhism).

## III. The Consideration and Fulfillment of Rules prescribed for Study and Teaching.

(With regard to the subject in question) there are four (principal points, which are to be treated separately,) as follows: —

A. The characteristic of the Doctrine, that is to be taught.
B. The characteristic of the methods of teaching, which are to be observed by the preceptor.
C. The characteristic of the methods of study (prescribed for) the pupils.
D. The instruction for realizing the aim of the Doctrine by both the teacher and the pupils [25 b].

*Characteristic of the Doctrine.*

III A. In order to become proficient in (the various) branches of science in general, the study of diverse kinds of scientific treatises is required. It is said in the Vinaya, that heterodox works etc. are likewise to be studied and that the Bodhisattvas especially must receive training in all (the various disciplines). However, those, that proceed on the Sublime Path, must (first of all) be keen upon the study and preaching of Buddha's Doctrine. The characteristic of this Doctrine is rendered by the *Prabhāvatī*[588]) as follows:

That, which perfectly teaches the three Disciplines,
is endowed with the three Seals,
and is virtuous in the beginning, in the middle and at the end —
is known by the wise as the Word of the Buddha.

Accordingly, (this Doctrine) demonstrates the three Disciplines, the training in which is to be (practically) carried out, and the three Seals, which are the distinctive mark, peculiar to the Scripture and philosophical system (of Buddhism). These are as follows: —

All elements of existence are impersonal,[589])
All phenomena[590]) are transitory,
All elements influenced by defiling agencies[591])
have mere phenomenal existence.

The essence of the Doctrine is characterised as "virtuous in the beginning, in the middle and at the end". The *Prati-mokṣa-sūtra* says:[592]) —

Do not commit any sin, in whatsoever it may be,
practise the complement of virtue, and
perfectly subdue your own mind, —
such is the Teaching of Buddha.

It is said in the Sutras: — The Highest Doctrine is: [593])

Virtuous in the beginning,[594])
Virtuous in the middle,[595])
Virtuous at the end,[596])
Of fine meaning,[597])
Endowed with fine words,[598])
Unique,[599])
Fully accomplished,[600])
Pure,[601]) and
Universally immaculate.[602])

As to the words "virtuous in the beginning, in the middle and at the end, Asanga and other authorities regard them as referring to study, investigation, and meditation.[603]) Others say that the introduction at the beginning of a discourse, the discourse itself in the middle, and the utterances of praise at the close of it are meant here. The teacher Kalyāṇadeva considers that the words in question concern the salutation at the beginning of an exegetical treatise, the main contents of the treatise in the middle and the blessings at the end. According to the interpretation given by the Vyākhyāyukti, [26 a] "the beginning", "the middle", and "the end", (respectively mean the aggregates of morality, profound meditation, and Highest Wisdom[604]) which are the complement of virtue, since they are indestructible.[605]) "Of fine meaning" refers to the complement of the subject-matter, since such is correct and incontrovertible.[606]) "Endowed with fine words" means — possessing the complement of (the means of) verbal expression, since (the subject-matter) is rendered completely intelligible. "Unique", has the meaning of "having nothing in common with other (Doctrines)".[607]) "Fully accomplished" (is the Doctrine), since it acts as an antidote against every kind of defilement.[608]) "Pure", as it is conducive to the liberation of an individual existence (from sin) through deliverance from the passions of this world of carnal desire.[609]) "Universally immaculate", since it leads to the complete deliverance of the stream (of elements constituting a personality), — by making it free from the dreaming residue of passions, that are peculiar to the other (higher) spheres (of existence).[610])

That, which is endowed with all these qualities, is known as the Highest Doctrine (of Buddha).

In short, Buddhism, the Highest Doctrine is 1) the Teaching, that harmonizes with all the three Vehicles,[611]) which is contained in the Sūtras on the four Truths of the Saint, appears as that, which subdues passion[612]) and is not in conflict with the laws of Causality[613]) and 2) (the Teaching) of the Great Vehicle as it appears in the *Uttaratantra*, the corresponding passage of which we have quoted above.[614]) Moreover, we read in the *Sūtrālaṁkāra*:[615]) —

This is the teaching of Virtue, —
since it is the cause of faith, felicity, and wisdom,

of twofold meaning,[616]) easy to apprehend,
and speaking of virtuous conduct, the merit of which is of four kinds: —

(It is) unique, as it is not in common with anything else,
bringing to accomplishment the annihilation of passions in the three spheres of existence,
pure by nature and free from defilement, — the conduct of virtue has fourfold merit.

As to the special theory of Mahāyāna, we read as follows: —

Relativity, that is one with Great Commiseration,
upon which the mind profoundly meditates, —
such is the Teaching, that refers to Buddha, the Doctrine and the Church.

Accordingly, Relativity, the essence of which is Great Commiseration[617]) is here [26 b] spoken of as (the true) Teaching of Buddha. This Teaching, — the Word of Buddha (proper) or the special exegetical treatises, — comprises the verbal part and the meaning. The *Sūtrālaṁkāra*[618]) says: —

Like a remedy, that smells bitter, but proves to be sweet if tasted, —

the Doctrine appears in two aspects, viewed from the standpoint of words and sense.

The complement (of the meaning of the Doctrine) is the conduct of virtue, which (as has just been said) is characterized by fourfold merit. As to the complement of the means of verbal expression, the *Sūtrālaṁkāra*[619]) speaks of it as follows:

Indicating and teaching correctly,
harmonizing with the three Vehicles, mild,
intelligible, dignified, conducive to Salvation,
and corresponding (to the Path of a Saint), —
such is the complement of the means of verbal expression familiar to the Bodhisattvas.

Moreover the *Vivaraṇa-saṁgraha*[620]) says: —

The body of a discourse is twofold, namely (its) words and (their) meaning. Of these two parts, — the words (are to be viewed as) receptacles, and the meaning, — as that, which is contained in them. Both parts combined together, form the subject of study. And in the abridged treatise of Dharmottara[621]) it is to be read: —

Twofold is the body of a scientific treatise, — (it includes) the words and (their) meaning.

Consequently, the Doctrine, that is to be taught is that, which has been exposed by Buddha, collected by the Compilers, commented by the great scholars,[622]) translated by the venerable Lotsavas and Paṇḍits, and supplied with instructions and precepts, delivered by one teacher to the other in regular succession,[623]) — the division of the Tantras, or that of the Sūtras, the Word of Buddha proper or the exegetical treatises, the three Codes, — of the Sūtras, the Abhidharma and the Vinaya. Each of these parts is a subject of teaching.

*Characteristic of the methods of teaching.*

III B. Three (principal points are to be distinguished here) as follows: —

a. The definition of the teacher, that expounds (the Doctrine).
b. The means of teaching resorted to.
c. The methods of teaching (proper).

*Definition of the teacher.*

III B a. In the various treatises many different characteristics of the (spiritual) teacher are given [27 a]

The *Çramaṇera-kārikā*[624]) says: —

Him that is morally pure, who knows the rules of religious Discipline,
is merciful to the distressed and (surrounded by) faithful adherents,
him, who is zealous in administering help by means of the Doctrine and of material objects,
and who teaches at due time, — you are to revere as your spiritual teacher.

The teacher Nāgārjuna says:[625])

Know thou in short the definition of the teachers:[626])
They are well versed in the rules of Discipline, endowed with Great Commiseration and pure morality,
and with the Highest Wisdom, that removes all defilement.
You must rely upon such teachers,
be full of reverence toward their wisdom.

Çāntideva has:[627])

(Never forsake) the Teacher, — him who is proficient in the meaning of the Great Vehicle.

And Candragomin:[628])

A teacher, that observes the vows, is learned and efficient,
must be chosen (as preceptor).

Moreover, we read in the *Sūtrālaṁkāra*:[629]) —

Rely upon the Friend[630]), that is well disciplined,
self-controlled and perfectly calming (all passions),
endowed with exclusive merits, energetic, and rich in (his knowledge) of Scripture,
perceiving the Absolute Truth, skilful in speech,
merciful by nature and never weary (to teach).

Here ten qualities are mentioned. (The teacher is): —

1) Well disciplined, being endowed with pure morality,
2) Self-controlled, since he practises profound meditation,
3) Perfectly calming all passions, through being endowed with Highest Wisdom,
4) Of exclusive merits, since his virtues are superior to those of others,
5) Zealous, as he is not indifferent toward the needs of others,
6) Rich in (his knowledge of) Scripture, through extensive study (of the latter).
7) Perceiving the Absolute Truth, that is to be cognized,
8) A skilful orator,
9) Merciful, since he does not look to profit, and
10) Never tired to expound the Doctrine.

And again:[631])

The Bodhisattva, the Highest of human beings,
is known to be greatly learned,
perceiving the Absolute Truth, eloquent,
full of compassion and free from lassitude. [27 b.]

Accordingly, (the teacher appears here) as endowed with five distinctive qualities. (He is): —

1) greatly learned, — an advantage as regards the theory,[632])
2) cognizing the Absolute Truth, — an advantage that concerns practice,[633])
3) an eloquent orator,
4) merciful, since his mind is not directed toward material gain,
5) free from lassitude in thought and action.

Moreover, four qualities are known, as follows:[634])

Extensive, clearing doubt, worthy of being heard to, demonstrating the Absolute Truth in two aspects, —
such do we know to be the complement of the teaching (administered by) the Bodhisattvas.

Here (the Bodhisattva is characterized as): –

1) Endowed with great knowledge, by having extensively studied,
2) Clearning the doubts of the converts, by (his) great wisdom
3) Worthy of being accepted as a teacher by being virtuous with regard to the three media (— body, speech, and mind),
4) Demonstrating the Absolute Truth, with a view to the (morally) defiling[635]) and purifying[636]) elements.

All these qualities are usually the (exclusive) attributes of a Saint and it is therefore not easy to become possessed of (all of) them. Three distinctive features, are however indispensable. These are: —

$a_1$) The High Wisdom, that characterizes a learned man,
$b_1$) A mind full of love and compassion,
$c_1$) Virtuous acts.

*The wisdom of a teacher.*

III $Baa_1$. (The teacher must be):

$a_2$) Well versed (in the Doctrine) that is to be expounded,
$b_2$) Skilful, as regards the way of expressing himself,
$c_2$) Experienced, as concerns his behaviour (toward the pupils and knowledge of the natural constitution of the latter).

*The teacher's knowledge of the subject to be taught.*

III B $aa_1a_2$. It is well if one knows thoroughly (all the different subjects of study, or otherwise the three Codes of Scripture, (but this is not all). We need (a teacher) who knows exactly what part (of the Doctrine) is to be taught, and who, with regard to words and sense, gives (good) instructions, that are based upon Scripture and Logic. Such (a teacher) is alone able to clear all the doubts of the pupils.

*Skill in the means of verbal expression.*

III B $aa_1b_2$. (The skill in the way of expressing oneself consists in using) grammatically correct speech, (observing) the three rules of verbal connection, — accordance with the sources, proportion to the compass of teaching[637]) and precision in regard of the contents, — and finally, sweet and agreable language, through which one is able to give pleasure to others. Moreover we read in the *Sūtrālaṁkāra*:[638])

1.[639]) Very eloquent through voice and style,
indicating, analysing, and clearing doubt,
communicating repeatedly, for those, that understand a brief indication,[640])
and those that need a description in detail,[641]) —

2.[642]) The teaching of the Buddhas is pure as regards its three aspects[643]) [28 a] and is known to be free from the following eight defects: —

3.[644]) Indolence, unclear speech, unappropriate speech, want of certainty,
impossibility to clear doubt and to confirm the absence of such,[645])

4.[646]) Lassitude and concealment of the Truth, — such are the defects in speech.
The teaching of the Buddhas, since in possesses none of them, is superior (to all other Doctrines).

(As shows this verse) the teaching must be free from the eight defects (just mentioned) and, consequently, pure, being viewed) from (its) three aspects. Otherwise, as says the *Vyākhyāyukti*,[647]) — twenty methods of communicating the Doctrine, which act as antidotes against eleven defects in speech are to be considered, — as follows: —

1) Teaching at due time. This is an antidote against that defect, which consists in preaching to a person, who by his immoral conduct is unworthy of being taught. This method is observed by teaching only after having become convinced, that (the hearer) really wishes to study and is worthy to receive instruction. My own means of teaching and studying are defective, as regards this (first method); they are therefore without real value and do not attain their aim.[648])

2) Teaching accurately, by admitting no carelessness in speech. This method is directed against the defect of incompleteness.

The following three methods are antidotes against the defect of broken, interrupted speech: —

3) Teaching in regular order,[649]) — by beginning with the communication of (subjects) which, as regards time, are to be mentioned first, namely charity etc., or of high, sublime matters.[650])
4) Teaching in due connection, — with a view to the Sūtra, that is to be explained, and replying to the awkward questions of opponents.
5) Teaching, with a regard (for one's hearers) by giving instructions in accordance with (their) questions, instructions in the form of one categorical answer[651]) etc.

The methods, which act against the defect of unintelligible speech are (likewise) three in number, as follows: —

6) Causing delight to those, that are devoted (to the Doctrine).
7) Arousing the desire (to study) in those that first meet (with the Doctrine) and are hostile to it. [28 b.]
8) Giving satisfaction to those, that are on the way toward apprehension, but are still full of doubt.

The defect in speech, that consists in disregard (for the Doctrine), has the two following antidotes: —

9) Not speaking so as to gratify those, that lead sinful lives, and are therefore unworthy of being pleased.
10) Not abusing (others) who through this become depressed.

An antidote against the defect of incorrect speech is —

11) Having recourse to Logic in never being in conflict with the modes of right cognition.[652])

That defect in speech, which consists in communicating matters of profound meaning to (a pupil) of weak intellectual faculties (unable to understand them) is avoided by —

12) Gradual progress — from the preceeding to the following. Then come: —
13) Precision, — an antidote against the defect of distraction, — by withholding from excourses on other subjects.
14) Dependence on the Doctrine, that is — being in harmony with (the teaching of) virtue. This is an antidote against the defect of (communicating) useless theories.
15) Accordance with the circle of adherents whosoever they might be, — an antidote against ill-suited speech.

The remaining five methods act against the defect of teaching, in being (at the same time) possessed of sinful thoughts. As to the latter, such may be of three kinds, namely, the consideration of oneself to be virtuous and trustworthy, the desire of being honoured and praised, and envy (with regard to the merit of others). The first of these has three antidotes: —

16) A mind full of love,
17) A mind full of desire to help, and
18) A mind full of compassion, — which manifest themselves in the desire (for others) to be happy, dispassionate, and free from suffering; otherwise, with regard to the virtuous, the vicious, and the indifferent, — by (words) full of love etc. respectively, and, in a third way, by wishing (others) to attain Nirvāṇa, to obtain full knowledge of the Path, that leads to it, and to understand completely the meaning of that, which is to be taught.

The antidote against sinful thoughts of the second kind is:

19) Not to look to profit, honour and praise [29 a], — in rejecting the desire (of such).

And of the third: —

20) Not to be inclined to arrogance and depreciation of others, — that is to abandon the desire of being regarded as trustworthy, and to become free from envy.

Of these twenty methods, each group of five, respectively, shows: how, for whose sake, in what form, and by what kind (of teacher) the Doctrine is to be communicated, or otherwise, the course of teaching, its work, the qualities of the speech, and those of the speaker. To follow these twenty methods and to avoid the (eleven) defects in speech is to be skilful in the way of expressing oneself.

### *The conduct and character of the teacher and the pupils.*

III $Baa_1c_2$. (A teacher must be) experienced as concerns his own behaviour, in order to be revered as one, that is virtuous in regard of the three media, — and must likewise perfectly know the natural constitution of (his) pupils, namely, their faculties, character, and inclinations,[653]) — for only by teaching in harmony with such will he attain his aim. It is said in the *Daçacakra-kṣitigarbha*:[654]) —

A worldling, with feeble faculties, and indolent,[655])
Who is not keen upon (the study of) the two Vehicles, —

Will never come to master the teaching[656]) of Mahāyāna,
For he is not worthy of it.

And further on: —

In the same way, if the adherents of the Çrāvaka Vehicle, unworthy of the Great one,
Come to hear the teaching of the latter, —
They will become confused, adhere to nihilistic views and fall into evil births.
For this reason you must teach the Doctrine, only after having examined the faculties of the hearers.

Again: —

It is not proper to preach Hīnayānistic Doctrines
To one that is worthy of the Great Vehicle.

And: —

(Speak not of) matters sublime and of profound meaning to one that adheres to the Small Vehicle.

As show (all these passages), thorough knowledge of the pupil's behaviour or character is needed.

*Love and compassion toward the pupils.*

III B a $b_1$. (The teacher must be) endowed with that quintessence of great Commiseration, which consists in the desire to secure Supreme Enlightenment for all living beings, or if not to such an extent, — at least of Commiseration in teaching without looking to profit and out of the mere wish, that the meaning of the subject, which is taught, might be perfectly understood and be of use (to the hearer). [29 b] By virtue of this Commiseration, one's teaching will attain its aim. It is said in the *Sūtrālaṁkāra:*[657]) —

The powerful ones,[658]) with a joyful heart, ever and anon give away their lives and property, which are hard to obtain and of no real value, for the sake of the suffering living beings, thus practising the highest form of Charity.

How much more will they do so in regard of the High Doctrine,[659]) which administers help to all that lives, always and in every way, is easy to obtain, increases the more you grant of it and never becomes exhausted.

Now, if the teaching has not such a character, a great sin will be committed, namely that of trading with the Doctrine. We read in the *Mañjuçrī-vikurvāṇa-parivarta:*[660]) — If the

Doctrine is expounded, but Commiseration with regard to the pupils is wanting, it will be an action of the Evil One, and if a teacher, being himself greatly learned, conceals (parts of) the Doctrine for fear that others should come to know them, this will be likewise an action of the Evil One.

The *Saṁdhinirmocana*[661]) says: —

Those that teach the Highest Doctrine out of desire (of gain),
Having got their wishes fulfilled, take again and gain.
These infatuated beings, though they are in poss:ssion of
the invaluable jewel of the Doctrine,
Roam about, as if they were beggars.

*Correct methods.*

III $Bac_1$. By endurance, that is by not being liable to depression as regards (the long) wearisome time of teaching and the difficulty of the task, by patiently entering upon all the questions of the pupils, and by resisting the challenges of adversaries in being able to answer them duly, the teacher will be of real help to his hearers. It is said likewise, that tolerance with regard to the faults made by the pupils is needed. This may be fulfilled if one is possessed of that supernatural insight through which one comes to know the amount of help that is to be administered to others. If (this insight) is wanting, one must abstain from preaching to those that are not devoted to the Doctrine and to those that wear insignia and the following five (categories of persons, the teaching to whom is prohibited by the Vinaya[662]) etc. Such persons will be always opposed to a teaching that humiliates them and become full of passion and hatred. Consequently, the preaching and study of the Doctrine, that has such an unfavourable result, cannot be of help for the attainment of felicity and salvation.

From all this we draw the conclusion, that if the Doctrine is communicated by a teacher, that proves perfect (with regard to all that has been said, — [30 a] the latter will be agreeable to the hearers and perfectly attain his aim.

The *Sūtrālaṁkāra* says:[663]) —

Accordingly the Bodhisattva, being wise, free from lassitude, full of compassion, greatly renowned, of virtuous behaviour and a good orator, —

shines, by (the lustre of his) teaching amongst all living beings, as if he were the sun.

*The means of teaching.*

III Bb. In the *Abhidharma-samuccaya,*[664]) fourteen, or from another point ef view, six media of teaching are mentioned, as follows: —

How is the explanation (of the Sacred Texts) to be conducted? (Answer): — In the manner, in which the Sūtras have been exposed (by Buddha), namely, by (communicating): — 1) The subject that must be fully apprehended (— the Truth of Phenomenal Existence)[665]) 2) the true character of it (— impermanence)[666]) 3) the factors conducive to full apprehension (— pure morality etc.)[667]) 4) complete apprehension itself — Enlightenment or the right philosophical view),[668]) 5) its final result (— Nirvāṇa),[669]) 6) Divine Wisdom (— an attribute of one that has attained it).[670])

The fourteen media of teaching are: —

1) The medium of abridged explanation,[671])
2) The medium of concentration (of teaching) upon one subject,
3) The medium of taking recourse to minute details,
4) The medium of (communicating the different degrees of perfection, each of which is respectively the foundation of) higher and still higher (virtues),[672])
5) The medium of exclusion (of all that does not come under the category in question),
6) The medium of changing the meaning of (ordinary) words (into termini technici),
7) The medium of demonstrating matters worldly and unworldly (in regard of each other).[673])
8) The medium of indicating the individual (to whom one intends to teach).
9) The medium of analysis of the stuff (by quadrilemmas etc.).
10) The medium of the six modes.[674]).
11) The medium of (enlarging upon) the full apprehension of the Truth etc.[675])
12) The medium of showing the power (of each word taken separately to indicate an idea) and the impotence, (if one word is omitted, of the others to render the contents intelligible.[676])

13) The medium of repeated teaching, and
14) The medium of evident proofs.

Some works explain (the subject in question) by indicating the aim, the subject-matter in abridged form, and the meaning of words, — others — by demonstrating the general meaning and the details. A certain teacher of the Chim-pa tribe in his turn distinguishes:

1) Demonstration of the meaning,
2) Explanation of (the verbal part of) the text [30 b].
3) Complete ascertainment (as regards both).

1) — First one gives a dry, brief account of the subject (treated in) the text, and then (the true meaning is) ascertained through the communication of the sources, the aim of the composition, and of its subject-matter. Through all this the students will get a clear aspect of the meaning of the text.

2) — Having become acquainted with the principal points by overlooking all the contents (of the text), one has to explain the Doctrine, that is made the subject of study, by removing all the doubtful points, and then to enter upon an investigation of the parts spoken of directly or indirectly. In this way the students will be able to understand completely the verbal part of the text.

3) — Although, in such a way, the meaning (of the text studied) will come to be thoroughly apprehended, nevertheless, some objection from the part of an opponent, who has not been refuted, may be met with, as (for instance): — "in that which has been said, there occurs such and such contradiction, tautology, and absence of (due) connection". Having in view an ignorant opponent, who thinks so, one ought to be ready to give him a due answer, which expells such thoughts, and then, by taking recourse to Scripture and to Logic, — to remove completely every suspicion, as to the opponent's objection being founded. We read in the *Vyākhyāyukti*:[677]) —

Those that communicate the meaning of the Sūtras,
Must explain it (having in view) the aim, the contents in abridged form,
The meaning of the words, the connection between the parts,
The objections (which may be met with) and the reply given to such.

The two last points are to be viewed together, in order that one may know, how to give a good reply. Having first come to know the aim of the Sūtras,[678]) he that is devoted to the study and observation (of the Doctrine) must indicate their aim. As such is to be understood from a brief indication of the contents, one must give such, that is, demonstrate the body of a discourse or an exegetical treatise, — the words and sense, — or, otherwise, the subject-matter condensed. The latter is in its turn apprehended through the knowledge of the (precise) meaning of each word. Therefore, on the basis of the four methods of elucidating the meaning of a word,[679]) one has to explain so as to remove all doubt and after having taken in to consideration all the questions and refutations. Otherwise, one may explain [31 a] the meaning of words by taking recourse to synonyms, homonyms, or to one of the many meanings of a word, by changing ordinary words into termini technici, or by changing the word itself, by omitting, for instance, negative particles etc. Moreover the *Vyākhyāyukti*[680]) says: — The meaning of words may be apprehended in four ways, namely by means of 1) synonyms, 2) definition, 3) etymology, and 4) the varieties (of the character of ideas expressed by such and such word).[681]) Synonyms are other names (given to the same object), the definition is (the indication of) the meaning in which the word is used, and the etymology, — that of the reason for using the term (in the sense which is applied to it). Some consider, that the etymology of a word does not explain its meaning, but this is not correct, because, according to Apraçibha(?), when a word is explained, this can be done in 8 different ways.

The due connection[682]) is the accordance between the preceeding and the following as concerns the meaning and the order (of the words); by it we know, (that our speech) is not contrary to the order in which one word is to follow the other, in regard of its meaning. The absence of contradiction with regard to Logic and disagreement between the preceeding and the following is to be known from the objections, that are made, and the answers, given in return; therefore, having (always) in view an opponent, who attacks words and sense, one must explain so, as to render the latter completely certain and incontrovertible.

*The character of teaching.*

III Bc. One must teach, having in view: —

$a_1$) The students,

$b_1$) The aim,

$c_1$) The manner of conducting the teaching.

*The character of teaching as concerns the students.*

III $Bca_1$. To students (possessed of) acute, mediocre and week intellectual faculties, one must, respectively, explain briefly, moderately, and in detail, just as we have three kinds of Sūtras, — the extensive, the intermediate, and the brief. In accordance with the (spiritual) family[683]) to which the student belongs, one has to teach Mahāyānistic or Hīnāyānistic Doctrines, and with regard to the different wishes of the pupils — that, which proves most suitable.

It is said in the *Samādhirāja*:[684]) —

1.[685]) If they entreat thee to grant the gift of the Doctrine[31b]
Thy first reply must be "I have not studied enough".

2.[686]) „ You all are wise and greatly learned, — how dare I speak
In the presence of such illustrious persons"? — so art thou to say.

3.[687]) Never speak at once, but only when thou seest, that (the hearer) is worthy.
But if thou knowest that, teach, even if they do not pray thee to do so.

4.[688]) If thou shouldst perceive, amongst thy hearers, many that are of immoral conduct,[689])
Do not preach to them abstinence,[690]) but sing the praise of charity.

5)[691]) If there be (others) with scant desire, but who live in pure morality, —
Arouse (in thee) thoughts full of love and speak of abstinence.

6.[692]) If those with sinful desires be few, and the virtuous are great in number, —
Then take thou the part (of the latter) and sing the praise of pure morality.

*The character of teaching as regards the aim.*

III $Bcb_1$. One must give a precise definition of the special aim (of the teaching) that is to be attained, aud teach so, as to lead to the attainment (of this aim).

*The procedure of teaching.*

III $Bcc_1$. (Here we have to distinguish): —

$a_2$) The preparations.

$b_2$) The teaching itself.

$c_2$) The conclusion.

*The preparations.*

III $Bcc_1a_2$. (The teacher must) make the due arrangements, address a prayer to the Three Jewels, and, having banished the Evil One (by means of the charm especially prescribed for this purpose),[693] manifest his great love with regard to all his hearers. It is said in the *Saddharmapuṇḍarīka*:[694]

1.[695] The teacher, when he thinks, that the time is come,
Is to enter the school-house, and, having closed the door,
And taken a review of the Doctrine, in all its parts, —
Is to teach with a mind free from dismay.

2.[696] The sage, always good-tempered and sitting at ease,
Preaches the Doctrine, after having erected
A spacious seat in a clean and agreeable spot.

3.[697] He dresses himself in a clean religious robe, well dyed with exquisite colours [32 a],
Puts on the black mantle and the spacious skirt.

4.[698] Then, on the seat, — a footstool covered with diverse garments, be seats himself,
And having well washed his feet, rises up, anoints head and face,

5.[699] And there, sitting on the preacher's seat, — to the people that have assembled and are full of attention, —
He is to deliver diverse sermons, — for monks and for nuns,

6.[700] For the devotees of the laity, male and female, and likewise for kings and princes.
The teacher must always be free from envy and teach with a sweet voice and on diverse subjects.

7.[701] He must reject all indolence and never be subjected to lassitude,
Become free from uneasiness and meditate upon the power of Love,
(Which he exercises) with regard to his hearers.

8.[702] By day and by night is he to preach the highest of Doctrines in the form of millions of diverse parables,

To gladden and to gratify the hearers, but never to desire anything for himself (in return).

9.[703]) Neither of food or beverage, of garments, a couch, a seat, a religious robe,

Nor even of a remedy, if he is ill, dare he think and accept such from his hearers.

10.[704]) Other must be his thoughts: — "may I and all these living beings attain Enlightenment;

To teach the Doctrine in order to help mankind, — this is the sole foundation of my happiness!"

Moreover we read in the *Sāgaramatiparipṛcchā*:[705]) — [32 b]

Çame! çamavati! çamitaçatrum! aṅkure! maṅkure! mārajiti! karāḍe! keyūre! tejovati! ojasvini viçiṣṭanirmale! malāsane! okhare! khage! grase! grasane! omukhe! parāṅmukhe! varammukhe! — all the bonds of the demons are removed, all the antagonists are vanquished, (we are) released from the chains of the Evil One and stamped with the seal of Buddha, and all the devils are annihilated. May all the works of Māra vanish by virtue of the perfect purity of the Immovable One! Such, o Sāgaramati,[706]) are the words, that vanquish the Evil One and remove all defilement. He, that expounds the Doctrine, must duly recite them and then, having occupied the preacher's seat, let his thoughts full of love (which manifest themselves in the desire) to secure supreme Enlightenment extend over all the circle of hearers. He must think of himself as of a physician, of the Doctrine, — as if it were a remedy, of those, that are to study, — as of patients, and of Buddha, as of the Highest of living beings. Moreover, he has to consider, that the rules of the Doctrine must be established so as to have a long existence. Now, if he teaches the Doctrine, having first uttered the charm (which has been mentioned), — the Evil One and his hosts will not dare to approach him, — in order to divest him from teaching, — within the reach of a hundred miles, and those, who still chance to come near, will not be able to make any disturbance.

And:[707]) — the teacher must be (morally) pure, of virtuous behaviour (outwardly) clean and neatly dressed.

*The teaching by itself.*

III $Bcc_1b_2$. The chief foundations of teaching must be six in number, corresponding to the six transcendental virtues,[708]) — as follows: —

1) Delivering the words and meaning according to one's own conception (=charity).[709])
2) Suppressing the sinful acts of the three media (= morality).[710])
3) Enduring heat, cold, and other odds (= patience).[711])
4) Perseverance in teaching (= energy).[712])
5) Concentration of the mind upon the subject of the latter (= concentration).[713])
6) Analysis in regard of the words and sense, as to their contradiction or right connection etc. (= analytic wisdom).[714]) [33 a]

The teacher Haribhadra[715]) says: — (The harmony with the six transcendental virtues is attained by): —

1) Granting the gift of the Doctrine etc. (= charity).
2) Becoming free from thoughts, that characterise a Hīnayānist[716]) (= morality).
3) Enduring harsh words from all those, with whom one chances to meet (= patience).
4) Arousing the desire to study (= energy).
5) Bringing about the concentration of mind (to a degree), which cannot be attained, if one is a follower of other vehicles (= concentration), and
6) Clothing those, that strive for Supreme Englightenment in the armour of Non-perception (of the reality of separate entities[717]) (= Highest Wisdom).

*The conclusion of study.*

III $Bcc_1c_2$. After having finished teaching, the preceptor must pray all his hearers to forgive the mistakes, which he may have made, pronounce a blessing that all might practise virtue and attain Supreme Enlightenment, and seal all with the seal of the Buddha.

*Characteristic of the methods of study.*

III C. (Here we have to distinguish): —

a) (The character of) the student,

b) The means of study, taken recourse to,
c) The manner of studying.

*The character of the student.*

III Ca. The students may be of three kinds, namely of: —
$a_1$) Acute,
$b_1$) Mediocre, and
$c_1$) Feeble intellectual faculties.

*The students of acute faculties.*

III $Caa_1$. With regard to the first kind we must show: —
$a_2$) The defects, that may be met with a student and are to be avoided, and
$b_2$) The definition of a student as he must be.

*The various defects.*

III $Caa_1a_2$. (We know): —
$a_3$) Thirteen,
$b_3$) Six, and
$c_3$) Three defects, that are to be avoided.

*Thirteen defects.*

III $Caa_1a_2a_3$. The *Vyākhyāyukti*[718]) mentions sixteen methods of study, that act as antidotes against thirteen defects. The latter are as follows: —

1) Disturbing the teacher, when he contemplates the subject to be expounded, and indecent behaviour (in general).
2) Showing arrogance, being proud of (one's own) high birth etc.
3) Showing no real desire to study.
4) Becoming oppressed at heart by disagreeing views.
5) Having no regard for the teacher, and
6) Thinking, how to make some objection in order to refute him, — both out of disrespect.
7) Want of reverence in having no consideration for the merits of the Doctrine and of him, that teaches it. [33 b]
8) Showing contempt for the Doctrine and the teacher by considering the former to be unconnected speech and, as regards the latter, by finding fault with him, his morals, behaviour, outward appearance, the way of expressing himself etc.
9) Using abusive language,
10) Looking to profit and honour,

11) Not listening duly, being distracted or plunged in apathy and sleepiness,
12) Not comprehending duly, by having incorrect views of the meaning and the essence of the Doctrine.
13) Not paying the due attention, — one's desire (to study) and efforts being to feeble.

*Six defects.*

III $Caa_1a_2b_3$. The *Vyākhyāyukti*[719]) says:

Arrogance, want of faith,
Absence of desire (to study),
Distraction, apathy,
And lassitude, such may be the defects[720]) of the student.

Otherwise[721]) (we distinguish): —

1) The defects in one's acts,
2) Absence of faith,
3) Disrespect,
4) Unappropriate thoughts,
5) Discord, and
6) The defects in apprehending.

As concerns the defects in one's actions, such may be corporeal, — immoral behaviour, oral and corporeal, — not making the due efforts with both body and speech, and mental — want of desire to study.

The defects, that consist in unappropriate thoughts, are, — to seek brawls and to think how to escape a controversy.

The defects (arising from) discord are five in number, — absence of reverence for the Doctrine by not taking it to be the Path, that leads to Salvation, and for the Word of it, considering such to be unconnected speech etc., disregard for the teacher, by finding fault with him, his conduct and the manner of teaching, contempt for (the teacher's) descent, and, last of all, self-deprecation, in thinking oneself unable to understand the meaning of the Doctrine and to act according to the latter.

The defects in apprehending are likewise five: — apprehending wrongly, getting no clear conception of the meaning, [34 a] misunderstanding the words, disregarding the grammatical forms, and getting no full apprehension (of the matter).

*Three defects.*

III $Caa_1a_2c_3$. A vessel, in which one intends to gather water, when it rains, may have three defects, which render it unable to exercise its function. It may 1) be turned downward or closed with a lid, the water having no entrance, 2) be dirty, so that the water, though it enters, will become polluted, and 3) may have a hole and through this be unable to retain the water. In the same way the vessel, that does not receive the rain of the Doctrine, when such descends, may be defective in three ways:

1) The hearer may not listen at all, being distracted or plunged in apathy, and (the Word of the Doctrine) will not reach him.

2) If one does not-listen with the due attention (the Words of the Doctrine), though they reach one, are in danger of being perverted.

3) If one is forgetful, that which has been heard, will not be retained in memory.

"As an antidote against all this", says the Lord, "study thoroughly and be attentive".

Otherwise, we may compare (those, that do not study as it is prescribed) to patients, who do not understand the directions of the physician, to those, that understand them wrongly, and to those, who, though they have understood them, waste the remedy, that is given to them. Again, they are like patients, that do not eat, when they should do so, like those, that eat what is unwholesome, and like those, who, though they have eaten wholesome food, vomit it back again. Therefore, the teacher, that knows the character (of his students) must, if they become distracted, speak so as to frighten them (in showing them the fatal consequences of their behaviour) as follows: —

The age of man, that dures a hundred years,
Is reduced to the half by night's sleep,
And if we sleep by day likewise, —
Even this half will be diminished.

And to such, that are overpowered by sleep, he must, in order to arouse their attention, tell curious and amusing tales, — of the ass and the foal, the lion and the fox, the elder-man and the woman, the old woman and the thief, of Paraçurāma etc.[722]).

*The definition of a student.*

III $Caa_1b_2$. It is said in the *Catuḥçataçāstra-kārikā*:[723]) —

One, that is sincere, desirous (to study) and intelligent,
Is fit to be called a good student.

Accordingly we have to consider: —

$a_3$) The intellectual power, through which one is able to understand (the subject studied),

$b_3$) The zeal of one, that strives (for knowledge),

$c_3$) The due reverence (with regard to the teacher and the Doctrine).

*The student's intelligence.*

III $Caa_1b_2a_3$. (The student) must (fully) understand the subject studied in order that the latter might (in reality) become an antidote against passions and lead to the attainment of Nirvāṇa. Vasubandhu[724]) says: —

Three factors render leather fit for use, namely, greasing, tanning, and drying (in the sun). In a like way the spirit (is rendered fit for entering upon the Path of Salvation) through study, analysis, and profound meditation. Consequently, in order to bring about such a state of the spirit, one must be keen upon study etc. By the aid of three expedients, travellers may easily make their journey by a rocky lofty mountain-road. These expedients are: —(sufficient) victuals, a (good) carriage, and a (trustworthy) guide. In the same way those, that travel on the hard, inhospitable path of this worldly existence, may easily do so, if they are endowed with the force of charity, morals, and High Wisdom. These three, in their turn, all of them depend on study.

*The desire to study.*

III $Caa_1b_2b_3$. It is said in the Sūtras: — By ten means must one strive to attain the virtues of the Bodhisattvas. — What are these ten? — (Answer: —) To seek for the Doctrine with a sincere mind, free from craft and deceit, — and so on.

*Reverence.*

III $Caa_1b_2c_3$. The great commentary (of Haribhadra on the *Aṣṭasāhasrikā*[725]) says: — One must study with the best intentions.[726]) This means, that one must take off the hat, seat oneself on a low seat, become free from the defect of distraction and study the Highest Doctrine with the desire to attain Salvation.

*The hearer of mediocre faculties.*

III $Cab_1$. These distinctive features (of a good student) cannot be found (with all the hearers). Still, if those, that are not possessed of them, come to hear the Doctrine and are able (to a certain extent) to understand its meaning, they will greatly profit [35a.].

The *Vyākhyāyukti*[727]) says: If those, that have accumulated all the factors (for the attainment of perfection), hear even a little (of the Doctrine), they will reap great merit. For instance, as the Saint Çāriputra was giving his instructions to the newly ordained monks, a certain Brāhmaṇa, sitting concealed in the neighbourhood, listened to him. Having heard the Saint's words: — "He, that enters the religious order, but still continues to lead an immoral life, will be subjected to suffering of twelve kinds," — the Brāhmaṇa abstained from his inclination toward sinful deeds. Moreover, (we know that) when Sangharakṣita preached the Doctrine, the anchorites who secretly listened to him, reaped the fruit of Arhatship.

*The hearer of feeble faculties.*

III $Cac_1$. (There may be such) that do not understand at all the meaning of that, which they hear. However, if they but listen full of devotion, they likewise attain great merit. It is said:[728]) Even those, that do not understand the words they hear, must devotedly listen to the word of Buddha. Indeed, if one but only listens full of faith, one becomes possessed of great virtues and gives increase to the element of Highest Wisdom (the germs of which exist in every being). How much more, consequently, will this be with one, who understands that, which he hears. We must only take the story[729]) of Nanda,[730]) the cowherd, who (unconsciously) trampled with his stick upon a frog (uttering all the while the name of Buddha. The frog, through hearing such, reaped merit in the following birth). And:[731]) — Dharmananda[732]) having been reborn as a sea-monster, shut his jaws, from merely hearing the name of

Buddha, (that was uttered by the mariners passing by, and did not swallow them up with their ship), because in his previous existence he was accustomed to make his salutation to Buddha. Therefore, since those, that have accumulated all the factors (for attaining perfection), greatly augment their virtues, even if they hear but a little of the Doctrine, — one must in any case devotedly listen to the word of Buddha.

*The means of study.*

III Cb. The *Bodhisattva-piṭaka*[733]) says: —

The two causes and the two conditions,
By which living beings attain (moral) purification,
Are agreeable speech with regard to others, [35 b]
And, as concerns oneself, the right philosophical point of view.

Accordingly, the external conditions are: — reliance upon the teacher,[734]) and providing oneself with the due necessaries of life. The internal conditions are, — to listen attentively, enter upon an analysis of the subject studied and render it completely clear with the help of the Sūtras and exegetical treatises, and by addressing questions to those, that are competent. Consequently one must bring study to complete achievement, and then exert oneself in profound meditation. We read in the *Vyākhyāyukti*:[735]) — As limestone is burnt with fire and then slaked by water, so is the stone of the residue[736]) of passions consumed by the fire of Highest Wisdom and then, slaked by the waters of profound meditation, is completely done away with. This High Wisdom cannot be obtained without having studied the Highest Doctrine, — therefore, listen devotedly to the Word of Buddha.

He, that merely bears the burden of words, without understanding (their) meaning, will never attain his aim, just as the boy, who had a paper with a testament (putting him in possession of) a treasury, fastened it to his neck (and did not know, what its contents was). Therefore, although one may have studied a great deal, still in order to get complete comprehension (of the subject), one must devotedly listen to (the explanation of) the meaning of the Sūtras. The sentinel, who does not look attentively about, but (contents himself) with saying: — I am awake, — is at length killed by robbers. Just in the same way one, that has studied much, but only pays attention to the words, without analysing (their meaning) will be soon overpowered by his enemies, the passions. As accurate analysis is itself impossible without the thorough knowledge (of the subject studied), one must strive to get a clear aspect of its meaning. We may give another example (to illustrate the failure of those, that pay attention only to the verbal part), namely musicians, who being afraid of robbers, sing in order to remain awake, and are nevertheless killed by the robbers. As a blind man, that holds a lamp, administers help only to others (but not to himself) [36 a], so is one, who has studied and knows the words, but has no clear knowledge of their meaning. Therefore, exclusively for the sake of apprehending this meaning, one must zealously listen to its explanation.

*The manner of studying.*

III Cc. (We distinguish): —

$a_1$) The preparations,
$b_1$) The study itself,
$c_1$) The conclusion.

*The preparations.*

III $Cca_1$. 1) (One must) first of all think, how to realize (the aim of) the Doctrine, as it is said (in the *Jātakas*:[737]) — The realization, which follows study, must be regarded as most important.

2) (The student's) behaviour must be characterized by devotion, in paying reverence (to the teacher and the Doctrine) by one's acts, speech and thoughts. We read in the *Jātakas*:[738]) —

Sitting on the lowest of seats, showing the splendour of self-discipline,
Looking with a sight full of joy, as one, that enjoys the nectar of the Word,
(The student), with thoughts full of reverence, concentrated, clear, and free from defilement,
Having made his salutations, — is to listen to the Doctrine as a patient to the instructions of the physician.

3) (One must) meditate upon that bliss, which is caused by the accumulation of (the factors and) conditions (for the attain-

ment of Nirvāṇa). It is said in the *Tathāgata-acintya-guhya-nirdeça*:[739]) —

Seldom does a Buddha appear in this world,
And seldom may birth in a human form be obtained as the result of previous virtue,
Alas! the study of the Doctrine, and faith are things (likewise) hard to obtain,
Even during a hundred aeons.

And the *Lalitavistara*[740]) says: —

Human birth and the appearance of a Buddha (in this world) is not easy to be met with,
And so are likewise the attainment of faith, avoidance of the eight unfavourable states of existence,[741]) and the opportunity to study the Doctrine.
At present, — the Buddha has appeared, and the favourable state of existence, faith, and the possibility to study the Doctrine are all of them secured.
Therefore — do away with all distraction.
There may come a time, whe[n] for millions and millions of aeons, —
It will not be [illegible] to hear (the word of) the Doctrine,
Therefore, since you may obtain it now, give up all distraction.

However, we read in the *Vyākhyāyukti*:[742]) —

The Word of Buddha, the opportunity to hear it,
The desire (to study) [36 b], wisdom, and the absence of impediments —
These four are hard to be obtained.
Therefore listen to the Word of Buddha (when it is possible).

And:[743]) —

If a living being dies, will he (in his next birth) meet with the Jewel of the Doctrine or not,
Will he come to study the Doctrine,
And will there be one, that explains it to him, — no one can tell.
Therefore, at present you must zealously listen to the words of the Teacher.

Again:[744]) —

If one exists in the phenomenal world,[745]) one is inevitably reborn,

But this new life usually passes away in vain, for
The Perfect Word (that shows us the right way) is seldom to be heard here.
It is rare as the flower of the Udumbara.

*The study itself.*

III $Cb_1$. (The study itself) must be in harmony with the six transcendental virtues. (One must): —

1) Consecrate the three media to the service of the Doctrine (= charity).
2) Suppress sinful inclinations and remove all the defects (that hinder one to become) a worthy receptacle of the Doctrine (= morality),
3) Endure odds (= patience),
4) Be zealous in study (= energy),
5) Concentrate the mind upon words and sense (= concentration),
6) (As concerns the Climax of Wisdom, distinguish): — The highest degree — the attainment of transcendental knowledge, the intermediate, — apprehension, preservation in memory and analysis, in following the word, and the lowest, — the five immeasurable feelings.

*The conclusion.*

III $Ccc_1$. (When the teaching is finished, the student must) pray the teacher to forgive his mistakes, pronounce a blessing, and render his thanks.

*The instructions for realizing the aim of the Doctrine.*

III D. In order that study and analysis might have an effective result, —

He, that has studied and gives himself up to analysis,
Must live in pure morality and practise profound meditation.

Accordingly, pure morals are needed, in order to act as a support (for him, that is to realize the aim of the Doctrine). It is said in the *Samādhirāja*:[746])

If he, that has become well versed in numerous works on the Doctrine,
Is proud of his knowledge and does not preserve his morals,
He will not be able to save others by his great learning,
And, morally impure, he is doomed to hell.

(Accortingly) extensive study must always be connected with pure morals and analysis of the meaning and profound meditation It is said in a passage of Scripture concerning the monks who have got a firm stand in the principles of the Doctrine[747]): — [37 a] By study and analysis only, without the practice of meditation, one is unable to get a firm stand in the Doctrine. Likewise is this impossible, if one merely practises meditation and does not take recourse to study and investigation. But if both parts (study on one side and analysis and meditation on the other) are resorted to and accepted as a foundation, one gets a firm stand in the Doctrine.

Moreover, the *Sūtrālaṁkāra*[748]) says: —

Therefore, the meditation of the Saints, can never be fruitless,
Therefore the teaching of the Buddhas can never be useless, —
Useless would be meditation, if reality were perceived through mere study, and
Senseless would be the teaching, if one could practise meditation without having studied.

Therefore, in order to have an antidote against perverse conduct, which is the foundation and the cause of much suffering, we must watch over our morals and make all our efforts, to become purified from sin. The gradual order in which this is to be attained is demonstrated by Çāntideva,[749]) as follows:

Be patient, strive to obtain study,
Then, betake thyself to the forest,
And, having concentrated thy mind,
Meditate upon the impurity (of all that arouses our passions).

Accordingly, first of all, we must become possessed of endurance (with regard to the odds that may be met with). If such endurance is wanting, the aversion (toward this worldly existence) will never arise and one will never enter upon the study (of the Doctrine that delivers from this existence). And, if one has not studied, one cannot come to know the means for doing away with all the passions, which is concentration of mind. Consequently, we must strive to obtain learning. But, if one is contented with having studied and leads a dissolute life, the concentration of mind can never be brought about, and, as says the *Candrapradīpa*[750]) —

— Addressed with words, that harmonize with the Doctrine,

Those that follow the usage of worldings, show (in return) wrath, hate, and disbelief [37 b]
And, though they understand the meaning (of the Doctrine), they have no faith in it.

Therefore one must abstain from making friends with the worldlings, and repair to a solitary forest, as we read (in the *Bodhicaryāvatāra*:[751]) —

In the woods, the beasts, the birds, and the trees do not utter harsh, abusive words,
O, when shall I come to live among them, with whom it is easy to make friends[752])!

Then, one must make all one's efforts to attain concentration of mind, for if one does not become free from distraction, one will never come to practise profound meditation. As the result of this meditation is to be the complete purification from all the passions, one must meditate upon the impurity etc. (of all that arouses them).

Again, if one, who has studied much, does not fulfill (the precepts of the Doctrine), he will commit a great sin. The *Ugraparipṛcchā*[753]) says: — If one, that is greatly learned, meets with the complement of conditions (for attaining salvation), but, nevertheless, continues to be attached to worldly property etc. and does not purify his mind, he will remain alone and will deceive all living beings, including the gods.

And in the *Ratnakūṭa*[754]) we read: — O Kāçyapa, just as some, that are borne by the waves of the ocean, may (at the same time) die of thirst, in a like way, O Kāçyapa, some Brāhmaṇas and ascetics, having studied many religious works and mastered them completely, are still unable to appease the thirst of desire, hatred and infatuation. Thus, although they are borne by (the waters of) the ocean of the Doctrine, they perish from the thirst, caused by passions and fall into evil births. — Consequently,[755]) since the preaching of the Doctrine with one's lips, without any practical application, as I do it, is worthless, one must regard this practical application, as the most important (part of the matter). It is said in the *Adhyāçaya-saṁcodana-sūtra*:[756]) —

1.[757]) Proud of one's great learning [38 a],
One is full of disregard (toward others),
Indulges in dispute and controversy,

Is forgetful and has no clear understanding.
Such are the defects of him, who takes delight in inane oratory.

2.[758]) One is far from having deep thoughts,
One's outward appearance and mind lose their serenity,
As one is (alternatively) subjected to great arrogance and humiliation[759]).
Such are . . . . .

3.[760]) The worldling loses all consideration for the Highest Doctrine,
Is harsh and has no thoughts of love,
And is far from (possessing) concentration of mind and transcendental knowledge.
Such are . . . . . . .

4.[761]) He is always irreverent with regard to the teachers,
And, finding pleasure in obscene tales,
Pays attention to that which is worthless,
And becomes destitute of High Wisdom.
Such are . . . . . . .

5.[762]) He is not esteemed by the gods and the spirits,
Nor has he any desire to obtain (such esteem),
And, as to correct knowledge, he possesses none.
Such are . . . . . . .

6.[763]) He is always reproved by the wise,
To whom his nature is perfectly clear;
His life passes away in vain.
Such are . . . . . .

7.[764]) The worldling laments at the hour of death,
(Saying): "I have not attained any positive result, what am I to do now?"
He suffers greatly by not having partaken of the deeper (sense of life).
Such are . . . . . . .

8.[765]) He is wavering like grass agitated (by the wind),
Is always full of doubt,
And never may call a firm conviction his own.
Such are . . . . . . .

9.[766]) Like an actor on the stage,
That speaks of the heroism of others, [38 b]

He has no prowess of his own.
Such are . . . . . . .

10.[767]) He becomes fraudulent and easily loses hope[768])
Again and again he enters upon dispute and controversy,
And draws far from the Highest Doctrine of the Saint.
Such are . . . . . . .

11.[769]) Feeble in strength, one rejoices to praise,
And, destitute of right knowledge, trembles when abused.
One's mind is fickle like a monkey.
Such are . . . . . . .

12.[770]) As one's mind is not possessed of correct knowledge,
One commits errors or depends on others,
And (finally) falls a prey to the passions.
Such are . . . . . . .

13. One's visual sense is deluded, and so is the auditory,
The olfactory sense errs and so does the gustatory,
The tactile sense and the intellect are likewise erring.
Such are . . . . . . .

14. One's mind being always in the power of auditory sensation,
One is intoxicated by (well-sounding) words and acquires no true knowledge,
Thinks incorrectly and enters upon evil paths.
Such are . . . . . . .

Having described (all these defects, the Sūtra continues): —

15.[771]) Having, for a long time, found pleasure in fine words,
One does not obtain real satisfaction, for
It is better to ponder over (the meaning of) one word,
Through which one may obtain infinite joy.

16.[772]) The bark of the sugar-cane (by itself) has no value, for
That which gives pleasure, its sweet juice, is contained within.
If one eats only the bark, one is not able
To taste the exquisite juice of sugar.

17.[773]) The (mere) words (by themselves) are like the bark,
And the meaning contained in them, — like the sweet juice.
Therefore, having ceased to find pleasure in (the mere sound of) fine words,
Ponder over the meaning and always be attentive.
All these methods (of studying and preaching the Doctrine),
Buton with the large mouth [39 a] who has studied much,
But has neither realized that, which he has learned

Nor accumulated the factors (for attaining salvation), — has written down.
May he (nevertheless) by (the force of) previous virtues,
After his death, which will soon take place,
Partake of Maitreya's religious feast in the regions of Tuṣita.

Finished the investigation of the methods of study and teaching, the first chapter of the History of Buddhism, entitled "The Jewellery of Scripture".

## Book II. (Part IV). [39 a. 2.]

### The History of Buddhism.

The main subject of this fourth subdivision will be the history of Buddhism, — (a description of): —

IV A. The way, in which the Doctrine took its origin in this world in general, and —

IV B. How it appeared in the country of Tibet — particularly.

### IV A. The Rise of Buddhism and its Development in India.

When the Bodhisattva brings to accomplishment the accumulation of merit, or, otherwise, when the sphere of his activity (as a Buddha[774]) has become completely pure, and when the roots of virtue in the converts have attained maturity, then the Buddha appears (in his chosen world) and expounds his Doctrine.

(There are many Buddhas, that have already appeared during the different aeons, and many that are still to come, so we have to distinguish): —

a) The aeons, in which the Buddhas appear — in general,
b) The rise of Buddhas during the Fortunate Aeon[775]),
c) The appearance of the Highest of Sages (the Buddha Çākyamuni) in this world of suffering,[776]) — the most particular (subject of our narrative).

*The different Aeons.*

IV Aa. The different aeons are to be divided into the bright and the dark ones. The former are those, that are marked by the appearance of Buddhas, and the latter, those, during which no Buddhas arise. In the bright aeon, which is called the Fortunate (that, in which we live), the (number of) Buddhas (that have already come and are still to appear), is 1000 or 1005.[777]) (The Fortunate Aeon) is to be followed by 60 great dark aeons. Then there will come a great bright aeon, named Mahāyaças[778]) and during it 10,000 Buddhas (will arise). Thereafter 10,000 dark aeons will pass away, and will be succeeded by the bright aeon, call the Starlike, with 80,000 Buddhas. 300 dark aeons will then follow, and, after they have passed away, the bright age named Guṇavyūha[779]) will come, during which 84,000 Buddhas are to appear. So says the *Bhadrakalpika-sūtra.*[780])

*The rise of Buddhas during the Fortunate Aeon.*

IV A b. (Here we meet with) two (versions): —

$a_1$) The rise of 1005 Buddhas according to the *Karuṇā-puṇḍarīka*[781]) [39 b], and

$b_1$) That of 1000 Buddhas according to the *Tathāgata-acintya-guhya-nirdeça.*[782])

*The version of the Karuṇāpuṇḍarīka.*

IV Aba$_1$. In olden times, when the great aeon named Dhāraṇa[783]) was lasting in this world, there lived a king, whose name was Araṇemi,[784]) — a universal sovereign,[785]) ruling over all the four continents. (This king) had a thousand sons, Animiṣa[786]) and the rest, and was the Lord Paramount of 84,000 tributary sovereigns. His chief household priest[787]) was the Brāhmaṇa Samudrareṇu,[788]) who had 80 sons and 1000 young Brāhmaṇas for his pupils. One of (the eighty) sons, the Brāhmaṇa Samudragarbha,[789]) attained Supreme Enlightenment (and became) a Buddha, known by the name of Ratnagarbha.[790]) The great sovereign Araṇemi worshipped (this Buddha uninterruptedly) for three months and so did each of his 1000 sons, 250 years and 3 months having passed away in this manner.

Then (the Buddha's) father, the Brāhmaṇa Samudrareṇu worshipped him for seven years, and after having heard the Doctrine from him, he had a dream.[791]) He saw, that the king Araṇemi was eating (the flesh of) many living beings and was (finally) himself devoured by wild beasts, tigers etc.[792]) He saw likewise some (of the king's) ministers who, mounted on chariots, were intending to travel by a wrong way.[793]) Having beheld these and many other (visions, Samudrareṇu) asked the Buddha the meaning (of each of them). The Buddha prophesied, that the king would be greatly attached to his royal power, commit sinful deeds, and through this fall into evil births and (perpetually) abide in the Saṁsāra, that his ministers would become Çrāvakas and Pratyekabuddhas[794]), and that others would attain Enlightenment. [40 a.] Thereupon, the Brāhmaṇa (went to the king) and said: "O Great Sovereign, it is not easy to become born in human form, meet with the appearance of a Buddha and with the favourable conditions (for entering upon the Path of Salvation). Therefore,[795]) make thy initial vow for the attainment of Supreme Enlightenment". The king, thus addressed, replied: — "I have no desire to attain Enlightenment and to become a Buddha. (I am too much attached to this worldly existence)[796])" — such was the motive, which he put forth for his refusing to make the initial vow. The Brāhmaṇa summoned him again and again, and the king finally promised to make the vow, if he could obtain a sphere of activity (as a Buddha), that would suit him.[797]) Thereafter, the Buddha Ratnagarbha became absorbed in the meditation called Ādarça-vyūha,[798]) and then, after he had (miraculously) demonstrated the great multitude of worlds of Buddhaic activity, (the Brāhmaṇa Samudrareṇu) summoned the king to choose the world, which pleased him most.[799]) The king, having obtained faith, (returned to his city), entered his palace, and, having forbidden the people to disturb him, gave himself up to thoughts, how to secure the world (in which he was to become a Buddha). His example was followed by all his 1000 sons.

In the meanwhile, the Brāhmaṇa Samudrareṇu converted a great number of living beings to (the teaching of) Highest Virtue.[800]) After seven years had passed away, the king, invited by the gods, set out with all his attendants, and, having come in the presence of the Buddha Ratnagarbha, he beheld his world of Buddhaic activity and made his initial vow. Then the Buddha uttered a prophecy (by the force of which) the king was to become the Buddha Amitāyus[801]) in the regions of Sukhavatī.[802]) (The king's) eldest son, Animiṣa,[803]) was, — after Amitāyus' attaining Nirvāṇa and on the very morn, that is to follow the eve, when his Doctrine would cease to exist, — [40b.] to be the Buddha named Samanta-raçmy-abhyudgata-çrīkūṭarāja.[804]) After his attaining Nirvāṇa the second son, —(prophesied up to that time to be the Bodhisattva) Mahāsthāmaprāpta[805]) — was to attain Buddhahood under the name of Supratiṣṭhita-guṇa-maṇi-kūṭa-rāja.[806]) The third son was to be (the Bodhisattva) Mañjuçrī, (and subsequently) — the Buddha Samantadarçin[807]) in the region called Çuddha-virajaḥ-saṁnicaya[808]). The fourth was to be Samantabhadra,[809]) the fifth — Padmottara[810]), the sixth — Dharma-vaçavartīçvara-rāja,[811]) the seventh — Prabhāsa-virajaḥ-samucchraya-gandheçvara-rāja[812]) and the eighth — Jñāna-vajra-viṣkambhiteçvara-ketu.[813]) At the same time 10,000 living beings likewise received the prophecy of future Buddhahood. Then came the ninth son, who was to be the Buddha Akṣobhya,[814]) the tenth — Suvarṇapuṣpa,[815]) and the eleventh — Jayasoma.[816]) In such a way all the 1000 princes, the 84,000 tributary sovereigns and 920,000,000 living beings more, the 80 sons of Samudrareṇu, his 1000 pupils and 30,000,000 Brāhmaṇas were foretold to become Buddhas, — (a long series ending with the Buddhas) Vipaçyin,[817]) Çikhin,[818]) and Viçvabhuj.[819]) Next came 1000 Brāhmaṇas, who recited the Vedas. The first of these having received the prophecy, such was likewise granted to the second, Jyotiḥpāla,[820]) who was to be Krakucchanda,[821]) the first Buddha of the Fortunate Aeon, to the third, Tamburu, who was to be Kanakamuni,[822]) to the fourth — Viçvagupta — the Buddha Kāçyapa[823]) [41 a] and to the fifth — Vimalavaiçāyana.[824]) The latter was to become the future Buddha Maitreya.[825]) In the same way all the other (Brāhmaṇa scholars) received the prophecy of Buddhahood, up to the 999th. Then the Brāhmaṇa Samudrareṇu said to the last of the scholars: — choose thy sphere of activity and make thy initial vow. The scholar (whose name was Mahābalavegadhārin) prayed him to wait a while, and after the five attendants[826]) of Samudrareṇu had chosen their spheres of activity, taken their vows, and were foretold to become Buddhas of the Fortunate Aeon, — he went to the Buddha Ratnagarbha and asked: — O Lord, will there be many Buddhas (that resemble) the sun (by their lustre) — in this Fortunate Aeon?[827]) The Buddha replied: — The Sages resembling the sun that are to appear, will be 1004 in number.[828]) (Mahābalavegadhārin) then made the following entreaty:[829]) — May I live as long as all these 1004 Buddhas resembling the sun, all of them taken together and may the number of my disciples be as great, as that of all of them, taken together. The Buddha Ratnagarbha) gave his approval, saying: — Well hast thou spoken, — and prophesied that (Mahābalavegadhārin) would become the Buddha Roca.[830])

After all this had taken place, the Brāhmaṇa Samudrareṇu began to ponder: — The great king and many other living beings have made their initial vow and accepted each their pure world of Buddhaic activity. The time is come for me to make likewise my initial vow.

So thought he, and, full of great commiseration, looked upon the impure world of suffering and the living beings therein harsh and cruel, living in the ten vices, committing the five inexpiable sins[831]) and hard to convert, — and made 500 great vows, that he would lead them to the Path of Salvation. And, his words being full of the power of truth, the Buddha Ratnagarbha approved them, saying: — Well said. — The energy of the Bodhisattvas manifests itself in four ways, and one of them is to make a vow (for the conversion of) a (suffering), impure world. [41 b.] Thou art a Bodhisattva, who resembles a white lotus, whereas the others are but ordinary flowers. — Thus he praised him greatly and prophesied him to be the fourth Buddha of the Fortunate aeon — Çākyamuni.[832]) Thereupon all the Buddhas in the ten quarters of the sky offered their gifts and all living beings, gods and men, worshipped (the future Buddha.

After that the Buddha Ratnagarbha passed away into Nirvāṇa and a monument harbouring his relics was erected and worshipped for 360,000,000 years. The Brāhmaṇa Samudrareṇu entered the religious order and lived in seclusion for twenty thousand years. Such is the account concerning the rise of 1005 Buddhas during the Fortunate aeon.

*The version of the Tathāgatācintyaguhyanirdeça.*

IV.Abb$_1$. In olden times, during the aeon of the Beautiful Light[833]) there appeared in the country, called Vibhūṣita (?))[834]) the Buddha Anantaguṇanānāratnavyūharāja (?)[835]). At that time, in his palace called Viçuddhimatī (?)[836]) — there dwelt a universal sovereign, Dhṛtarāṣṭra,[837]) whose power extended over all the four continents and who had 700,000 queens and 1000 sons.[838]) This king zealously worshipped the Buddha and his congregation of monks for 10,000,000 years and made to each of the monks a present of three slaves.[839]) At that time the young princes (became full of the desire to attain Enlightenment) and amongst them the following verse became current:[840]) —

Seldom does a Buddha appear in this world,
Birth in human form is hard to be secured,
And as to friends, that have faith and study the Doctrine,
Such may scarcely be met with, even during 100 aeons.

And once, when the king, with his wives and sons was sitting in his palace, built of the finest sandal wood[841]), [42 a] he was (miraculously) raised up to the skies and came to sit in the presence of the Buddha, who expounded his doctrine to him[842]) saying: — O great monarch, thou must never lose faith and constantly abide on sublime paths.[843]) The king, after having heard him, returned to his palace, and at the time when the moon was in full glance, his two wives Aninditā (?)[844]) and Anupamā (?)[845]) bore him each a son, the former — Dharmacetas (?),[846]) and the latter — Dharmamati.[847]) With these two (new born sons) the king continued to listen to the Doctrine delivered by the Buddha. Once the following thought came to the king: — All these my sons will certainly attain Enlightenment, but I am still eager to know, who of them will first become a Buddha. Accordingly, he wrote down the names of all the young princes and deposited (the billets) in a precious urn, made of the seven kinds of jewels. Seven days the king abided in uninterrupted prayer, and then, in the presence of the queens, the 1000 sons and the two newlyborn infants, a near relative of the king drew out the billets, containing the names of the princes.[848]) The name of Viçuddhamati[849]) was the first to appear and the trembling of the earth and sounds of (celestial) music announced, that he was to become the Buddha Krakucchanda.[850])

Next came: —

The prince Vijayasena[851]) who was to be Kanakamuni.[852])
,, ,, Çāntendriya (?)[853]) who was to be Kāçyapa.[854])
,, ,, Sarvārthasiddha[855]) who was to be Çākyamuni.[856])
,, ,, Mekhalin (?)[857]) who was to be Maitreya.[858])
,, ,, Çreṣṭhamati (?)[859]) who was to be Siṁha.[860])

The prince Vidyuddeva (?)[861] who was to be Ketu.[862]
„ „ Bhadrarāja (?)[863] who was to be Puṣpottama.[864]
„ „ Prabhāçrī (?)[865] who was to be Puṣpa.[866]
„ „ Vairocanapadma (?)[867] who was to be Nakṣatrarāja.[868]
„ „ Vimalaprabha[869] who was to be Sulocana.[870]
„ „ Virajas[871] who was to be Subāhu.[872]
„ „ Matirāja[873] who was to be Prabha.[874]
„ „ Puṇyavyūharāja (?)[875] who was to be Jyotīrāma.[876]
„ „ Digbhūti (?)[877] who was to be Abhyudgata.[878]
„ „ Viçuddhavyūharāja (?)[879] who was to be Guṇottama.[880]
„ „ Çrīgupta[881] who was to be Dhanaçrī.[882]
„ „ Suvibhaktakāya[883](?) who was to be Jñānākara.[884]
„ „ Ugra[885] who was to be Ratnākara,[886] and
„ „ Ratnakīrti[887] who was to be Samantaprabhāsa.[888]

(Thus the names appeared one by one) up to Uṣṇīṣālaṁkṛta,[889] who was to be the Buddha Anantaguṇakīrti[890] and the two youngest sons — the princes Anantabuddhikīrti[891] and Anantamati.[892] The elder relatives and brothers said to the latter: — What will there remain for thee to do, after we have converted all the living beings and brought to accomplishment all the Buddhaic achievements? — Thus they scorned him, but he replied in return:[893] —

The virtues of the Buddhas are (as infinite) as the skies,
And as to the number of living beings, such, I think, will never be exhausted.
May I, by virtue of pure morality, be able to make my vows
And ye all (that are present) listen to them.
O kings of virtue, may I live as long,
As will be the lives of all of you (taken together).
And fulfill all the vows, which you all are to observe.
May the congregation of my disciples be as great in number,
As (all your congregations) taken together.

Thus speaking, he, the youngest of the 1000 princes, (secured future Buddhahood) under the name of Rocana[894] — the Desirous. He was to be called so, because he wished a duration of life and a number of converts equal to that of 999 Buddhas. Thereupon the 1000 princes asked the two infants [43 a], — Dharmacetas and Dharmamati, — of what kind would be their vows. Dharmacetas, in return, made the following entreaty: — may I become the Bearer of the Sceptre of all of you, act in secret, prevent the exposition of all, that is to remain concealed as regards the Buddhas, and study, believe in and fully apprehend all the exoteric and esoteric doctrines (of the Buddhas.[895]) He was thus destined to become the Bodhisattva Vajrapāṇi, the compiler of Scripture for all the 1000 Buddhas, and in a future aeon, called the Completely Enlighted, in the country named the perfectly pure, — the Buddha Vajravikrāma.[896])

Dharmamati, in his turn, expressed the wish, that he might exhort all the 1000 Buddhas to teach their Doctrines. He was accordingly to be Brahma, the Crest-bearer.[897]) As to the king Dhṛtarāṣṭra, he was to become the Buddha Dīpaṁkara.[898]) Thus 1000 Buddhas (were foretold to appear in the Fortunate Aeon), and those, who maintain their number to be 1002 and (who say) that Vajrapāṇi is the same as Rocana, are fools, that deserve no belief.

Now, for what reason is this aeon called the Fortunate? The *Mahākaruṇāpuṇḍarīka*[899]) says: — At the time, when this world was destroyed by a flood, 1000 golden lotuses arose from the ocean. They were seen by the gods, who knew them to be an omen, that 1000 Buddhas were to appear. — O, this aeon is a fortunate one, -- said the gods, and from there comes the name of our aeon. And in the *Jñānavaipulyasūtra*[900]) we read: The name of the Fortunate is given to that aeon, (at the beginning of which) 1000 lotuses were to be seen.

As to the rise of 1000 Buddhas, such takes place in the period of stability,[901]) at the time of regress, from the age, when human life lasts 80,000 years, and ending with the age, when it will be only 100 years. [43 b.] (At the time) preceeding this period, there is no opportunity for the Buddhas to appear, since (among living beings) the aversion (to this wordly existence) is not great, and the Doctrine is not required for. After human age becomes reduced to 100 years, the Buddhas likewise cease to appear, because there follows a period of (complete degeneration), characterized by the following five features:[902]) (diminishment of) lifetime, (deterioration of the character) of living beings, (predominance of) passions, incorrect views, and low spirits. Neither are they to appear at the time of progress (that is to follow), for all, that is sinful will cease to exist, and, since all things will be in growth, no aversion (toward worldly existence) can take place. It is said accordingly:

They (the Buddhas) appear —

In the period of regress up to the time, when human age is to be 100 years.

Now, all that has just been said, concerns only the Fortunate Aeon, but not all the aeons in general, for the *Karuṇā-puṇḍarīka*[903]) tells us of the region of Anguṣṭhā — the thumb-sized, — where men live only 10 years and are in size not larger than a thumb. This region, (says the Sūtra), is presided by the Buddha Jyotīrāma,[904]) whose size is that of one cubit and seven fingers. We are likewise told of many Buddhas, appearing in the time previous (to the period when human life) lasts 80,000 years. As concerns this our age, (we know that) Krakucchanda appeared when men lived 40,000 years,[905]) Kanakamuni, — when human age dured 30,000 years,[906]) Kāçyapa,[907]) — when it was 20,000, and Çākyamuni, when it was reduced to 100. (The future Buddha), Maitreya, will come, when it will again be 80,000 years.[908])

The *Bhadrakalpikasūtra*[909]) indicates, with regard to each Buddha, his native country, caste, nimb, father, mother, son, favourite attendant, the two foremost disciples, (to whom the Buddha transfers his) high Wisdom and miraculous powers, the circle of adherents, lifetime, duration of the Doctrine, and, finally, the quantity of the Buddha's relics. If the two foremost disciples are counted separately, there will be altogether 13 subjects. Some authorities count 14, adding (the Buddha's) descent. As to the circle of adherents, such is (with some of the Buddhas) scarce and with others — numerous. The relics are likewise different: — with some they are abundant, and with others they may be contained in a pill. If we take for instance our Teacher, as He Himself told to Uttararāmarāja (?),[910]) — his birthplace [44 a] was Kapilavastu,[911]) his caste — that of the Kṣatriyas, his descent, — from Gautama, his nimb — a fathom in breadth; his father was called Çuddhodana, his mother — Māyā, his favourite attendant — Ānanda, his chief disciple, to whom he delivered his teaching of Highest Wisdom—Çāriputra, the foremost of his disciples endowed with miraculous powers — Maudgalyāyana, his congregation at the beginning numbered 1250 monks, his life dured 100 years, the Highest Doctrine is to exist for 500 years, and for the next 500 — (only) a resemblance of it. As to our Teacher's relics — such are known to be abundant.

Now, there may arise an objection as to human age being spoken of as infinite at the time, when the Buddha Rocana is to appear. This will be in conflict with the statement, that before human age, (in its regress), has attained the limits of 80,000 years, no Buddhas are to appear. This is right, but since this infinity of human age is the desire of a Buddha, it is a thing inconceivable to our mind.

Again: — if one thousand Buddhas are to be regarded as a definite number, this will disagree with the ***Aṣṭasāhasrikā***, where it is said, that 10,000 ascetics will, during the Fortunate Aeon, attain Supreme Enlightenment. This is also true, but, says the Saint Vimuktasena, although it is admitted that 1000 Buddhas are to arise during this Fortunate Aeon, this statement concerns only the foremost, and it does not mean, that the coming of others is denied. It is said in the ***Pañcaviṁçatisāhasrikā-ālokā***,[912]) that the definite number of 1000 Buddhas is given in order to make it known, that such a number is usually admitted as relating to the Fortunate Aeon, but those, that are competent as regards the subject, neither affirm, nor deny the appearance of others.

Again, it is admitted, that, after this world has undergone destruction, those that are to attain Enlightenment, become Buddhas likewise at the time of formation of a new world [44 b] (at such times as), for instance that, when the aeon Mahādhāraṇa began, after the age called Dhāraṇa had passed away. Moreover 1000 or 1005 Buddhas are mentioned with reference to the 12 Buddhaic achievements directly exhibited by them, and as to other works mentioning a greater number, (such statements) concern in general all those, who during this Fortunate Aeon attain Enlightenment. Otherwise, the previous incarnations (of Buddhas) are likewise taken into consideration, such as for instance (that of our Lord, when he was existing as) a teacher and Brāhmaṇa's son (in the times of Buddha Kāçyapa). It will not however be possible to draw from this the (false conclusion, that one Doctrine may have two (and more) teachers, for, at the time, when one Buddha is active, another, though he may (likewise) have (already) assumed the character of a Buddha, — does not preach his doctrine. Now, may it be said, if it is maintained, that, previous to the four Buddhas, there were none in this Aeon, it will be contrary to the *Kāla-cakratantra*,[913]) where it is said, that in the Fortunate Aeon seven Buddhas, Vipaçyin etc., up to Çākyamuni, have already appeared, — and to the usual belief, that the Buddhas, who have passed away, are seven in number. There is no mistake in this, for since (the seven) are Buddhas that have arisen in this world and are now extinct, (the Tantra etc.) view them only from such a standpoint.

(As to the difference of names) we may say, indeed, that in different Sūtras, the names of the Buddhas are not the same, that Ketu is sometimes called Pradyota, and Rocana — Roca or Ruci, but these are mere synonyms and, above all, differently translated. We need not, therefore, have any doubt as concerns this subject.

*The Rise of the Buddha Çākyamuni in the world of Endurance (Sahālokadhātu).*

IV Ac. (Now, first of all, we must see) for what reason this our world is called Sahā-loka-dhātu. The word *Sahā*[914]) is a synonym of "endurance", (and this name has been given to the world in which we live) because (the Buddhas and Bodhisattvas, that appear therein) do not fall a prey to the three sources of evil, the causes of defilement, but endure (the hardships caused by them) and, morally, resist (to the passions). It is said in the *Karūṇā-puṇḍarīka*:[915]) — Why is this world called the World of Endurance? It is called so, because the living beings therein are endurin g(hardship caused by) desire, hatred, [45 a] infatuation, and by all the bonds of the passions. In this World of Endurance a great aeon called the Fortunate is to come. Why is it to bear this name? Because during it, amongst living beings, that indulge in lust, hatred, and infatuation, 1000 fully accomplished Buddhas, endowed with great Commiseration are to appear. Moreover, our world has its name (of the Word of Endurance), because the Bodhisattvas (that act therein) are endowed with the virtue (of resistence) or because the Buddhas (appearing therein) are likewise characterised by it. It is said in the *Mañjuçrī-buddha-kṣetra-guṇa-vyūha*:[916]) — The followers of the Bodhisattva Vehicle have performed acts of great devotion in regard of the Buddhas of former ages, engendered the roots of virtue, worshipped many hundreds and thousands of Buddhas and were possessed of great endurance, self-discipline, and faith. They were abused, menaced, beaten and wounded by all the living beings, but they patiently endured (all these odds), however harsh they may have been, and did not fall a prey to lust, hatred, and infatuation. O noble youth, this (our world) has got its name from those holy men and is called the World of Endurance. Similarly (this world has derived its name) from the Buddhas, who were endowed with the virtues just mentioned.

As to the rise of our Teacher in this world, we read in the Master Nāgārjuna's Salutation to the Ten Monuments:[917])

I worship the Lord, the (Man —) Lion,
Who, having first made his Creative Effort for the attainment of Supreme Enlightenment,
Has amassed merit during three immeasurable periods of aeons[918])
[45 b] And vanquished the four mischief-doing demons.[919])

Accordingly, we have to distinguish: —

$a_1$) The Creative Effort.

$b_1$) The Accumulation of Merit.

$c_1$) The attainment of Buddhahood, — and take into consideration, with regard to each of these points, respectively, —

$a_2$) the Hīnayānistic, and

$b_2$) the Mahāyānistic tradition.

### *The Initial Vow according to Hīnayāna.*

IV $Aca_1a_2$. In olden times there lived a king named Prasannakīrti,[920]) who made one of his attendants, skilful in the art of taming elephants, — the keeper and tamer of (the royal) elephants. The keeper, after having completed the task of taming one of the elephants, made it known to the king and the latter ordered him to bring the animal to him. When the elephant was brought, the king mounted, intending to go for a ride, but the beast, having smelt the scent of a female elephant, which aroused its passions, ran headlong through woods and valleys and there was no possibility to stop it. The king, terrified, asked the keeper what to do and the keeper told him to snatch the branches of a tree. The king did so, fell down, and fainted.

After the keeper had made him recover from his swoon, the king, enraged said, that he, the keeper, since he had boasted with taming the elephant, when this was not, really, the case, was to be punished with prison. But the keeper said: — I have tamed the animal's body, but it was impossible for me, to do the same with its mind. — What proof canst thou give, that thou hast tamed its body, — asked the king in return. — In a week, after the elephant has come back, — replied the keeper, — you shall see. After seven days had passed, the elephant returned, and the keeper, having made an iron hammer red-hot, placed it before the beast, saying: — Eat, eat! [46 a] The beast, notwithstanding (the terrible pain) began to eat. This (the keeper) showed to the king and said: — I have not been able to subdue the elephant's mind. The king believed, (and having from this example come to the insight, that he must subdue his own mind), made his Initial Vow and uttered the following entreaty: —

May I, by virtue of my charity, be reborn in the Çākya Clan,
Attain (the state of a) Buddha, that will harmonise with my (future) merits, family, and descent,
And convey great peace, deliverance from fear and salvation,
To all living beings, including Brahma, who are stricken with distress.

*The Accumulation of Merit according to Hinayāna.*

IV $Acb_1a_2$. From that time and up to (the age of) the Buddha Rāṣṭrapāla[921]) (our Master) worshipped 75 000 Buddhas and accumulated merit during immeasurable aeons thus bringing to accomplishment the first period, as it is said in Scripture: —

From the time of Buddha Çākyamuni[922])
And up to the age of Rāṣṭrapāla,
I have worshipped 75,000 Buddhas.

Then, beginning with the Buddha Sādhukara (?)[923]) and up to Indradhvaja,[924]) our Master worshipped 76,000 Buddhas more, thus completing the second period, as follows: —

I have worshipped the full number of 76,000 Buddhas,
Beginning with Sādhukara and up to the Sage Indradhvaja.

Thereafter, from the time of Dīpaṁkara and up to Kāçyapa He worshipped 77,000 other Buddhas and terminated the third period, as it is said in Scripture: —

From the age of Dipaṁkara
And up to the Buddha Kāçyapa
I have worshipped the full number of 77,000 Buddhas.

And the *Abhidharmakoça*[925]) says [46 b], that the first period of aeons ends with the Buddha Ratnaçikhin, the second — with Dīpaṁkara, and the third — with Vipaçyin, as follows: —

Vipaçyin, Dīpaṁkara, and Ratnaçikhin,
Appeared (each of them) at the end of each of the three periods of aeons.
And the first (of the Buddhas who received the homage of our Teacher) is Çākyamuni.

Thereupon, during 100 great aeons, (the Master) brought to accomplishment all the factors for attaining the sublime character of a Bodhisattva and (from that time, uninterruptedly) abided as such. Then, during the remaining 100 aeons He 1) circumambulated the Buddha Nakṣatrarāja for seven days, all the while chanting a verse and by this energy accumulated the merit, (usually) attained in the period of nine great aeons, and 2) up to the time, when the other 91 aeons had passed away and He was born in the age of the Buddha Kāçyapa as a teacher and Brāhmaṇa's son, — brought to accomplishment all the factors (for attaining Buddhahood). Finally he was born as Çvetaketu and after that came to perform the 12 achievements of a Buddha, as we know in detail from Scripture, and, particularly, from the Abhiniṣkramaṇa-sūtra. As to the special tradition (of the Hīnayāna, such is as follows: —

The Teacher and the solitary Pratyekabuddha[926])
Have, on the basis of the Highest degree of mystic absorbtion,
Attained (all the virtues) up to Enlightenment.

Accordingly, (Buddha), by accumulating merit, equal to that, attained by ordinary worldlings during three immeasurable periods of aeons, has, in the evening, vanquished the four demons. Then, at midnight, having taken recourse to the four stages of mystic meditation, he acquired (all the virtues), up fo (those attained on) the Path of Training.[927]) And, finally, in the morning, from daybreak till sunrise, he has in one moment brought to accomplishment all the six transcendental virtues, as follows: —

(Buddha), guided by mercy toward all (living beings),

Has, by His gifts, completed (the transcendental virtue of) charity,
By freeing himself from the members (of the causal nexus) connected with passions —
(The virtues of) unflinching patience and pure morality,
By praising Nakṣatrarāja — the virtue of energy,
And, immediately after [47 a] — those of Trance and Highest Wisdom.

*The Attainment of Buddhahood according to Hīnayāna.*

IV $Acc_1a_2$. Thus he attained the six transcendental virtues, became a Buddha, possessed of the spiritual[928]) and physical[929]) body (characterizing such), revealed his Doctrine to (His disciples) — Ājñātakauṇḍinya etc. up to Bhadrika and then passed away into final Nirvāṇa.

As regards the Mahāyānistic tradition concerning Buddha, we distinguish: —

IV $Aca_1b_2$. The Creative Effort for Enlightenment.

IV $Acb_1b_2$. The Accumulation of Merit during three immeasurable periods of aeons.

IV $Acc_1b_2$. The victory over the four demons and the attainment of Buddhahood.

*The Creative Effort according to Mahāyāna.*

IV $Aca_1b_2$. (Here we have to consider) five points: —

$a_3$) The character of the Creative Effort,
$b_3$) Its cause,
$c_3$) Its merit;
$d_3$) Its varieties, and
$e_3$) The different traditions concerning Buddha's first Creative Effort.

*The character of the Creative Effort.*

IV $Aca_1b_2a_3$. We read in the *Sūtrālaṁkāra*:[930]) —

Great by its energy, great by its achievements,
Great by its aim, and great by its result,
Is the thought of the Bodhisattvas, —
A manifestation of their spirit, directed toward the double aim (of human activity).

Thus the Creative Effort may be defined as "a manifestation of the spirit (of the Bodhisattva), which, endowed with due associates, expedients, and active energy, has for its result the fulfillment of one's own aim and that of others, and is founded upon altruism and the desire of Enlightenment".

And the *Abhisamayālaṁkāra* says:[931]) —

The Creative Effort is a desire of Supreme Enlightenment in pursuit of the welfare of others.

It is exposed briefly and in detail, in harmony with the Sūtras.

(Ratnākaraçānti) in his Commentary *Çuddhimatī*[932]) has: The Creative Effort is to be defined as a desire of Supreme Enlightenment, based upon altruism.

*The Causes of the Creative Effort.*

IV $Aca_1b_2b_3$. The *Bodhisattvabhūmi* mentions four causes, four conditions, and four forces, through which the Creative Effort is produced. And in the *Sūtrālaṁkāra*[933]) we read: —

The Creative Effort, that is originated by foreign influence —
By the grace of a teacher, by the efficiency of the cause (— adherence to the Mahāyānistic family)[934])
By the agency of the roots (of virtue, that are caused to thrive),[935]) —
Through study and the practice of virtue, — manifests itself in a powerful or feeble form. [47 b.]

— Such are the causes of the Creative Effort relating to Empirical Reality. As to the factors, that refer to Absolute Reality, we read as follows:[936]) —

If the Supreme Buddha has been duly worshipped,
And the Accumulation of virtue and wisdom fully accomplished,
Then it (the Creative Effort) is regarded as relating to the Absolute Reality,
Since it produces unflinching, true knowledge as regards all elements of existence.

And in short we have:[937]) —

The seed of Great Commiseration having first been aroused to life,
By the efficiency of the (Mahāyānistic spiritual) family,
The Creative Effort for Enlightenment, —
As a result of the Complement of sublime thoughts and deeds — is made.

*The Result (Merit) of the Creative Effort.*

IV $Aca_1b_2c_3$. The direct result (of the Creative Effort) is a miracle, the intermediate is the attainment (of that supernatural power) of the mind, (through which one, as if possessed of) a wish-fulfilling gem, (may cause) all the desired objects to come down like rain, and the final is Buddhahood, and the like, all of which is inconceivable to our mind.

The *Vīradattaparipṛcchā*[938]) says: —

If all the merits of making the Creative Effort
Could assume a visible form,
They would fill all the regions of the sky
And even extend beyond them.

*The Varieties of the Creative Effort.*

IV $Aca_1b_2d_3$. From the stand point of its essential character the Creative Effort is to be viewed as 1) the Vow[939]) and 2) the action according to it.[940]) If regarded from the point of its more rough or more subtle character, it may be 1) conventional (produced by foreign agency)[941]) and 2) absolute.

As concerns the different stages of Enlightenment, the Creative Effort manifests itself in four ways, (as says the *Sūtrālaṁkāra*)[942]) —

The Creative Effort is, on the different stages, characterized
By faith, the purest and best intentions, maturity, and the
absence of all obscurations.

Further on, as regards its associates and that, with which it may be compared, the Creative Effort is considered to have twenty-two forms, as we read (in the *Abhisamayālaṁkāra*):[943])

It is like the earth, like gold, the moon, or fire etc., (and in the *Sūtrālaṁkāra*):[944]) —

The Creative Effort is regarded as ressembling the earth etc.

The *Nirṇaya-saṁgraha*[945]) mentions in its turn ten varieties, as follows: —

The Creative Effort is of ten kinds: —

1) Conventional,
2) Absolute, [48 a]
3) Uncertain,
4) Sure,
5) Not perfectly ,pure,
6) Perfectly pure,

7) Feeble,
8) Powerful,
9) With incomplete result, and
10) With complete result.

The *Conventional* Creative Effort is that, characterizing all the Bodhisattvas, who are not able to act (by themselves) surely and infallibly.

The *Absolute* is made by those, that act correctly and without mistakes and by the Çrāvakas, that have devoted themselves to Supreme Enlightenment.

The Creative Effort may be regarded as *uncertain*, when it is made by those, who do not belong to the (Mahāyānistic) family and by such members of it, who may relapse (into sin).

It is *sure*, if made by such, who are known by characteristics reverse to those just mentioned.

It is *not completely pure*, wh en made (out of desire of) imitating others, from fear of worldly power, rapine, judgement, of (being drowned in) a river (and similar calamities), or, — out of self-conceit, without consideration and accurate analysis, — for the sake of (prolonging one's) life, obtaining gain and renown, and in order to be praised and spoken of. The Creative Effort, made out of such and similar motives, cannot be regarded as completely pure. (On the contrary), it is *perfectly pure*, when it may be recognised by its motives being the reverse of (those mentioned).

The Creative Effort is *feeble* if the Bodhisattvas, after having made it, fall a prey to desire, hatred, and infatuation, and overpowered by (these three sources of evil) [48 b] are unable to act correctly and commit errors.

The Creative Effort, the consequences of which are reverse to these, is, on the contrary, to be considered as *powerful*.

The *result* of the Creative Effort is *incomplete* with those, who are on the (different) stages of Bodhisattva perfection, beginning with the Stage of Faith[946]) and up to the tenth Stage.[947])

The *full result* is attained after (the Bodhisattva's) having become a Buddha, as the Lord, Himself, says: — After I had finished the practice of asceticism,[948]) I attained Enlightenment, according to my sublime vows.

*The different traditions as to Buddha's Creative Effort.*

IV.Aca$_1$b$_2$e$_3$. In the *Karuṇā-puṇḍarika*[949]) it is said, that the first Creative Effort was made by the Brāhmaṇa Samudrareṇu.

In the *Bhadrakalpikasūtra*[950]) we read: —

In former times, when I was in an inferior state of existence,
I, having sacrificed to the Buddha Çākyamuni,
First made my Creative Effort for Enlightenment.

The tradition of the *Anukampā-pratikaraṇa-sūtra(?)*[951]) is as follows: —

Our Teacher, in the time of his previous existence, was once, through the influence of former deeds, reborn in the infernal region of Red-hot Iron, as an athlete, who had to draw a heavy vehicle. As his companions, feeble in strength, were constantly beaten by the ward, that surveyed them, (Buddha) became full of great commiseration and made his Creative Effort for Enlightenment (in order to help all the suffering living beings). After that he said to the keeper: — Be thou a little more merciful (toward these unfortunate beings). — The keeper, enraged, struck him with his trident, and (Buddha) dying, was delivered from infernal existence, as the drawer of a fiery vehicle and became purged from the guilt of sin (previously committed by him) during eight aeons.

According to the *Traiskandhaka*,[952]) the Teacher, whilst he was abiding in the form of Abhinanda,[953]) the son of a merchant, made his first Creative Effort in the presence of [49 a] the Buddha Mahāsundara (?)[954])

And still another tradition says, that the Teacher, when he was existing as a potter's son, named Ābhākara (?)[955]) presented the great Buddha Çākyamuni with a vase of porcelain, five chowries, a pair of boots and a parasol, and made the following entreaty: —

O Buddha, may I become just like thee
By corporeal ressemblance and by (the n umber of) disciples,
By duration of life, native country,
And by the high name, thou bearest.

Thus spoke He and made His Vow.

*The Accumulation of Merit according to Mahāyāna.*

IV Acb$_1$b$_2$) (Here we distinguish): —

a$_3$) The character of the Accumulation of Merit,

$b_3$) The period of time, during which it is brought about,
$c_3$) The way in which it was completed (by Buddha).

*The Character of the Accumulation.*

IV $Acb_1b_2a_3$. (The Accumulation of Merit) is to be viewed from the following eight points: —

$a_4$) Essence,
$b_4$) Connection with the six Transcendental Virtues,
$c_4$) Etymology (of the word *saṁbhāra*) — its appelation in Sanscrit,
$d_4$) Action,
$e_4$) Modes,
$f_4$) Result,
$g_4$) Sphere of activity,
$h_4$) The different subjects with which (the Accumulation) may be identified.

*Essence (definition) of the Accumulation.*

IV $Acb_1b_2a_3a_4$. We read in the *Sūtrālaṁkāra*:[956]) —

The Accumulation of Merit of the Bodhisattvas
Consisting of virtue and Transcendental Wisdom is incomparable.
The first (virtue) leads to bliss during this worldly life,
And the second (Transcendental Wisdom) conveys an existence free from defilement.

Accordingly we may define the Accumulation as: — "Virtue influenced[957]) and uninfluenced[958]) (by passions), which is the cause of a blissful existence[959]) (in the Saṁsāra) and of the super-bliss[960]) (of Salvation).

*The Connection of the Accumulation with the six Transcendental Virtues.*

IV $Acb_1b_2a_3b_4$. It is said):[961]) —

(Charity and Morals form the Accumulation of Virtue,
And High Knowledge, — that of Transcendental Wisdom.
The other three (Patience, Energy and Concentration) represent the Accumulation of both,
And the first five, moreover, that of Transcendental Wisdom likewise.

*Etymology (!!) of „saṁbhāra."*

IV $Acb_1b_2a_3c_4$. (The *Sūtrālaṁkāra*[962]) says: —

An amassing, again and again, of virtue,

(Practised) uninterruptedly and leading to concentration of mind

(Such is *saṁbhāra*, the Accumulation of Merit of the Bodhisattva

Accordingly, in the word *saṁbhāra*, which is the Sanscrit name for Accumulation, — (*sam* means) *saṁtānena* (or *saṁtatyā*) — uninterruptedly, (*bhā* stands for) *bhāvanā* — concentration, and (*ra* for) *āhāra*[963]) — (amassing) again and again. Consequently, (the Accumulation of Merit) is called *saṁbhāra*, since it is a repeated (practice of virtue), that goes on uninterruptedly [49 b] and leads to concentration of mind.

*The Function of the Accumulation.*

IV $Acb_1b_2a_3d_4$. (The *Sūtrālaṁkāra*[964]) says):

The Accumulation of Merit of the Powerful Ones
Leads to the fulfillment of all their projects.

*The Modes of the Accumulation.*

IV $Acb_1b_2a_3e_4$. (We read further on): — [965])

The Accumulation of Merit is made by the Powerful Ones,
For the sake of entering (upon the stages of Enlightenment),
(Rising up) to the state of non-differentiation,[966])
Attaining impassibility,[967]) receiving the consecration[968]) (for Buddhahood),
And (ultimately), for reaching the final goal.

Thus, the Accumulation of Merit appears in diverse forms, in harmony with the different stages of the Bodhisattva, viz. the (preliminary) Stage of Faith,[970]) the first six stages, the seventh[971]) stage, the eighth[972]), the ninth[973]) and the tenth. (The different degres in accumulating merit on each of these stages) respectively lead to: — the entrance upon the (ten main) stages (of the Bodhisattva), (the full monistic conception and) cessation of all differentiation, — on the seventh stage, complete impassibility — on the eighth, the consacration for Buddhahood), on the tenth, and the attainment of the final result (Nirvāṇa), — when one is already a Buddha.

*The Result of the Accumulation.*

IV.$Acb_1b_2a_3f_4$. It is said in the *Ratnāvalī*:[974])

The physical form[975]) of the Buddha
Is a result of the Accumulation of Virtue,

And, as to his spiritual body,[976] o King[977])
Such, to speak briefly, is a product
Of the Accumulation of Transcendental Wisdom.

And in the *Yukti-ṣaṣṭikā*[978]) (the master Nāgārjuna) says: —
May I attain the two sublime (forms)
Which are a result of virtue and Transcendental Wisdom.

Accordingly, (the result), viewed from the standpoint of the principal cause, may, plainly, be characterized as follows: — It is the (attainment of) the two forms (of a Buddha), as the consequence of the two kinds of Accumulation.

*The Spheres of the Accumulation.*

IV $Acb_1b_2a_3g_4$. The sphere of activity of the Accumulation of Virtue is Empirical Reality or the world as it seems, and that of the Accumulation of Transcendental Wisdom, — Absolute Reality or the world as it is (sub specie aeternitatis).

*The Accumulation of Merit from different points of view.*

IV $Acb_1b_2a_3h_4$. We distinguish here twelve forms: —

1) According to the Mahāyānistic theory (the Accumulation of Merit manifests itself as): — the means (of attaining Bodhisattva perfection and Buddhahood), and high, analytic wisdom. The latter puts an end to the conception of plurality,[978a]) and the former brings together all the roots of virtue. It is said in the *Gayāçirṣa-sūtra*:[978b]) — The means is knowledge as regards the amassing (of the roots of virtue), and Highest Wisdom, — discriminative knowledge, (containing an analysis of existence). Of these two, Highest Wisdom[979]) [50 a] is founded upon Relativity and represents the full notion (of it). As to the means, — such is the fulfillment of all the projects of living beings out of commiseration, as it is said:[980])

(The attainment of Enlightenment is, with some, based upon)
Relativity, endowed with the essence of great Commiseration.

2) All the virtuous qualities are comprised in the six Transcendental Virtues, through the practice of which the Teaching of Buddha is fully realized, (as we read in the *Sūtrālaṁkāra*):[981])

All the pure qualities are to be viewed as
Distracted, concentrated and mixed,
They are (respectively) comprised in each pair of Transcendental Virtues.[982])

And:[983]) —

Absence of inclination to objects of worldly enjoyment
Strict observation (of the rules of Discipline)
Absence of lassitude in regard of two points,[984])
And meditation, free from distracted thoughts, —
This is the whole of the Great Vehicle taken in short.

The Great Vehicle is thus demonstrated as contained in the six Transcendental Virtues.

Now, may it be asked, do not the six Transcendental Virtues likewise exist with the Çrāvakas and Pratyekabuddhas? No. — We read in the Commentary on the *Mahāyāna-saṁgraha*:[985])

With the solitary Pratyekabuddhas[986])
The six Transcendental Virtues do not exist even by name,
Only (the Buddha) our Lord
Abides on the summit of these virtues.

But, may it be said, in the Çrāvaka Code we have the six Virtues and all that relates to the conduct of a Bodhisattva clearly demonstrated. (To this we answer): — They are only briefly indicated, and as to their full analysis, such is nowhere to be found (in Hīnayānistic Scripture).[987]) *The Ratnāvalī*[988]) says: —

The vows, that characterise the Bodhisattvas
And (the precepts) for devoting oneself to the practice (of their virtues)
Are not treated in the Çrāvaka Vehicle.
How is it then possible (for an adherent of it) to become a Bodhisattva?

And the *Sūtrālaṁkāra*:[989]) —

The Teaching of the Çrāvakas,
Being incomplete, contradictory,
Affording no sure means and unable to give the due instructions,
Is not that, which may be called the Doctrine of the Great Vehicle.

3) The Accumulation of Merit has various degrees, corresponding to the stages (of Bodhisattva perfection). We read in the *Ratnāvalī*:[990]) —

Just as the Vehicle of the Çrāvakas,
Mentions eight stages (of perfection attained by) its saints,
In the same way the Great Vehicle [50 b]

Has ten stages (of Enlightenment) for the Bodhisattvas.
And the *Triçaraṇa-saptati*[991]) says: —

Just as the Complete Wisdom of a Hinayānist saint[992])
Is preceded by seven (preliminary) stages,
In the same way the Divine Wisdom of the fully accomplished Buddha
Has ten stages, that go before it.

The stages of Çrāvaka perfection are accordingly as follows:[993])

The stage of Pure Vision,[994])
" " " (entering the Çrāvaka) family,[995])
" " " Entering the Stream,[996])
" " " Illumination,[997])
" " " Refinement,[998])
" " " Deliverance from Passions,[999])
" " " Full Exposition (of the Truth),[1000])
" " " a Pratyekabuddha.[1001])

Similarly, the Great Vehicle has its ten stages, that of Joy[1002]) and the rest, which are in coordination with the ten Transcendental Virtues respectively.[1003]) These are the principal stages, but by entering those, that are subservient to them, (the Bodhisattva) when he is still a worldling, likewise becomes purified, as it is said: —

These (the ten) are the chief stages,
But the ordinary man, that abides on the stage of devotion etc.

Here we have, accordingly, the stage of devotion,[1004]) (attained) on the Path of Accumulating Merit.[1005]) And further on: —

He, that attains the (chief) stages,
Must (first abide in) that of Faith.[1006])

According to this passage, the stage of Faith lasts till the end of the Path of Training.[1007])
Moreover, the *Bodhisattva-bhūmi*[1008]) mentions seven other stages, namely: —

The stage of (entering) the Family,[1009])
" " " Faith,[1010])
" " " Purest and Best Intentions,[1011])
" " " Assurance,[1012])
" " " Activity,[1013])
" " " Sure Action,[1014]) and
" " " Attainment of the Final Result.[1015])

4) (The Accumulation of Merit) viewed from the standpoint of the four methods of propaganda[1016]) is characterized by the *Sūtrālaṁkāra*[1017]) as follows: —

(Of the four methods of propaganda)
Charity is equal (to the Transcendental Virtue of that name).
And as to fine, pleasant speech, favourable acts and common interest, —
Such are to be viewed as the teaching (of the Transcendental Virtues),
Incitation (of others to practise such),
And the conformity of one's own acts.

Accordingly, the four methods of propaganda are: — Charity,[1018]) that harmonizes with the corresponding Transcendental Virtue, sweet and pleasant speech,[1019]) by means of which (the teaching of) the six Transcendental Virtues is communicated to others, fulfillment of the projects (of others)[1020]) by inducing them to practise the said Virtues and common interest,[1021]) — by being oneself devoted to this practice.

5) The Accumulation of Merit regarded from the point of the four methods of action, is [51 a] as says the *Sūtrālaṁkāra*:[1022]) —

The activity of the Powerful Ones (manifests itself) according to the Sūtras, in four ways: —
With regard to the living beings, that are devoted to the Great Vehicle,
To those, who found their belief in the Small One,
And, in behalf of the adherents of both Vehicles,
For the sake of Discipline and to arouse the energy (of the converts).

Thus, for those, who are followers of the Great Vehicle (the Bodhisattvas) act on the basis of the Transcendental Virtues,[1023]) (their actions being characterized by the essence of these ten virtues); in regard of the adherents to the Small Vehicle, (their activity is founded upon) the characteristic features of Enlightenment,[1024]) 37 in number. With reference to those, who found their belief in both the Vehicles, in order to arouse, forcibly, the zeal of such persons, (the Bodhisattvas) have, in their action, (recourse to) supernatural perception,[1025]) of which there are six forms.

And in order to lead to spiritual maturity the converts,

that adhere to all the three Vehicles, (they) act so as to bring all living beings to this maturity by the aid of innumerable expedients. Such are the four ways of action, according to the *Ratnacūḍa-sūtra.*[1026]) And the *Bodhisattva-bhūmi*[1027]) says: — All the activity of the Bodhisattvas is to be regarded as comprised in the four methods of action.

6) As to the coordination of accumulated merit with the 80 imperishable things[1028]) we read in the *Çuddhimati*:[1029]) —

The Creative Effort, sublime thoughts and deeds, the best intentions,

The six Transcendental Virtues, the (four) immeasurable feelings,

The (five) forms of supernatural perception, the four methods of propaganda,

The (four) methods of correct discrimination, the points of reliance, and the two accumulations,

The characteristics of Enlightenment, concentration etc.

The power of memory, and so on,

The (four main) aphorisms, the uniform concentration of the Bodhisattvas,

And their skill in expedients.

Thus we have: —

The Creative Effort, (1)
(Sublime) thoughts,[1030]) (2)
Activity,[1031]) (3)
The best intentions,[1032]) (4)
The six Transcendental Virtues, (5—10)
The four Immeasurable Feelings,[1033]) (11—14)
Five forms of supernatural perception,[1034]) (15—19)
The four methods of propaganda, (20—25)
The four methods of correct discrimination,[1035]) (24—27)
Reliance upon the elements of existence and not upon the personality[1036]) (28)
" " " meaning and not upon the words,[1037]) (29)
" " " direct meaning and not upon the conventional,[1038]) (30)
" " " Transcendental Wisdom and not upon ordinary human knowledge,[1039]) (31)
The two Accumulations (32, 33)

The thirty-seven characteristics of Enlightenment,[1040]) (34—70)

Concentration[1041]) and Transcendental Knowledge,[1042]) (71,72)

Power of memory[1043]) and readiness of wit[1044]) (73, 74)

The four aphorisms of the Doctrine: —

All active[1045]) elements are impermanent, (75)

All elements influenced (by defiling agencies)[1046]) have mere phenomenal existence, (76)

All elements (whatsoever) are impersonal,[1047]) (77)

Every form of Nirvāṇa is Quiescence, (78)

The uniform concentration (of the Bodhisattvas),[1048])(79)

(Their) skill in expedients.[1049]) (80)

These 80 subjects are mentioned in the *Akṣayamati-nirdeça-sūtra*,[1050]) and the *Munimatālaṁkāra*[1051]) says, that all the Mahāyānistic Path is contained in them.

7) As to the varieties of the Accumulation of Merit, viewed from the standpoint of the 22 forms of the Creative Effort, we read in the *Abhisamayālaṁkāra*:[1052]) —

The Creative Effort has 22 forms,
Since it may be like the earth, like gold, the moon, or fire,
Like a treasury, a jewel-mine, or like the ocean,
Like a diamond, a mountain, a remedy, a teacher,
Like the wish-fulfilling gem, like the sun, or like a song,
Like a king, a jewellery, a great road,
A Vehicle, a fountain, a pleasant sound, a river, and a cloud.

As to the subjects, meant by these examples, the Saint Vimuktasena and the teacher Haribhadra[1053]) consider them to be the associates, connected with the Creative Effort, namely zeal,[1054]) sublime thoughts, activity, the ten Transcendental Virtues (respectively), the two Accumulations of Merit, the 37 characteristic features of Enlightenment, Commiseration, Transcendental Knowledge, power of memory, readiness of wit, the triumph of the Doctrine,[1055]) the uniform concentration of the Bodhisattvas, and the Cosmical Body of Buddha.

(Vasubandhu's) Commentary on the *Sūtrālaṁkāra*,[1056]) the *Çuddhimatī*, and the *Munimatālaṁkāra* enumerate, instead, all the 80 imperishable subjects, the 6 Transcendental Virtues etc., in accordance with each (of the examples), and place them in the due succesive order. These 22 forms of the Creative Effort [52 a], comprise, according to the opinion of the teachers Haribhadra and Abhayākaragupta, — the Mahāyānistic Path and its result.[1057]) Others, in their turn, consider, that they include (only) the Paths of Discipline.

8) (The Accumulation of Merit) has likewise various forms corresponding to the four methods of intuition, which are as follows: —

The thorough knowledge of all the forms of the 3 Kinds of Wisdom and of their respective objects,[1058])

The Culminationz of the Process of Illumination,[1059])

The Progressive Process of Illumination,[1060]) and

The Final, Momentary Intuition[1061]).

It is said accordingly: — The cause (of perfection) is endowed with the essence of the four methods of intuition.

Otherwise the various forms of the Accumulation harmonise with the four Actions,[1062]) that of the Outfit,[1063]) Access,[1064]) Accumulation (proper),[1065]) and Issue.[1066])

9) In harmony with the teaching, that is common to all the Vehicles, the Accumulation of Merit differs in regard of the four Paths which are:

The Path of Accumulating Merit (proper,[1067])

" " " Training,[1068]) (2)

" " " Illumination,[1069]) (3)

" " " Concentration[1070]). (4)

As to the Final Path[1071]) such, being identical with the result, is not taken into consideration. (The first) two (— the Paths of) Accumulation and Training represent the practice (of virtue), which is founded upon faith in the Absolute Truth, but not upon direct perception of the latter; they are, therefore, (only) preliminary stages of the Path. On the contrary, the Path of Illumination and that of Transcendental Concentration are characterized by the full intuition of the Truth, which is directly perceived (by the Saint). Consequently, the first two, being still influenced (by passions)[1072]) and based upon the knowledge of Empirical Reality,[1073]) are but subservient degrees and not the Truth of the Path proper. Now, (if this is so), how is it then said in the *Nirṇaya-saṁgraha*:[1074]) — Of what kind is the Truth of the Path? (Answer): — That, which represents the Path of Accumulating Merit, that, which is called the Path of Training, and that, which we know as the Path of complete Purification.[1075]) All these, taken together,

form the Truth of the Path. And in the *Abhidharma-samuccaya*[1076]) we read, that all the five subdivisions of the Path represent the Truth of that name. There is no mistake in this, for (the first two Paths) are viewed as subservient to the Path (proper), or as the stages, that aid (in its realization). It is said in the *Abhidharma-samuccaya-bhāṣya*:[1077]) —
(In speaking of) "The fivefold Path", (the author of the *Abhidharmasamuccaya*) has in view the five different stages of the Path. These are the Truth of the Path proper and the subservient degrees. [52 b.] The Paths of Accumulation and Training are thus regarded as preliminary. Moreover, the *Nirṇayasaṁgraha*[1078]) says: —
There are such elements, which, in spite of their relation to this world are such, which put an end to the thirst for repeated births, being antidotes against it, and to the Path for passing out of this world. Why are these elements, nevertheless, counted amongst those relating to the Truth of the Origin[1079]) (of phenomenal existence)? (Answer): — (The elements spoken of) are, indeed, by their nature, antidotes against the thirst for repeated births. Still, since they are connected with the actions, however virtuous, of body, speech, and mind, which three are all subjected to rebirth, the said elements must be regarded as relating to the Truth of the Origin. (Some authorities say), that the Paths of Accumulation and Training are, as regards their essential character, uninfluenced (by passions)[1080]) and, therefore, belong to the Path (proper). This is not right, for it is said in the *Nirṇayasaṁgraha*:[1081]) — By means of analytic wisdom, which is a result of study and investigation, (the Bodhisattva) exerts himself in the (four) acts of intense mindfulness.[1082]) This kind of knowledge relates to the Empirical Reality, and, notwithstanding its virtuous character, is influenced by passions. On the basis (of this knowledge, the Bodhisattva) practises meditation through which he becomes prepared for the (four) degrees conducive to Illumination[1083]) and is keen upon the acts of intense mindfulness, connected with this form of meditation. This is likewise Empirical Knowledge, virtuous, but still influenced by passions. Then, on the basis of the said knowledge, (the Bodhisattva) manifests his energy in regard of the four acts of mindfulness, connected with the four degrees conducive to

Illumination, through which he is prepared for the Path of Illumination. However, this form of knowledge too is empirical, and, in spite of its virtuous quality, influenced (by passions). Finally, having such a basis (for further activity the Bodhisattva) attains the "Highest Virtues of the worldly being",[1084]) which (degree) is included in the Unobstructed Path,[1085]) leading directly to the Path of Illumination (and the direct perception of the Truth). But even this (wisdom of the Bodhisattva) is based upon Empirical Reality, and its virtues still bear the stain of passion.

10) The Accumulation of Merit may be likewise viewed from the standpoint of the three Disciplines, which are:
Moral Discipline,[1086])
Mental Discipline,[1087]) and
The Training in Highest Wisdom.[1088]) [53 a]

We read in the *Sūtrālaṁkāra*:[1089]) —

The (Teaching of the) six Transcendental Virtues has been preached by the Buddhas
In regard of the three Disciplines.
The first (of these Disciplines)[1090]) corresponds to the (first) three (Transcendental Virtues),[1091])
The last two (Transcendental Virtues)[1092]) are connected with two (of the Disciplines,[1093])
And one (Transcendental Virtue)[1094]) relates to all the three Disciplines.[1095])

11) (We may further on distinguish) the three forms of virtue[1096]) namely that of Charity, Morals, and High Wisdom. The first of these is identical with the Transcendental Virtue of Charity, the second with that of Morals and the third includes Patience, Energy, Concentration, and the Climax of Wisdom.

12) (Finally we may view the Accumulation of Merit as) the seven subdivisions of the Path of the Bodhisattva[1097]) or as the thirty-seven characteristic features of Enlightenment in their successive order. In such a way it is possible to explain the whole of Buddha's Teaching.

*The time of Accumulation.*

IV $Acb_1b_2b_3$. Scripture gives us many different versions as regards this subject. It speaks of three, seven, ten, and thirty-three immeasurable periods of aeons. Some of the discourses have, moreover, the number thirteen. However, in the majority of cases, Scripture mentions three immeasurable periods. As concerns the meaning of the term "Immeasurable Period"[1098]) (its interpretation is likewise different). The Commentary on the *Abhidharmakoça*[1099]), the *Munimatālaṁkāra*,[1100]) and other works say, that the word (*asaṁkhya*: innumerable, immeasurable) has not in this case the meaning of "beyond calculation", but that it is (the name of a definite number), which has its place in the decimal system[1101]) as one of its sixty members, (that are usually met with in scientific works). The numbers are as follows:[1102]) —

1, 10, 100, 1000, 10.000,[1103])
100.000,[1104]) 1.000.000,[1105])
10.000.000,[1106]) 100.000.000.[1107])
1.000.000.000,[1108]) 10.000.000.000,[1109])
100.000.000.000,[1110]) 1.000.000.000.000.[1111])
10.000.000.000.000,[1112]) 100.000.000.000.000,[1113])
1.000.000.000.000.000,[1114]) 10.000.000.000.000.000,[1115])
100.000.000.000.000.000,[1116])
1.000.000.000.000.000.000,[1117])
10.000.000.000.000.000.000,[1118])
100.000.000.000.000.000.000,[1119])
1.000.000.000.000.000.000.000,[1120]) [53 b]
10.000.000.000.000.000.000.000,[1121])
100.000.000.000.000.000.000.000,[1122])
1.000.000.000.000.000.000.000.000,[1123])
10.000.000.000.000.000.000.000.000,[1124])
100.000.000.000.000.000.000.000.000,[1125])
1.000.000.000.000.000.000.000.000.000,[1126])
10.000.000.000.000.000.000.000.000.000,[1127])
100.000.000.000.000.000.000.000.000.000,[1128])
1.000.000.000.000.000.000.000.000.000.000,[1129])
10.000.000.000.000.000.000.000.000.000.000,[1130])
100.000.000.000.000.000.000.000.000.000.000,[1131])
1.000.000.000.000.000.000.000 000 000.000.000.000,[1132])
10.000.000.000.000.000.000.000.000.000.000.000,[1133])
100.000.000.000.000.000.000.000.000.000.000.000,[1134])
1.000.000.000.000.000.000.000.000.000.000.000.000,[1135])
10.000.000.000.000.000.000.000.000.000.000.000.000,[1136])
100.000.000.000.000.000.000.000.000.000.000.000.000,[1137])
1.000.000.000.000.000.000.000.000.000.000.000.000.000,[1138])
10.000.000.000.000.000.000.000.000.000.000.000.000.000,[1139])
100.000.000.000.000.000.000.000.000.000.000.000.000.000,[1140])
1.000.000.000.000.000.000.000.000.000.000.000.000.000.000,[1141])
10.000.000.000.000.000.000.000.000.000.000.000.000.000.000,[1142])

100.000.000.000.000.000.000.000.000.000.000.000.000.000.000,[1143])
1.000.000.000.000.000.000.000.000.000.000.000.000.000.000.000,[1144])
10.000.000.000.000.000.000.000.000.000.000.000.000.000.000.000,[1145])
100.000.000.000.000.000.000.000.000.000.000.000.000.000.000.000,[1146])
1.000.000.000.000.000.000.000.000.000.000.000.000.000.000.000.000,[1147])
10.000.000.000.000.000.000.000.000.000.000.000.000.000.000.000.000,[1148])
100.000.000.000.000.000.000.000.000.000.000.000.000.000.000.000.000,[1149])
1.000.000.000.000.000.000.000.000.000.000.000.000.000.000.000.000.000,[1150]).

After this number eight members more of the decimal system are mentioned.[1152])

It is said, further on, in the *Bodhisattvabhūmi*:[1153]) —

There are two methods of counting the immeasurable periods of aeons. (According to the first of these methods), the periods derive their name from the years, months, and moments, which, as regards each aeon, are immeasurable. Otherwise (one may explain the term) "immeasurable period" as — „extending beyond every imaginable number." Those who are of the opinion, that many "immeasurable" periods are required for the attainment of Buddhahood, admit the first system. On the contrary, those, who hold three immeasurable periods to be sufficient, consider the second (system to be the right one). Indeed, it will be in harmony with the Sūtras, where it is said: — Extending beyond the number of aeons, equal to that of the sands of the Ganges. In the Commentary on the *Aṣṭasāhasrikā*[1154]) we read: — The mentioning of three immeasurable periods is conventional.[1155])

From the standpoint of (the Sūtras of) direct meaning,[1156]) the number is in reality thirty-three, as it is said: — Indeed, the first period begins with the (primary) stage of Accumulation and ends with the first stage of Enlightenment.[1157]) The second commences with the Immaculate[1158]) stage and lasts till the seventh.[1159]) Otherwise, the three immeasurable periods last [54 a] from the stage called the Immovable[1160]) and up to the attainment of Buddhahood. Thus, may it be said, if it is stated, that Buddhahood may be attained in three immeasurable periods, it will be in conflict with the Sūtras of direct meaning.[1161]) (To this we answer: — This is quite right). Indeed, (the time of Accumulating Merit is generally divided into) three equal portions, and this is the reason, that three immeasurable periods are (frequently) spoken of in Scripture. This, however, is by no means the true state of things, and consequently it is quite right, that the version of the Sūtras of conventional meaning proves to be contradictory. Indeed it has been said by Vasubandhu himself: —

The first period of aeons passes away the while (the Bodhisattva) brings to termination the (preliminary) stage of Accumulating Merit. Thereafter the Stage of Faith is brought to completion and in the meantime the second period of aeons elapses. Finally (the Bodhisattva) enters upon the ten main stages, (rising higher and higher) from the Stage of Joy and up to the final stage (of Bodhisattva perfection), — that of the Clouds of the Truth.[1162]) Each of these stages is brought to accomplishment during three immeasurable periods and after they are all terminated, the stage of Buddhahood, — that of the All-pervading Light is reached. Consequently, the state of a Buddha is attained after thirty-three immeasurable periods of aeons.

As to the tradition of the *Lalitavistara*[1163]) such is as follows: (Buddha) has brought to maturity all the roots of virtue during seven immeasurable aeons. This tradition, consequently, considers seven periods to be the time required for the attainment of Buddhahood).

According to Vinītadeva's *Nikāya-bhedopadarçana-saṁgraha*[1164]) some of the Hīnayānist sects admit, in their turn, ten periods. We have thus a great many different traditions and interpretations (as regards the time of accumulating merit). It has, moreover, been said by Maitreya:[1165]) —

This is regarded as the first stage;
(Attained) after immeasurable aeons.[1166])

And: [1167]) —

The end of the Path of Concentration,
Is attained after the termination of two immeasurable periods.

According (to these two verses) three periods are likewise admitted. Now, these immeasurable periods of accumulating merit [54 b] do not begin immediately after (the Bodhisattva's Initial Vow. It is said in the *Ratnameghasūtra*:[1168]) — O noble youth, the state of a Buddha is completely attained (only) after many immeasurable aeons. O noble youth, the Buddha is unaccessible to measure, thought and investigation. — The Bodhisattva Sarvanīvaraṇaviṣkambhin[1169]) asked: — O Lord, is it not possible (for us) to become Buddhas after three immeasurable periods? — The Lord replied: — O noble youth, how canst thou ask (such a question)? The attainment of the sphere of a Buddha by a Bodhisattva is a thing inconceivable to the mind, and it is not possible to reach this goal within the time of three immeasurable aeons. The periods (of Accumalation) commence, when the Bodhisattva has come to (the conception of) the unity of the universe. From that time the aeons are to be counted and not from (the Bodhisattva's Initial Vow).

And in the *Mahāyānasaṁgraha*[1170]) we read: —

Endowed with the power of good (qualities) and with that of his solemn oaths,
And, with a firm mind, venturing on Sublime Paths,
The Bodhisattva begins (his Accumulation of Merit)
For three immeasurable periods of aeons.

The *Mahāyāna-saṁgraha-upanibandhana*[1171]) comments (this verse) as follows: — The good qualities mean the same as virtue, and (the Bodhisattva) being possessed of the power of virtue is spoken of as "endowed with the power of good qualities". He is likewise regarded as possessing the power of (his) solemn oaths (and of prayer), since this power makes itself manifest in him. The first of these powers is concluded from the Bodhisattva's being unaccessible to harm from the part of hostile agencies, and the second — by his invariably meeting with a teacher,[1172]) (who guides him in precepts). The firmness of (the Bodhisattva's) mind (shows itself) by his never giving up the thoughts directed toward Enlightenment, in spite of the attempts of bad friends to divert him. "Venturing on Sublime Paths" means, [55 a] that (the Bodhisattva) in this life[1173]) and in the future states of existence gives increase to all the virtuous qualities and never becomes destitute of any of them. Consequently, when he becomes possessed of the force of the roots of virtue and with that of his vows, obtains a firm mind, which it is impossible to divert, and is no more contented with slight, insignificant merits, — from that time the Bodhisattva begins (the Accumulation of Merit) for three immeasurable periods of aeons.

Some authorities say, that the immeasurable periods begin from the Path of Training, since it is said in the *Bodhisattva-bhūmi*:[1174]) —

During the first immeasurable period one abides on the Stage of Faith,[1175] and, the latter having been terminated, the entrance upon the Stage of Joy is secured. And in the Commentary[1176] it is to be read: — Because (the commencement of) this (first) immeasurable period from the Stage of Faith is made known by the Bodhisattva's being firmly rooted in virtue through his persistent, fiery energy.

All this requires accurate examination. If it is said, that (the first period) begins from the Stage of Faith, this does not mean, that it commences only with the Path of Training. In the same *Bodhisattva-bhūmi*[1177] we read, that the Stage of Faith begins directly after the Initial Vow (of the Bodhisattva). And the *Abhidharma-samuccaya-bhāṣya*[1178] says: —

The Bodhisattva, who has attained the Stage of Faith and got a firm position in the Mahāyānistic family, is not, however, able, — (during the period, that lasts from the moment of) his first great vow, and up to his entering the Stage of Joy, — to attain, alone and by himself, the passage out of this world. (Consequently, the first immeasurable period begins long before the Bodhisattva has entered upon the Path of Training), for, if this were otherwise, there would be a disagreement with Scripture as we have seen above, and with the statement of Abhayākaragupta[1179] that the first immeasurable period begins with the Path of Accumulating Merit and lasts till the end of the first stage. Therefore, the first period (in reality) commences, when (the Bodhisattva, abiding) onl the Path of Accumulation, has become possessed of the power of virtue etc. [55 b].

Again, we read in the *Nirṇaya-saṁgraha*:[1180]

How is it possible to attain Supreme Enlightenment during one single state of existence, if even the attainment of Arhatship requires not one life, but a long succession (of births)? (Answer): — It is possible by (miraculously) prolonging (the activity of) the vital force. And the Mādhyamika Dharmamitra[1181] says: — By the force of the (supernatural) faculties and the energy of the Bodhisattva, the three immeasurable periods may lose their obligatory character.

*The Mahāyānistic traditions concerning the Buddha's Accumulation of Merit.*

IV $Acb_1b_2c_3$. The tradition of the *Bodhisattva-piṭaka*[1182]) on this subject is as follows: — (Our Teacher) when he was existing in the form of the prince Caritavīrya, the son of the king Vijitāyus in the palace called Vijayadhvaja, worshipped the Buddha Mahāskandha, who had come into this world, and, having engendered the roots of virtue, accumulated merit for. one immeasurable period of aeons and attained the first stage of Bodhisattva perfection.

Thereafter, having been born as the merchant Prajñābhadra, the minister of king Sundarāloka (?)[1183]) in the city called Jambunadīsuvarṇa[1184]) (?) he worshipped the Buddha Ratnānga, who had appeared in this world, and took the latter's precepts to heart. From that time he began to accumulate merit for another immeasurable period and through this reached the seventh stage. Then, reborn as Megha, the son of a Brāhmaṇa, he studied the Vedas with the Brāhmaṇa Ratna, and after that set out to search for an object of worship. After having passed through many cities of Central India, he reached the market place of Padmavatī, the residence of the king Arindama(?)[1185]) At that time the son of a Brāhmaṇa, Dīpapati, had just attained Buddhahood under the name of Dīpaṁkara, and as he manifested himself in this world (as a Buddha), the gods appeared in the skies to greet him, with flowers, lutes [56 a], and cymbals in their hands and singing songs (of praise). This (Megha, the Brāhmaṇa's son) saw and asked the gods: "What are you doing there?" (The gods replied): — How doest thou not know? The Buddha Dīpaṁkara is residing here. Upon hearing this, (Megha) thought: — O, it is not easy to meet with the appearance of a Buddha. Therefore, I should well do, if I repay afterwards the money (which I have to bring) to my teacher and, with the hundred karṣapaṇas I have collected, to sacrifice to the Buddha. Having thus thought, he bought five blue lotus-flowers from the Brāhmaṇa's daughter Bhadralābhikā[1186]) and promised, that she, as a reward (for aiding him in his pious action) would (henceforth) in all her births have a good husband. Then he strewed the flowers to the feet of the Buddha Dīpaṁkara, and having spread the skin of a black antelope before him, (addressed him as follows): — O Dīpaṁkara, thou all-seeing Buddha, take thou to heart my best intentions and deign to place thy feet on this deer-skin. And, as the Buddha descended, Megha, delighted, prepared for him a seat, covered with a lion's skin of the colour of gold, and said: O Dīpaṁkara, thou all-seeing, if thou shalt not place thy feet on this and grant me thy prophecy, my body shall wither away on the spot. The teacher thus earnestly requested, sat down and spoke: O brethren, ye art not to tread upon the head of this youth, for he is (to become) the object of reverence for all living beings including the gods. In times to come is he to be Çākyamuni!

Thus he prophesied, and Megha, full of the highest delight, suddenly grew to the height of seven Tala-trees and, having practised 100,000 forms of meditation, attained the eighth stage, as it is said: —

Having presented the Buddha Dīpaṁkara with five lotus-flowers,
And made for him a seat out of a lion's skin,
I came to master the Teaching of Relativity,[1187]) [56 b]
And was foretold to be the foremost of the Çākyas.

Moreover, in Scripture, we read: —

At the time, when I received the prophecy of the Buddha Dīpaṁkara,
I attained the eighth stage (of a Bodhisattva)
And became possessed of the ten powers.

A certain teacher of the Chim-pa tribe says: —

The end of the three immeasurable periods coincides with the appearance of the Buddha Nakṣatrarāja. At that time Buddha had brought to accomplishment the Accumulation of Merit, but not completely, in all its forms. Therefore, (even) during this aeon, up to the time, when (human age in its regress had attained the limits of) twenty thousand years, and he was reborn as a teacher and Brāhmaṇa's son in the city of Ñer-ldan (?), he continued to accumulate merit. During the whole of this (immeasurable) period of time, the Teacher worshipped an infinite number of Buddhas and studied their Doctrines, as it is said in the *Candra-pradīpa*:[1188]) —

I have worshipped hundreds of millions of Buddhas,
And even more, — (a number infinite), — like that of the sands of the Ganges,

And al' these highest of living beings I have adored,
Sitting here on the Vulture's Peak.[1189])

*The Attainment of Buddhahood according to Mahāyāna.*

IV Acc$_1$b$_2$. (This paragraph deals with) the attainment of Supreme Enlightenment (by Buddha).

We have here to distinguish:

a$_1$) The essential character of Buddhahood,

b$_1$) The special narrative of the achievements performed by the Teacher,

c$_1$) The investigation of the essence of the (three) different forms of the Doctrine.[1190])

*The Essence of Buddhahood.*

IV Acc$_1$b$_2$a$_3$. The state of a Buddha is (in the diverse canonical works) differently characterized: —

1) (Some) take in consideration three distinctive features: (the Buddha's) Body as the substratum, (His) Transcendental Wisdom as the quality of this substratum, and the acts (of the Buddha).

2) (Others) view five subjects, namely (the Buddha's) Body, Word, Mind, qualities and actions.[1191])

3) (Still others) admit three characteristics: the removal (of the obscurations), the perception (of the Truth) and the (Buddha's) activity.

4) (And finally) there are authorites who characterize Buddhahood by two or three complements. As to the ***Buddha-bhūmi-sūtra***[1192]) — the version rendered by it considers the state of a Buddha to have five distinctive attributes. These five are as follows: —

1) The perfectly pure Absolute,[1193])
2) The (quiescent) Transcendental Wisdom resembling a mirror,[1194])
3) The Altruistic [57 a] Transcendental Wisdom[1195]) (characterized by equal treatment of oneself and others),
4) The Discriminiative Transcendental Wisdom,[1196])
5) The (active) Transcendental Wisdom pursuing the welfare of living beings.[1197])

Moreover, (the state of a Buddha) is viewed from the standpoint of His three of four[1198]) Bodies.

Here we have to distinguish five points: —

$a_4$) The essential character of the three Bodies,

$b_4$) The etymology (of their Sanscrit names — *dharma-kāya, saṁbhoga-kāya* and *nirmāṇa-kāya)*,

$c_4$) The definite number of the Bodies (as corresponding to to the aim of each),

$d_4$) By what sort of intellect each of these Bodies is perceived,

$e_4$) Varieties (of the Bodies).

*The Essence of the three Bodies.*

IV $Acc_1b_2a_3a_4$. It is said in the *Sūtrālaṁkāra*:[1199]) —

The Essential Cosmical Body, the Body of Bliss, and the Apparitional,
Such are the different forms of the Buddhas, — their immaculate Absolute Essence.
The varieties of the Bodies of the Buddhas are:
The Essential Body, the Body of Bliss,
And another form is the Apparitional,
The first form being the substratum of the other two.

Thus we have first of all the Essential Body, which is otherwise called the Fundamental or the Cosmical. (This form represents the (monistic) Absolute in its perfectly pure nature and the (quiescent) Transcendental Wisdom, that resembles a mirror.

The Body of Bliss includes two other forms of Divine Wisdom, — the Altruistic, abiding in the Altruistic Nirvāṇa,[1200]) which is a result of the contemplation of equality in regard of oneself and other living beings, — and the Discriminative Transcendental Wisdom, perceiving everything cognisable without hindrance. The Apparitional Body is the Wisdom, acting in behalf of others, which conveys the fulfillment of all the projects of living beings by manifesting itself in various (miraculous) transformations.

The *Sūtrālaṁkāra*[1201]) says: –

The immeasurable transformations of the Buddhas are regarded as their Apparitional Body;
The complement of the double aim is thus founded upon two of the Bodies.[1202])

*Etymology of „dharma-kāya", „saṁbhoga-kāya" and „nirmṇāa-kāya".*

IV $Acc_1b_2a_3b_4$. The Sanscrit name for the Cosmical Body is *dharma-kāya.* The word *kāya* is derived from the verbal root *ci*, — to collect, accumulate. (The Cosmical Body) is thus regarded as the accumulation, the aggregate of (all) the elements, uninfluenced (by defiling agencies).[1203]) The *Satya-dvaya-vibhanga*[1204]) accordingly says: —

The Cosmical Body is thus called,
Being the aggregate of all the elements,
The substratum of all the unthinkable virtues,
And the essence of all things, the nature of which agrees with Logic.

The Cosmical Body is thus viewed from the standpoint of its being all-pervading,[1205]) [57 b], a receptacle of virtues, and demonstrable, as the essence (of all things).

The name for the Body of Bliss is *saṁbhoga-kāya*. The word *saṁbhoga* means "bliss, enjoyment", and this appelation has been given to this Body, since it represents (an existence characterized by) the full enjoyment of the Truth of the Great Vehicle,[1206]) as it is said: —

Perfectly enjoying the Truth.

Or: —

Since it takes delight in the Truth.

And: —

As it represents the complete enjoyment of the Truth.

The Apparitional Body is called *nirmāṇa-kāya*. It is Apparitional, since it neccessarily changes, has no stabile existence, and constantly assumes new forms, as says the *Sūtrālaṁkāra*:[1207]) —

By means of innumerable transformations, inconceivable to the mind,
(The Wisdom of the Buddha) brings about the fulfillment of all the projects of living beings.

***The definite number of the Bodies in correspondence with their aim.*** —

IV $Acc_1b_2a_3c_4$. (We read in the *Sūtrālaṁkāra*):[1208]) —

(All) the forms of the Buddhas are contained in the three Bodies,
Which represent the substratum, the fulfillment of one's own aim,
And that of others (respectively).

Thus we have the Body of Bliss as (the complement of) one's

own aim, the Apparitional, — as (that of) the welfare of others, and the Cosmical, — as the substratum of the former two.

*The different kinds of Intellect, perceiving the Bodies.*

IV $Acc_1a_2d_3$. The Cosmical Body in its complete form is accessible to the knowledge of the Buddha alone.[1209]) Those, who have attained the eighth or the first stage, are capable of intuiting its refractions. And (the Bodhisattvas), who abide on the Stage of Faith, have but a general notion of it. As to the Body of Bliss, — there are two opinions, as to whose element it might be: — that, which considers it to be perceived exclusively by the Bodhisattvas, that have attained the tenth stage, and that, which admits it to the sphere of all, who have reached the main stages.

The first opinion is expressed in the *Ratnāvalī*[1210]) (in the passage, that ends with the verse:

The Lord of the region of unthinkable Divine Wisdom,
Is the Great Supreme God,[1211]) —

and by the Mādhyamika Dharmamitra,[1212]) who likewise says, that the Body of Bliss (proper) is perceived by those, who have attained the tenth stage.

As to the second version, we read in the *Triçaraṇa-saptati*:[1213])

Emerged from the immeasurable Accumulation of Virtue,
The sons of the Buddhas,[1214]) abiding on the ten stages,
Behold that Body, which [58 a] completely enjoys the Truth of the Doctrine.

This Body becomes thus the element of such Bodhisattvas.

As concerns the Apparitional Body, — its highest form, when needed, manifests itself after the Degree of Heat[1215])but, in general, the manifestations of the Body begin with the great Path of Accumulation, as says the *Sūtrālaṁkāra*:[1216]) —

The Buddha, whom it is not easy to behold, may thus be seen.

And: —

It is possible to see him even before.

As to (the manifestations of the Apparitional Body) in the form of) incarnations etc. (we read in the *Abhisamayālaṁkāra*:[1217]) —

If all the factors (of perfection in the converts) are brought to maturity,
Wherever and whenever His help is needed,
At that place and time He manifests Himself.

To those, that are not converted, as well as to the converts, that are unworthy,[1218] the Buddha does not appear.

The *Sūtrālaṁkāra* says:[1219] —

As in a broken water-pot
The reflection of the moon cannot be seen,
In the same way to those, that are evil,
The Buddha does not manifest Himself.

*Varieties of the Bodies.*

IV $Acc_1b_2a_3e_4$. In regard of the varieties of the Bodies, we first of all take into consideration the Cosmical Body. The *Suvarṇa-prabhāsa* says: — The Cosmical Body is that, which represents the Absolute Truth and the unerring Transcendental Wisdom. — The Cosmical Body may thus be viewed as the substratum and the essence of all the elements, as the Absolute and the Divine Transcendental Wisdom, and as either active[1220] or immutable[1221]. As concerns the Body of Bliss, we quote the opinion of the Mādhyamika Dharmamitra:[1222] — The great Body of Bliss (proper) is perceived only by (the Bodhisattva) who has attained the tenth stage, but that, which, being (in reality) a special form of the Apparitional Body, seen already by the Bodhisattva, who has reached the first stage, — is likewise known as the Body of Bliss. The first of the varieties has five definite characteristics, which are as follows: — 1) The definite place, — is (the region) Akaniṣṭha.[1223] It is said in the Madhyama-āgama-pariccheda(?)[1224] that Akaniṣṭha forms a part of the Pure Spheres.[1225] And in the *Lankāvatāra*[1226] we read: —

In the delightful region Akaniṣṭha,
Shining with diverse jewels [58 b]
In the highest of the Pure Spheres,
The Supreme Buddha has come to full Enlightenment,
And as to the incarnate forms, —
Such attain Buddhahood here (in this world).

And in the Tantras: —

If the Pure Spheres are abandoned etc.

The teacher Kamalaçīla says: — Akaniṣṭha is (the realm of) the gods. One part of it is the residence of the gods of the Pure Spheres and there only the Saints have their dwelling. Above them there is a region, called the Abode of the Great Supreme God,[1227] where the Bodhisattvas that are on the tenth stage, have their last birth. The incarnations of such Bodhisattvas (at the same time), manifest themselves here in this world. So is it said in Scripture. — The Mādhyamika Dharmamitra[1228]) considers the abode of the Body of Bliss to be the region Ādhāra-garbha-puṣpa-alaṁkṛta (?)[1229]). He says: — 1.000.000.000 worlds of four continents[1230]) form the three chiliocosms.[1231]) The latter, taken 1.000.000.000 times are equal to one Prasara-anusaṁdhi(?)[1232]). 1.000.000.000 such aggregates of worlds form one Prasara-tantu (?)[1233]). This one, being in its turn taken 1.000.000.000 times constitutes one Madhya-prasara-tantu (?)[1233a]) (Finally), the latter, multiplied by 1.000.000.000 is that, which is called the Puṣpa-ādhāra-garbha-alaṁkāra-vyūha(?), the sphere of Vairocana,[1234]) on the palm of whose hand, in a minute particle of it, may be placed the Great Frozen Lake. This Vairocana is viewed as the Body of Bliss.

2) The definite Essence. (The Body of Bliss) is endowed with the (32) characteristic marks (of a Buddha)[1235]) and with the (80) secondary features.[1236])

3) The definite circle of adherents is formed by the Bodhisattvas, who have attained the tenth stage.

4) The definite character of enjoyment is: — Taking delight in the Truth of the Great Vehicle.[1237])

5) The definite time is: — Eternity.

As regards the Apparitional Body, we read in the Sūtrālaṁkāra:[1238]) —

By constantly showing acts of great dexterity,
Birth (in an individual form), the attainment of Enlightenment, and that of Nirvāṇa, —
This Apparitional Body proves a sure means of final deliverance.

Thus (we see the Apparitional Body) in four aspects. First of all it manifests itself as Viçvakarman[1239]) or a Gandharva [59 a], then it appears in the form of birds and the like, furtheron — as a (human) incarnation (like that of) Çākyamuni, and, finally, as passing away into Nirvāṇa. Dharmamitra, in his turn, speaks of two forms, — that, which has and which has not attained complete maturity.

(From all that has been said, we see), that the numerous Bodhisattvas, who have attained the state of a Buddha, can neither be regarded as (coalesced into) one single substance, nor may they, on the other hand, be viewed as a plurality of forms. — The ideas of unity and plurality cannot be applied (to Buddhahood). This is expressed by the *Sūtrālaṁkāra*[1240]) as follows: —

With the Buddhas, in the aspect of the Absolute,
There is neither unity nor plurality, —
Since (from one point of view) they are bodiless like space,
And (from the other) still adhere to their previous bodily forms.

And:[1241]) —

(From the standpoint of) the Absolute Essence,
Buddhahood is not a unity,
For (the Bodhisattvas that have come to Enlightenment)
Belong to different families,
(The Accumulation of Merit) of each of them cannot be rendered fruitless,
Their moral feats are summarized and the course of moral progress is beginningless.
Neither is it a plurality, the Cosmical Body being an undifferentiated whole.

***The Acts of the Buddha.***

IV $Acc_1b_2b_3$. Although the acts of the Buddha are so numerous as to be inconceivable to our mind, still, having in view those, who demand a definite number, and, moreover, in order to examine more closely the principal achievements of the Buddha, the learned (usually) mention twelve acts. Kamalaçīla says: — It is necessary to remove the impediments in regard of the thoughts, that concern the Buddha's Body and his twelve acts. And the Mādhyamika Dharmamitra[1242]): — by means of (the narrative of) the twelve acts of the Buddha, beginning with his descent from Tuṣita,[1243]) the converts are brought to maturity.

The *Ratnāvalī*[1244]) speaks of the Buddha's acts as follows: —

(The Buddhas), guided by mercy, manifest (their achievements),
The coming (into this world), birth, enjoyment of life,
Departure from home, practise of asceticism,
The proceeding toward Enlightenment,
The victory over the Evil One and his hosts,

The exposition of the Doctrine,
The descent from the abode of the gods,
And, in a like way, the passing away into Nirvāṇa.

According to this and similar passages, the Buddha's descent from the realm of the gods is regarded as one of his achievements. When he was residing in the city of India called Keçavatī[1245]) the Lord [59 b] rose up to the realm of the gods in order to convert His mother, (who was reborn there). Thencefrom he descended, by means of a staircase of lapis-lazuli, and this His return is known as "the descent from the abode of the gods".

In the *Upāyakauçalya* and other Sūtras[1246]) the fact of (Buddha's) fixing the time of the decline of His Doctrine is likewise considered to be one of His acts. (Buddha said) that the Doctrine would cease to exist, when there would be no need in it. He made this in order to prevent the arising of guilt, connected with the (forcible) rejection of the Doctrine. The *Suvarṇa-prabhāsottamā*[1247]) says: —

The Buddhas do not pass away,
And their Doctrines do not cease to exist,
But, in the process of converting living beings,
They, (from time to time), show the passing away into Nirvāṇa and the like.[1247])

Some count the descent from the Tuṣita heavens among the acts of the Buddha, but others object to this, saying, that, since it is said in the Commentary on the *Sūtrālaṁkāra*:[1248]) —

Showing the dwelling in the region of Tuṣita, —

In the Commentary on the *Abhisamayālaṁkāra*:[1249]) —

By manifesting oneself as residing in the abode of Tuṣita, —

and the *Uttaratantra*:[1250]) — He became born etc., —

the Buddha's residing in Tuṣita is regarded as previous to His twelve acts. This, however, disagrees with the geat Commentary on the *Saṁdhi-nirmocana-sūtra*,[1251]) where it is said: — (The Buddha) in His Apparitional form exhibits, simultaneously, in all the regions of the world, His twelve acts, to begin with the first — His descent from Tuṣita, and up to the last — the Great Nirvāṇa. Now, there may arise the question, as to which of the said acts being peculiar to the Buddha, and which — to the Bodhisattva. It is said in the *Pitṛ-putra-samāgama-sūtra*,[1252]) that the Highest of Sages, has, an immeasurable period of aeons before, attained Enlightenment in the world called Indraketu, and that now He (constantly) manifests Himself in the form of a Buddha or a Bodhisattva, pursuing the welfare of living beings. [60 a] It is said as follows:

O Lord, in eight milliards of forms,
Thou hast manifested thyself as a Buddha,
Nevertheless, not satisfied with this,
Thou hast again directed Thy mind toward Enlightenment;
For skilful in the way of exercising Thy power,
By bringing to purification thousands of Buddhaic worlds,
Thou, o Buddha, art searched for by all living beings.
And at present, having made Thy first Initial Vow,
Here and there Thou doest appear.
And even now, Thou, o Greatest of Leaders,
Showest Thyself in innumerable hosts of Buddhas.

And in the *Saddharma-puṇḍarīka*[1253]) we read: —

For hundreds and thousands of aeons,
The duration of which cannot be measured,
I have attained Supreme Enlightenment (again and again)
And have constantly preached the Doctrine.

From all this we see, that (the Teacher) has attained Buddhahood long before (His manifesting the twelve acts), which, consequently, are all to be equally viewed (as those of the Buddha). However, there are other points of view, as regards this subject, which are to be found with the different schools. Of these the Hīnayānist tradition has been mentioned by me before. According to the versions of (especially) Mahāyānistic character, the Buddhas, having attained Enlightenment in the regions of Akaniṣṭha, exhibit, subsequently, their twelve acts here, in the world of gross bodies. It is said in the *Lankāvatāra*:[1254])

In the world of gross bodies and in the immaterial sphere,
The Buddhas cannot attain Enlightenment,
Only in Akaniṣṭha, the sphere of pure matter,
Free from passions, thou canst become a Buddha.

In the *Ghanavyūha-sūtra*:[1255]) —

All the Buddhas (attain Enlightenment) in Akaniṣṭha,
And those, who have not become Buddhas (there),
Cannot exhibit the twelve acts in the world of gross bodies.

The *Uttaratantra*[1256]) says: —

The Wisdom of the Universe, having mercifully looked down upon all living beings,
Has, without changing His Cosmical Essence,
Manifested Himself in the form of diverse incarnations. [60b]
He assumed the birth (in an individual form),
Descended from the region of Tuṣita,
Entered His mother's womb, became born,
Showed His skill in arts and sports,
Led a merry life amongst women,
Then, departed (from home), practised asceticism,
Came to Bodhimaṇḍa, vanquished the Evil One and his hosts,
Attained Supreme Enlightenment,
Turned the Wheel of the Doctrine,
And passed away into Nirvāṇa.
These acts He demonstrated in the impure spheres,
As long as He was abiding in this world.

(The twelve acts) are, consequently, ascribed to the Apparitional Body. It is said, moreover, in the *Vyākhyāyukti*:[1257]) — From the time of His existence as a teacher and Brāhmaṇa's son, Buddha manifested Himself only in one of His Apparitional forms. How that? (Guṇamati)[1258]) comments this passage as follows: — The Lord, in the times of the Buddha Kāçyapa, manifested himself in one of His Apparitional forms, as Brahmacārin, a teacher and Brāhmaṇa's son. Thereafter He was reborn as Çvetāketu in the Tuṣita heavens, and then became Sarvārthasiddha, the son of Çuddhodana. He dwelt in a royal palace, from which He (ultimately) departed, went to Ārāḍakalāma[1259]) and other (heretical teachers) in search of the Path for Attaining Enlightenment. After that He gradually attained the state of a Buddha, preached His Doctrine, and then, gradually passed away into Nirvāṇa. During all this time He showed only one of His Apparitional forms.

Vagīçvarakīrti says: —

Victorious be He, who, having perceived the Absolute Truth in Akaniṣṭha,
Has assumed the form of Çvetaketu, to act in behalf of the denizens of Tuṣita,
And after that, for the sake of the living beings of this world,

Has manifested Himself as the Highest of the Çākyas,
Has vanquished the Lord of Death and showed His miraculous feats.

Thus, according to this and many other similar traditions, the Teacher, having accomplished the Accumulation of Merit [61 a], attained the tenth stage and the uttermost limits of phenomenal existence, became a Buddha in Akaniṣṭha and after that demonstrated in the world of gross bodies His twelve acts, which are, consequently, all of them, to be viewed as solely those of the Buddha.

Çākyamitra and others, who hold the doctrine of the Guhyasamāja, say, that the Teacher, when He was practising asceticism, left His worldly frame on the banks of the Nairanjanā river, and, in His spiritual form, rose up to the Akaniṣṭha heavens, where He became a Buddha in the form of the Body of Bliss. Thereupon the spirit again descended into the Body wearied by penance, and after that, the other acts, the arrival at Bodhimaṇḍa etc. were performed. Consequently, to speak with the said authorities, the acts preceding the practice of asceticism are to be regarded as those of the Bodhisattva, and those, performed subsequently, — as the acts of the Buddha. The great translator, the Incarnation (of Atīça) — Ratnabhadra, in his Refutation of the incorrect spells, shares the same opinon. The Mādhyamika Dharmamitra in his turn says, that the Buddha, having attained Enlightenment in Akaniṣṭha, exercises his activity there, and that the Buddha in such a form, and He, who has demonstrated the twelve acts in the world of gross bodies exclusively, are to be regarded as two (separate manifestations).

The tradition in common with all the Vehicles is rendered, by the ***Abhidharma-samuccaya***[1260]) as follows: — Who is He, the Buddha, inconceivable to our mind? (Answer) It is the individual, who, from the time of His residing in the Tuṣita heavens and, up to that of the great Nirvāṇa, has demonstrated in the world of gross bodies all the acts of the Boddisattva and those of the Buddha.

The ***Abhidharma-samuccaya-bhāṣya***[1261]) gives the following explanation: — In saying "all the acts of the Bodhisattva", the author of the main work means those exhibited in the period, beginning with the Teacher's abiding in Tusita and up to His victory over the Evil One. "The acts of the Buddha" are those, that begin with the attainment of Enlightenment and end with the final Rest. [61 b] Such is the direct meaning of the words.

As concerns this narrative of ours, (the order of the Buddha's acts, given by it) is founded upon the verses of the *Uttaratantra*. After the Brāhmaṇa's son had died, the Teacher was reborn in Tuṣita as Çvetaketu and preached His Doctrine to the gods. At that time, by the force of His own virtues, and that of the blessing of (all) the Buddhas, He came to hear, from the sounds of celestial music, the following words:[1262]) —

O Thou, treasury of boundless virtues,
Displaying the light of High Wisdom, knowledge, memory and understanding,
And endowed with matchless powers, —
Remember Thou the prophecy of Dīpaṁkara.
Although,[1263]) Highest of living beings,
This abode of Tuṣita shines with the splendour of Thy virtues,
Still, as Thou hast a mind full of great mercy,
Let the rain of it descend (on earth) from the miraculous banner of Commiseration.
The time is come, be Thou not indifferent,
And, as Thou art merciful, grant Thy ear to this prayer.

## Notes.

1 These translations are in need of revision, since there are considerable mistakes in which both translations always agree.

2 Bod-Chos-ḥbyuṅ.

1 Tib. *bdun-ldan* = Sanscr. *Saptāçva, Saptāçva-vāhana,* — «possessed of seven» — the seven horses of the sun's chariot.

2 tib. *thugs-bskyed* = *(bodhi-) citta-utpāda*; definition cf. below 47 a. 5. Cf. also Bodhicaryāvatāra I 15. 16.

3 tib. *dge-tshogs* = *kuçala-saṁbhāra* — "Accumulation of Merit", consists of *bsod-nams-kyi-tshogs* = *puṇya-saṁbhāra* "Accumulation of Virtue" and *ye-çes-kyi-tshogs* = *jñāna-saṁbhāra* — "Accumulation of Transcendental Wisdom"; cf. below 49 a. 3 ff.

4 Tib. *sku-gsum* "The Three Bodies (of Buddha)" — *saṁbhoga-kāya* — the Body of Bliss — Buddha in the heaven Akaniṣṭha (cf. below 57 a. 4, 58 a. 6—b. 5), *nirmāṇa-kāya* — the Incarnate Form (in the person of Çākyamuni

etc. cf. 57 a. 45, — b. 2, 3), and *dharma-kāya* — the Cosmical Body, representing the Universe sub specie aeternitatis. On the *dharma-kāya* and its identification with the Absolute cf. below 57 a. 3, 58 a. 4. Cf. also "Conception of Buddhist Nirvāṇa" p. 33.

**5** tib. *gzuṅ-ḥdzin-gos-bral-ba* = *grāhya-grāhaka-rahita*. This passage refers to Buddha viewed as the Absolute. Cf. Vasubandhu's Commentary on Sūtrālaṁkāra VI. 7. — "*dharma-dhātoḥ pratyakṣato gamane dvaya-lakṣaṇena viyukto grāhya-grāhaka-lakṣaṇene' yaṁ darçana-mārga-avasthā*". Cf. also Aṣṭasāhasrikāpiṇḍārtha Tg. MDO. XIV 333 a. 7. The Sanscrit text of this verse, preserved in Haribhadra's Abhisamayālaṁkārālokā (MS. Minaev 23 b. 4.) is als follows: *Prajñāpāramitā jñānam advayam. sa Tathāgataḥ* — The Climax of Wisdom is the unique (undifferentiated) Divine Wisdom. This is the Buddha. A more theistic conception of Buddhahood is to be found in the Uttaratantra (Tib. Rgyud-bla-ma) of Maitreya-Asanga, where the Buddha is spoken of as eternal (*ḥdus-ma-byas* = *asaṁskṛta*, — which term is explained as *thog -ma -dbus-mthaḥ-med-pa* — having neither beginning, middle nor end), — and endowed with Wisdom, Love, and Power (*mkhyen-daṅ-brtse-daṅ-nus-pa-ldan* = *jñāna-kṛpā-sāmarthyavān*) (Tg. MDO. XLIV 55 a. 3-7).

**6** Tib. *bya-lam* "the path of birds".

**7** Tib. *chu-ḥdzin* = *jaladhara* "the bearer of water".

**8** Tib. *ñon-moṅs-kyi-sgrib-pa* = *kleça-āvaraṇa* — the Obscuration of Passion and *çes-byaḥi-sgrib-pa* = *jñeya-āvaraṇa* — the Obscuration of Ignorance.

**9** An allusion to the *Apratiṣṭhita-nirvāṇa*. On the latter as the form of existence peculiar to the *saṁbhoga-kāya* and Buddha in this form regarded as the Supreme God, cf. below 57 a. 4 and 57 b. 4.

**10** Tib. *raṅ-byuṅ* = *Svayaṁbhū*. The xyl. has "*rab-byuṅ*".

**11** Tib. *sbyin-dgra* = *Yajñāri* "The enemy of sacrifices".

**12** Tib. *gtsug-na-zla-ba* = *Candraçekhara* — "with the moon in his diadem". **13** tib. *log-ḥdren* = *Vinayaka*.

**14** Tib. *skem-byed*.

**15** Tib. *mig-stoṅ* = *Sahasrākṣa* — "endowed with 1000 eyes".

**16** Tib. *ḥtsho-byed* = *Jīva*.

**17** Tib. *ston-par khas-ḥche che-bar mṅon-rlom* etc. "*khas-ḥche che-bar*" is a form of alliteration corresponding, in Indian poetics, to the Chekānuprāsa; cf. Alaṁkārasarvasva.

**18** tib. *srid-gsum* = *tribhuvana* — the human world, the realm of the gods and the infernal regions, or = *khams-gsum*. Cf. below p. 17, note 131.

**19** tib. *ḥdren-byed ñams-byed*. *ḥdren-byed* is a literal translation of the Sanscrit *netra* or *nayana* — "the eye".

**20** Gautama.

**21** tib. *rig-byed-gžuṅ-ḥdzin*.

**22** tib. *nam-mkhaḥi-gos-can* cf. Nyāyabindu B. B. 62. 19, 63. 10, 93. 1.

**23** The Çrāvakas, Pratyekabuddhas and Bodhisattvas are respectively compared to the bees that are satisfied by merely beholding the flower, those that enjoy its odour, and those striving to obtain from it honey — the true essence of Buddha's teaching.

**24** Tib. *ñer-ži* = *upaçama* "Pacification", "Quiescence".

**25** Tib. *chos-rnams-sdud-mdzad*. These are: —

a) Of Hīnayānistic Scripture: —
Ānanda — the Compiler of the Sūtras cf. below 92 b. 2—93 b. 3.
Upāli — the Compiler of the Vinaya cf. below 93 b. 4—94 a. 2.
Mahākāçyapa — the Compiler of the Abhidharma cf. below 94 a. 2—3.
b) Of the Mahāyāna: —
the Bodhisattva Mañjuçrī — Compiler of the Abhidharma,
" " Maitreya — " Vinaya,
" " Vajrapāṇi — " Sūtras cf. below, 101 a. 4.

26 Tib. *rtag-chad smra-baḥi-lta-ba* — *çāçvatavāda* and *uccheda-vāda.*

27 Tib. *dkar-phyogs-lha-rnams* "the gods of the light (white) quarter", according to the Tibetan tradition "those that rejoice in virtuous deeds". They are opposed to *nag-phyogs-kyi-lha-rnams* — "the divinities of the dark quarter, those that rejoice in deeds of sin.

28 cf. M. V. § 125.

29 Tib. *ṅag-gi-yul-las ḥdas* "passed beyond the sphere of words".

30 The celebrated Teachers of Buddhism in India — Nāgārjuna, Āryāsanga, Āryadeva etc. The prophecy, as rendered by the Lankāvatāra and Mañjuçrīmūlatantra cf. below — with regard to Nāgārjuna — 105 b. 3—6, and to Asanga 105 b. 6—106 a. 3.

In this verse there are 12 varieties of Chekānuprāsa:

(a) *rgyal-ba mchog-gis mchog-tu* "by the Highest of Buddhas as great" (*mchog-gis* — "by the Highest"; *mchog-tu* — "as great").

(b) *luṅ-bstan-bstan-pa* — "...foretold, of the Doctrine..." (*luṅ-bstan* "foretold"; *bstan-pa* "the Doctrine");

(c) *dar-mdzad mdzad-pa dri-med* — "...the Propagators, the stainless work..." (*dar-mdzad* — "the Propagators"; *mdzad-pa dri-med* — "the stainless work");

(d) *mṅaḥ; mṅaḥ-bdag* — ..."apprehending, of the Lord..." (*mṅaḥ* mastering, apprehending"; *mṅaḥ-bdag*" — the Lord";

(e) *dam-paḥi dam-paḥi-chos* — "... the Great One, the Highest Truth..." (*dam-paḥi* — "of the Great One"; *dam-paḥi-chos* = *sad-dharma* — "the Highest Truth..." lit. — "Doctrine").;

(f) *kun kun-tu bzuṅ-phyir* — "...all of it completely possessing..." (*kun* — "all"; *kun-tu* — "completely");

(g) *theg-pa-gsum-gyi-tshul tshul-bžin* "...of the three Vehicles the systems duly..." (*tshul* — "system"; "*tshul-bžin*" — "duly");

(h) *rab-ston ston-paḥi* — "...well expounded; the Teacher's..." (*rab-ston* — "well expounded"; *ston-pa* — "the Teacher");

(i) *gsuṅ-rab rab-tu* etc. — "...Word perfectly etc...." (*gsuṅ-rab* — "Word (Scripture);" *rab-tu* — "perfectly");

(k) *mṅaḥ-baḥi-thugs; thugs-rjes* — "...with powerful mind, mercifully ..." (*mṅaḥ-baḥi-thugs* — "powerful mind"; *thugs-rjes* — "out of mercy");

(l—m) *dgoṅs-ḥgrel ḥgrel-bçad bçad-pa* — "...primary and secondary comments uttered..." (*dgoṅs-ḥgrel* = Sanscr. *vṛtti* — "primary commentary"; *ḥgrel-bçad* = Sanscr. *ṭippaṇī* — "secondary Comment"; *bçad-pa* — "uttered, spoke").

31 The Hīnayāna is sometimes regarded as consisting of two independent parts: — the Vehicle of the Çrāvakas and that of the Pratyekabuddhas.

32 cf. note 2 l—m.

33 The fundamental Scripture of Buddhism (*pravacana*), the Tibetan translation of which is the *Bkaḥ-ḥgyur*.

34 The division of Çāstras — tib. *Bstan-ḥgyur*.

35 Tib. *bslab-pa-gsum*. (a) *tshul-khrims-kyi-bslab-pa* = *adhiçīla-çikṣā* — the Discipline of Morals.

(b) *sems-kyi-bslab-pa* = *adhicitta-çikṣā* — the Discipline of the Mind, otherwise termed *tiṅ-ṅe-hdzin-gyi-bslab-pa* = *adhisamādhi-çikṣā* — the Discipline of Meditation.

(c) *çes-rab-kyi-bslab-pa* = *adhiprajñā-çikṣā* — the Discipline of high (analytic) Wisdom.

36 Tib. *bsdu-ba-bži* = *catvāri saṁgraha-vastūni*: —

(a) *mkho-ba-sbyin-pa* = *dāna* — charity.

(6) *sñan-par-smra-ba* = *priya-vāditā* — fine, polite speech.

(c) *don-spyod-pa* = *artha-caryā* — favourable acts.

(d) *don-mthun-pa* = *samāna-arthatā* — common interest. cf. below 50 b. 5 and M. V. § 35.

3? Tib. *byin-zas* = *havirbhuj* or *hutāçana* — "the devourer of oblations".

3? Tib. *brda-sprod-tshig* — grammatically correct words.

40 Xyl. corrupt. Read *gzuṅ-gnas* for *gzur-gnas*.

41 Tib. *dam-paḥi-chos* = *saddharma*. For definition cf. below.

42 Tib. *rdzu-ḥphrul-gyi-rkaṅ-pa-bži* = *ṛddhipāda* cf. M. V. § 40.

43 Tib. *chu-srin-rgyal-mtshan-can* = *Makaradhvaja* — "the Owner of the Crocodile Ensign."

44 Tib. *smin-grol-gyi-žiṅ* — "the field of Conversion and Salvation".

45 cf. above p. 6 note 36.

46 Tib. *chos-kyi-ḥkhor-lo-bskor-ba* = *dharma-cakra-pravartana* — "Turning the Wheel of the Doctrine".

Three divisions of Scripture are known, with regard to time and contents: —

(a) Early Scripture (tib. *bkaḥ-daṅ-po*) — the Hīnayāna.

(b) Intermediate (tib. *bkaḥ-bar-ba*) — the Mādhyamika Doctrine and the Prajñā-pāramitā.

(c) Latest (tib. *bkaḥ-tha-ma*) — the Yogācāra Doctrine. cf. below 76 b. 6—80 a. 3.

47 cf. below 97 b. 3—4, 104 b. 4—6.

48 Tib. *Byaṅ-chub-sems-dpaḥi-sde-snod*. Kangyur DKON. III. 160 b.5., quoted in the Vyākhyāyukti 136 b. 3—4.

49 Tib. *Rnam-bçad-rigs-pa*, The work of Vasubandhu, one of his Prakaraṇas; tib. translation — Tangyur MDO LVIII 136 b. 4—137 a. 8 (condensed).

50 cf. p. 6 note 35. 51 ibid. 52 ibid.

53 Tib. *kun-nas-ñon-moṅs-pa* = *saṁkleça*.

54 Tib. *las-kyi-kun-nas-ñon-moṅs-pa* = *karma-saṁkleça*.

55 Tib. *ñon-moṅs-paḥi-kun-nas-ñon-moṅs-pa* = *kleça-saṁkleça*.

56 Tib. *skye-baḥi-kun-nas-ñon-moṅs-pa* = *jāti-saṁkleça*. Guṇamati in his Vyākhyāyuktiṭīkā (Tg. MDO. LX. 16 b. 5—8) enlarges upon this subject as follows: — *ñon-moṅs-paḥi-kun-nas-ñon-moṅs-pa daṅ las-kyi-kun-nas-ñon-moṅs-*

*pa dan skye-baḥi-kun-nas-ñon-mons-pa-ste; ñon-mons-pa-ñid kun-nas-ñon-mons-pa-yin-pas ñon-mons-paḥi-kun-nas-ñon-mons-pa-ste. las dan skye-baḥi-kun-nas-ñon-mons-pa-gñis kyan de-bžin-no. de-la yan-lag gsum-po ma-rig-pa dan sred-pa dan len-pa-dag-ni ñon-mons-paḥi-kun-nas-ñon-mons-pa-yin-no. ḥdu-byed dan srid-pa dan yan-lag-gñis-ni las-kyi-kun-nas-ñon-mons-pa-yin-te. rnam-par-çes-pa-la-sogs-pa yan-lag lhag-ma-rnams-ni skye-baḥi-kun-nas-ñon-mons-pa-yin-no.* Accordingly, the members 1, 8, and 9 of the formula of Evolution (i. e. *avidyā, tṛṣṇā* and *upādāna*) form "the defilement of passion" (*kleça-saṁkleça*), — the members 2, 10 (*saṁskāra* and *bhava*) — the defilement of former deeds, and the remaining seven (*vijñāna, nāma-rūpa, ṣaḍ-āyatana, sparça, vedanā, jāti,* and *jarā-maraṇa*) — the "defilement of birth" (*jāti-saṁkleça*).

**57** Tib. *dban-poḥi-sgo bsruns-pas* — "by guarding the doors of the senses".

**58** Tangyur MDO LVIII 135 b. 6—7.

**59** Tib. *thos-pa yons-su-byan-bar ḥgyur-ba* — "Complete purification of the matters studied".

**60** Prajñāpāramitā. Xyl. corrupt. Read according to Tg. *çes-rab-kyi-don* etc. for *çes-rab-kyis.*

**61** This and the following is condensed from the Vyākhyāyukti. Ibid. 135 b. 7—136 a. 8.

**62** cf. "Conception of Buddhist Nirvāna" p. 17. Correct *bden-pa-rtogs-pa* for *bden-par-rtogs-pa.*

**63** Tib. *thos-pa-las-byun-baḥi-çes-rab* = *çrutimayī prajñā.* cf. M. V. § 65.

**64** Tib. *bsam-pa-las-byun-baḥi-çes-rab* = *cintamayī prajñā.* Ibid.

**65** Tib. *bsgom-pa-las-byun-baḥi-çes-rab* = *bhāvanāmayī prajñā.* Ibid. This passage is likewise condensed from the Vyākhyāyukti. (Tg. MDO. LVIII 136 a. 8—b. 3).

**66** Tangyur MDO LVIII. 142 a. 3—5.

**67** Tg. *yon-tan-lna* for *phan-yon-rnam-pa-lna.*

**68** Tib. *ḥphags-paḥi-çes-rab-kyi-mig sbyon-bar-byed-pa* — "Purification of the vision of Highest Wisdom, the attribute of a Saint". This *ḥphags-paḥi-çes-rab* is synonymous with *ḥjig-rten-las-ḥdas-paḥi-çes-rab* = *lokottarā prajñā* and with *yogipratyakṣa.* Cf. "Conception of Buddhist Nirvana" p. 16—20.

**69** Tg. LVIII. 141 a. 4—8.

**70** Tib. *byan-chub-kyi-phyogs* = *bodhi-pakṣa.* These are (thirty seven in number): —

*dran-pa-ñe-bar-gžag-pa-bži* = *catvāri smṛtyupasthānāni.*
*yan-dag-par-spon-pa-bži* = *catvāri prahāṇāṇi.*
*rdzu-ḥphrul-gyi-rkan-pa-bži* = *catvāra ṛddhi-pādāḥ.*
*dban-po-lna* = *pañca indriyāṇi.*
*stobs-lna* = *pañca balāni.*
*byan-chub-yan-lag-bdun* = *sapta bodhy-angāni.*
*ḥphags-paḥi-lam-yan-lag-brgyad* = *ārya-aṣṭānga-mārga.*

**71** Tg. MDO. LVIII. 141 a. 8—b. 3.

**72** Tib. *rgyud-smin-pa-rnams-la.* Tg. has *rgyu-smin-pa.*

**73** Tg. 141 b. 3—7.

**74** cf. Meghadūta, Pūrvamegha v. 33 (*toya-krīḍā-nirata-yuvati* etc.).

**75** Correct, according to Tg. (141 b. 5) *yan-ḥbyun-baḥi-sred-pa* for ... *srid-pa.*

76 Tib. *bsam-gtan* = *dhyāna* (of four kinds cf. M. V. § 67).

77 Tbi. *mṅon-par-çes-pa* = *abhijñā* cf. M. V. § 14.

78 Tib. *tshad-med-pa* = *apramāṇa* ibid. § 69.

79 Tib. *rnam-par-thar-ba* = *vimokṣa* ibid. § 70.

80 Tib. *ḥjig-tshogs* = *satkāya*, defined as *zag-bcas-kyi-phuṅ-po-lṅa* — *sāsravāḥ pañca skandhāḥ* — the five groups of elements influenced by passions.

81 Tib. *gzuṅs* = *dhāraṇī*.

82 Tib. Byams-pa-seṅ-ge-sgraḥi-mdo. Kg. DKON V. 82 a. 4—5. The Kg. has: *mi gaṅ-gis-ni Gangāḥi bye-sñed-kyi ḥjig-rten-khams-mchog rin-chen gaṅ-byas-te dgaḥ-mchog-sems-kyis* etc.

83 Tib. *saṅs-rgyas-žiṅ* = *buddha-kṣetra*.

84 Kg. DKON. V. 82 a. 1—2. —

*Stoṅ-chen-khams-ni rin-chen gser-dag-gis*
*bkaṅ-ste gaṅ-la sbyin-pa byed-pa-ni*
*tshig-bžiḥi tshigs-su-bcad-pa-gcig brjod-pas*
*ji-ltar phan-ḥdogs de-ltar ḥgyur-ma-yin.*

85 Tib. Seṅ-ges-žus-paḥi-mdo. Kg. DKON. VI. 27 b. 4. Quoted in the Çikṣā-samuccaya BB. 53. 8 — *jāti-smarā, dharma-dānāt.*

86 Tib. Kluḥi-rgyal-po rgya-mtsho žus-paḥi-mdo. Kg. MDO. XIV, 125 a. 4.

87 Tib. Rin-chen-phren-ba. The Work of Nāgārjuna Tg. MDO. XCIV, 143 a. 2. The Tg. has: *chos-gžuṅ-don-dag dran-pa* for *gžuṅ-gi-don-dag dran-pa.*

88 Tib. Lhag-paḥi-bsam-pa-bskul-baḥi-mdo. Quoted in the Çikṣā-samuccaya B. B. 351. 1—8: — *yathoktam Ārya-adhyāçaya-saṁcodana-sūtre-viṁçatir ime Maitreya anuçaṁsā nirāmiṣa-dāne yo lābhā-satkāram apratikāṅkṣan dharma-dānaṁ dadāti (dadāmi?). Katame viṁçatiḥ yaduta smṛtimāṁç ca bhavati matimāṁç ca bhavati buddhimāṁç ca bhavati gatimāṁç ca bhavati dhṛtimāṁç ca bhavati prajñāvāṁç ca bhavati lokottarāṁ ca prajñām anuvidhyati alpa-rāgo bhavati alpa-dveṣo alpa-mohaḥ. Māraç ca asya avatāraṁ na labhate buddhair bhagavadbhiḥ samanvāhriyate amanuṣyāç cai' naṁ rakṣanti devāç ca asya ojaḥ kāye prakṣipanti amitrāç (sic) ca asya avatāraṁ na labhante mitrāṇi ca asya abhedyāni bhavanti ādeya-vacanaç ca bhavati vaiçāradyāṁç ca (sic) pratilabhate saumanasya-bahulaç ca bhavati vidvat-praçastaç ca anusmaraṇīyaṁ ca asya tad dharma-dānaṁ bhavati ime Maitreya viṁçatir anuçaṁsā iti.*

89 Tib. *blo* = *buddhi.* 90 Tib. *blo-gros* = *mati.*

91 Tib. *ḥjig-rten-las-ḥdas-paḥi-çes-rab* = *lokottarā prajñā* is the same as *ḥphags-paḥi-çes-rab* cf. above p. 10 note 68.

92 Tib. *glags* = *avatāra.* 93 Tib. *mi-ma-yin-pa* = *amanuṣya.*

94 Tib. *mdaṅs* = *ojas.* 95 Tib. *mi-ḥjigs-pa*=*vaiçāradya* cf. M. V. § 8.

96 Tib. Bslab-btus, B. B. p. 350. 24 — *dharma-dānaṁ nirāmiṣaṁ puṇya-vṛddhi-nimittaṁ bhavati* and *Kārikā* XXVI — *sarvāvasthāsu sattvārtho dharma--dānaṁ nirāmiṣaṁ bodhi-cittaṁ ca puṇyasya vṛddhi-hetuḥ samāsataḥ.*

97 *Çrāvaka-yāna-abhisamaya-gotra, pratyekabuddha-yāna-abhisamaya-gotra, tathāgata-yāna-ābhisamaya-gotra* — M. V. § 61.

98 Tg. MDO. LVIII 141 a. 1—2. 99 Tib. mṅon-pa-kun-las-btus-pa. The Work of Āryāsanga. Ibid. LVI, 123 b. 5.

100 Correct *ḥdzin-pa daṅ kha-ton-byed-pa daṅ bçad-pa-ni...* for .... *kha-ton-byed-pa dan bçad-pas.*

101 Tib. Luṅ-rnam-ḥbyed. Kangyur ḤDUL. VI—IX.

102 Tib. *phuṅ-po* = *skandha*. 103 Tib. *khams* = *dhātu*.

104 Tib. *skye-mched* = *āyatana*.

105 Tib. *rten-ciṅ-hbrel-par-ḥbyuṅ-ba* = *pratītya-samutpāda*.

106 Jātakamālā (ed. Kern, Harvard Series 1891) p. 214. 14—215. 2 (Sutasoma-jātaka).

107 *dīpaḥ çrutaṁ moha-tamaḥ-pramāthī caurādy-ahāryaṁ paramaṁ dhanaṁ ca*
*saṁmoha-çatru-vyathanāya çastraṁ nayopadeṣṭā paramaç ca mantrī* (verse 32).

108 Māra.

109 *paraṁ nidhānaṁ yaçasaḥ çriyaç ca* (end of verse 33) correct *grags daṅ dpal-gyi-gter* for *grags daṅ dpal daṅ gter*.

110 *satsaṁgame prābhṛta-çībharasya sabhāsu vidvaj-jana-rañjanasya, para-pravāda-dyuti-bhāskarasya* (*viçeṣahetuḥ*) ... (pada 1, 2, 3 of verse 34).

111 *vinīta-dīpta-pratibhojjvalasya prasahya kīrti-pratibodhanasya, vāk-sauṣṭhavasyā' pi viçeṣahetuḥ yogāt prasannārthagatiḥ çrutaçrīḥ* (verse 37).

112 *artha* is here in the sense of *bhūtaḥ sadbhūto' rthaḥ cf.* Nyāyabindu B. B. p. 11. 18. ff. (on yogipratyakṣa).

113 In tib. *bsgoms* (= *bhāvanā*) stands for *yoga* of the original. Prof. J. Speyer's translation of this passage is quite wrong.

114 *Çrutvā ca vairodhika-doṣa-muktaṁ trivarga-mārgaṁ samupāçrayante Çrutānusāra-pratipatti-sārās taranty akṛcchreṇa ca janma-durgam.* (verse 38).

115 Tib. *ḥkhor-gsum* = *trivarga* i. e. *dharma, artha, kāma* — religion, wealth and love.

116 Tg. MDO. LXIII. 27 a. 8—b. 1.

117 Tib. De-bžin-gçegs-paḥi-gsaṅ-ba-bstan-pa. Kg. DKON. I. 130 b. 7—131 a. 1.

118 Tib. Blo-gros-rgya-mtshos-žus-paḥi-mdo. Kg. MDO. XIV, 51 b. 1 (Ist and 2nd verse) and 52 a. 1. (3d verse) quoted in the Çikṣāsamuccaya p. 43—44.

119 *Parigṛhīto bhavatī* (sic) *jinebhir*
*devebhi nāgebhi ca kiṁnarebhiḥ* (sic) *puṇyena jñānena parigṛhītaḥ*
*saddharmadhāritva* (sic) *tathāgatānām.* p. 43. 6—9.

120 Omitted in the Çikṣāsamuccaya.

121 *Çakro 'tha Brahmā tatha* (sic) *lokapālo*
*manuṣya-rājā bhuvi cakravarttī*
*sukhena saukhyena ca bodhi* (sic) *budhyate*
*saddharmadhāritva tathāgatānām.*

122 Sic according to the passage in the Prajñāpāramitā quoted below. To speak with the Lamas, not merely a *theg-chen-gyi-grub-mthaḥ-smra-ba* (expounder of Mahāyānistic teachings) is meant here, but a Bodhisattva, one who belongs himself to the family of the High Vehicle — a *theg-chen-gyi gaṅ-zag*.

123 Here the first four subdivisions of the Path — the *saṁbhāra* —, *prayoga* —, *darçana* —, and *bhāvanā-mārga* are meant.

124 The *mi-slob-lam* = *açaikṣa-mārga*.

125 Çikṣāsamuccaya B. B. 351. 13—352. 1 ... *ye trisāhasra-mahā-sahasre lokadhātau sattvās te sarve arhattvaṁ prāpnuyus teṣāṁ ca arhatāṁ yad dānamayaṁ puṇya-kriyā-vastu çīlamayaṁ puṇya-kriyā-vastu bhāvanāmayaṁ*

*puṇya-kriyā-vastu tat kiṁ manyase Ānanda api tu sa bahu* (sic) *puṇyaskandhaḥ. āha bahu bhagavan bahu sugata bhagavān āha...* (351. 18.) ... *ato'py Ānanda bahutaraṁ puṇyaskandhaṁ prasavati yo bodhisattvo mahāsattvo' parasya bodhisattvasya prajñāpāramitā-pratisaṁyuktaṁ dharmaṁ deçayati antaça eka-divasam api.*

126 *dānamayaṁ puṇya-kriyā-vastu, çīlamayaṁ puṇya-kriyā-vastu, bhāvanāmayaṃ puṇya-kriyā-vastu* cf. M. V. § 93.

127 Çikṣāsamuccaya 352. 2—4. ... *idam Ānanda tasya bodhisattvasya mahāsattvasya dharma-dānaṁ sarva-çrāvaka-yānikānām api sarva-pratyeka-buddha-yānikānāṁ ca pudgalānāṁ kuçala-mūlam abhibhavati.*

128 Lit. the Vehicles of the Çrāvakas and Pratyekabuddhas.

129 Tg. MDO. XLIV 73 a. 4—b. 1. 130 Tg. corrupt *ñid-re.*

131 Tib. *srid-gsum* = *khams-gsum*: —

a) *ḥdod-paḥi-khams* = *kāma-dhātu* — the sphere of gross bodies,

b) *gzugs-kyi-khams* = *rūpa-dhātu* — the sphere of ethereal bodies, and

c) *gzugs-med-kyi-khams* = *arūpa-dhātu* — the sphere of immaterial bodies.

132 Cf. Conception of Buddhist Nirvāṇa p. 12—13 and Index 6 s. v. Yoga II.

133 Tib. Mdo-sde-rgyan XII 21—23. (Ed. Prof. S. Lévi.)

134 *yo granthato' rthato vā gāthā-dvaya-dhāraṇe prayujyeta sa hi daça-vidham anuçaṁsaṁ labhate sattvottamo dhīmān.*

135 *kṛtsnāṁ ca dhātu-puṣṭim prāmodyaṁ co' ttamaṁ maraṇa-kāle janma ca yathābhikāmaṁ jāti-smaratāṁ ca sarvatra.*

136 cf. above p. 13 and note 97. Vasubandhu, commenting this line, says: *kṛtsna-dhātu-puṣṭiḥ sarva-mahāyāna-adhiṣṭhānāya dhātu-puṣṭis tad āvaraṇa-vigamāt sarvatra mahāyāne' dhimukti-lābhataḥ* — Full increase of the elements (of virtue) means increase of all the elements, that cause one's perpetual abiding in the Mahāyāna, for, all the obscurations having been (through this) removed, adherence to the family of the High Vehicle at all times is secured.

Prof. S. Lévi translates: L'alimentation des Plans intégrale c'est l'alimentation des Plans pour dominer intégralement le Grand Véhicule, car, ces obstructions une fois quittées, on arrive à la croyance dans l'intégralité du Grand Véhicule. (?)

137 *buddhaiç ca samavadhānaṁ tebhyaḥ çravaṇaṁ tathā' grayānasya adhimuktiṁ saha buddhyā dvaya-mukhatām āçu bodhiṁ ca.*

138 Tib. *saṅs-rgyas-rnams-daṅ-phrad-pa* = *buddha-samavadhāna.*

139 *samādhi-mukhatā dhāraṇī-mukhatā ca* — the medium of deep meditation and that of memory.

140 Tg. MDO LVIII 34 a. 1—2. 141 Correct *thos-na* for *thos-nas.*

142 Ibid. 40 b. 2—3.

143a Cf. Abidharmakoça-bhāṣya B. B. 6. 2—3. — *don-dam-paḥi-chos mya-ṅan las-ḥdas-pa.* Cf. also Rosenberg Problems p. 87 "dharma par excellence".

143b Lit. an object of mental faculty (*yid-kyi-yul* = *mano-viṣaya*).

144 This and the following is condensed from the Vyākhyāyukti (Tg. MDO. LVIII 40 b. 3—41 a. 2).

145 Tib. *ḥdus-byas* = *saṁskṛta.* 146 Tib. *ḥdus-ma-byas* = *asaṁskṛta.*

147 Tib. *çes-bya* = *jñeya.*

148 Tib. *yaṅ-dag-paḥi-lta-ba* = *samyag-dṛṣṭi, the* first of the eight subdivisions of a Saint's Path (*ārya-aṣṭāṅga-mārga* cf. MV. § 44.)

149 The Vyākhyāyukti (40 b. 5.) says: *de-ni-yid-kho-naḥi-yul-yin-žiṅ yul-kho-na-yin-gyi rten-ni ma-yin-no* — it (*dharma* as a non-sensuous element) is an object of the intellectual faculty only, and only the object, but not that which forms the support (of mental faculty). And Guṇamati (Vyākhyāyuktiṭīkā, Tangyur MDO. LX 14 b. 2—24.) comments: — *de-ni yid-kho-naḥi yul yin-žiṅ žes-bya-ba-ni mig-la-sogs-pa-nas lus-kyi-dbaṅ-po-la-thug-pa-rnams-kyi ma-yin-pa-ste. de-ltar-na gsugs-la-sogs-pa bsal-ba-yin-no. mig-gi-rnam-par-çes-pa-la-sogs-pa-dag-kyaṅ de-ltar thal-bar-ḥgyur-na mi-ruṅ-bas yul-kho-na-yin-gyi rten-ni ma-yin-no žes-bya-ba-ḥdi smos-te. mig-gi rnam-par-çes-pa-la-sogs-pa-ni yid-kyi-rten-yaṅ yin-pas-so*: — the words "an object of intellectual faculty only" mean that it is not one corresponding to any of the sensuous faculties, to begin with the visual and ending with the tactile. Accordingly, (such elements as those of) Matter etc. are excluded. In such a case (the different kinds of) consciousness — the visual etc., — could be likewise meant (here). This would be a mistake; therefore, (the Author) says: "only the objects of mental faculty but not its supports", for visual consciousness and the other (five) are the supports of mental faculty. Cf. Central Conception of Buddhism p. 8. 6—12.

150 Tib. *ḥbyuṅ-ḥgyur* = *bhavana*. The Vyākhyāyukti (40 b. 8) says with regard to this meaning of *dharma*: *ḥbyuṅ-bar-ḥgyur-ba-la-ni ḥdu-byed-kyi-rdzas-rnams-ni deḥi-chos-so* — the attribute (quality) of things that are subjected to the influence of (active, originating) forces. In both the Xyl. and the Tangyur text of the Vyākhyāyukti we have *lus-ḥdi-ni-rgas-paḥi* (or: *rga-baḥi*) *chos yin-no*. This is evidently a mistake made by the Lotsavas in translating from the original which must have been *jarā-dharmo' yaṁ kāyaḥ* — a *bahuvrīhi* which they mistook for a *tatpuruṣa*. Guṇamati's Commentary (Tg. MDO. LX 14 b. 5) has correctly - - *rga-baḥi-chos-can*.

151 Cf. M. V. § 269. 152 Tib. *raṅ-gi-mtshan-ñid* = *svalakṣaṇa*.

153 Tib. *gzugs-su-ruṅ-ba* = *rūpaṇā*, has the same meaning as *sapratighatva* cf. Central Conception of Buddhism p. II.

154 Tg. MDO. LVIII 32 a. 4.

155 Tib. Ched-du-brjod-paḥi-tshoms. Tg. MDO. LXXI. 7 b. 5. The Tg. has *bde-ba thob* for *bde-bar ñal.*

156 Cf. M. V. § 82.

157 Tib. *gzugs-med-kyi-tiṅ-ṅe-ḥdzin*. Is the same as *samāpatti* cf. M. V. § 68.

158 Tib. *naṅ-paḥi-skyabs* lit: the interior (i. e. Buddhist) refuge. Cf. M. V. § 267 2.

159 Tib. *ḥkhor-daṅ-bcas-pa* together with (its) retinue.

160 Tib. *raṅ-bžin-med-pa* = *niḥsvabhāvatā*.

161 Tib. *sñiṅ-rje-chen-po* = *mahākaruṇā* cf. below p. (Xyl. 26 a. 6—b. 1.): *stoṅ-ñid-sñiṅ-rjeḥi-sñiṅ-po-can* = *karuṇā-garbhā çūnyatā* — Great Commisera.-tion — the Essence of Relativity. cf. Conception of Buddhist Nirvāṇa p. 83

162 *srid-žir-ltuṅ-ba. srid-pa* = *bhava* is the phenomenal world. *ži-(ba)* = *çama* "Quiescence" means here the Hīnayānistic Nirvāṇa. The idea of altruism and love in connection with the Doctrine of the Mahāyāna is expressed in the Abhisamayālaṁkāra I. 10 as follows: — *prajñayā na bhave sthānaṁ kṛpayā*

*na çame sthitiḥ* — by being possessed of High Wisdom, one does not remain in the phenomenal world, and being full of love, one does not abide in the (egoistic) peace.

163 Tib. *gźi-mthun-pa* = *sāmānādhikaraṇya.*

164 *rtogs-paḥi-chos* = *adhigama-dharma.*

165 *luṅ-gi-chos* = *āgama-dharma.* The quotation is from the Abhidharmakoça: Tg. MDO. LXIII. 27 a. 8.

166 Tg. MDO. XLIV. 55 b. I.

167 Tib. *ḥgog-pa* = *nirodha.*

168 The following passage is repeated twice: — a) as the definition, made by Buston himself, and b) as a quotation from the Abhidharmasamuccaya Tg. MDO. LVI 108 a. 1—2. The Absolute is here termed *de-bźin-ñid* = *tathatā.*

169 Tib. *slob-paḥi-(spaṅs-pa).* 170 *mi-slob-paḥi* = *spaṅs-pa.*

171 Tib. *lhag-med-kyi-myaṅ-ḥdas* = *anupadhi-çeṣa-nirvāṇa.*

172 Tg. MDO. XLIV 55 b. 1.

173 Tib. *mthoṅ-lam* = *darçana-mārga.*

174 Tib. *sgom-lam* = *bhāvanā-mārga.*

175 Tib. *mi-slob-lam* = *açaikṣa-mārga.*

176 Tib. *tshogs-lam* = *sambhāra-mārga.*

177 Tib. *sbyor-lam* = *prayoga-mārga.*

178 Tib. *ḥkhor* — retinue, followers (*parivāra*).

179 Tib. *bag-chags* = *vāsanā.* 180 Tib. *[illegible]os-pa* = *prapañca.*

181 Tib. *chos-kyi-dbyiṅs* = *dharma-dhātu.*

182 cf. below p. 31—33.

183 Tib. *chos-ñid* = *dharmatā.*

184 Tg. MDO. XLIV, 43 b.

185 Tib. *rgyu-mthun-(paḥi-ḥbras-bu)* = *niṣyanda-phala.* Haribhadra's Abhisamayālaṁkārālokā (MS. Minaev 29 a. 13—29 b. 2.) has: *tathāgata-dharma-deçanāyā evo' pacāra-nirdiṣṭa-puruṣa-kāra-svabhāvāyā eṣa sadṛçah syando niṣyandas tad-anurūpaṁ phalaṁ yat sūtrādi....* (*āgama-dharmaḥ*).

186 Xyl. *Sunyaçrī.*

187 Of the Çrāvakas, Pratyekabuddhas, and Bodhisattvas.

188 Tib. *gzuṅ-ba-b[illegible]ag-med* = *grāhya-nairātmya,* the same as *dharma-nairātmya.*

189 Tib. *myaṅ-ḥdas* (=*Mahāparinirvāṇa.* Kg. MDO. VIII, IX, X).

190 This and the following is condensed from the Pratītyasamutpāda-ādi-vibhanga-nirdeça-ṭīkā of Guṇamati. Tg. MDO XXXVI,75 b. 4—7 b. 7

191 Cf. MV. § 112.

192 Xyl. corrupt.: *yod-pa-ma-yin-pa*; correct — *yon-po-ma-yin-pa.*

193 Tib. *dran-pa-ñe-bar-gźag-pa* =*smṛty-upasthāna.* Cf. above p. 10 note 70.

194 The defilement (*sgrib-pa*) spoken of here is the same as *kun-nas-ñon-moṅs-pa* (= *saṁkleça*) on page 9 note 56.

195 Tib. *khams-gsum* cf. above p. 7 note 31.

196 Tib. *bdag-rkyen* = *adhipati-pratyaya.*

197 Tg. MDO. XLIV 74 a. 1. 198 Ibid. LVIII 137 b. 1. ff.

199 Sic according to Tg. — *yaṅ-dag-par-bslaṅ-pa-ñid-kyis.* Xyl. — *yaṅ-dag-par-blaṅ-pa-ñid-kyis.*

200 Tib. *dbaṅ-du-mdzad-pa-ñid-kyis.*

201 *rab-tu-ldan-pa-ñid-kyis.* Tg. has *rab-tu-bstan-pa.*

202 Read according to Tg. — *bar-chad-ma-byas-par bar-chad-med-par yaṅ-dag-par* etc. Xyl. has — *ḫar-chad ma-byas-par yaṅ-dag-par* etc.

203 According to Vyākhyāyukti (Tg. 133 b. 7) a) *ḥbrug-sgra-ltar-zab-pa* — deep as thunder, b) *sñan-žiṅ-ḥjebs-la-rna-bar-sñan-pa* — charming and agreeable to the ear, c) *yid-du-ḥoṅ-žiṅ-dgaḥ-bar byed-pa* —pleasing and causing delight. d) *rnam-par-gsal-žiṅ-rnam-par-rig-par-bya-ba* — perfectly clear and intelligible, e) *mñan-ḥos-çiṅ-mi-mthun-pa-med-pa* — worthy of being heard to and free from contradiction.

204 The Tg. text of the Vyākhyāyukti and Guṇamati's Commentary (Tg MDO LX 171 b. 7—8) have both... *ji-sñed-pa-la-thug-par-go-bar-mdzad.* Xyl. — *ji-sñed-pa-la-go-bar-mdzad.*

205 *çāçvatavāda* and *ucchedavāda* — Eternalism and Nihilism. Guṇamati's Vyākhyāyuktiṭīkā says (172 a. 1—2) — *ḥdi-ltar-rtag-pa-daṅ-chad-pa-la-sogs-paḥi-mthaḥ spaṅs-paḥi ḥphags-paḥi lam gsuṅs-pas-so* — "as it speaks of the Path of a Saint, through which the extremities of Eternalism and Nihilism come to be rejected".

206 The following passage occurs in the Vyākhyāyukti (Tg. MDO. LVIII 138 a. 1—139 b. 6.) and in Vasubandhu's Commentary on Sūtrālaṁkāra XII. 9, where we have the original sanscrit text. Both these works refer to the Tathāgata-guhya-nirdeça (Guhyaka-adhipati-nirdeça according to Vasubandhu) — *punar aparaṁ Çāntamate Tathāgatasya ṣaṣṭy-ākāra-upetā vāṅ niçcarati* "moreover, o Çāntamati, the Word of Buddha appears in sixty aspects". Cf. also MV. § 20.

207 *snigdhā sattva-dhātu-kuçalamūla-upastambhikatvāt.* The Xyl. has *dge-baḥi-rtsa-ba ñe-bar-ston-par-mdzad* etc. Correct according to Vyākhāyuktiṭīkā (Tg. MDO LX 171 a. 2 and the Sanscrit — (*upastambhikatvāt*) — *dge-baḥi-rtsa-ba rton-par-mdzad.*

208 *Mṛdukā dṛṣṭa eva dharme sukha-saṁsparçatvāt.*

209 *Manojñā svārthatvāt.* 210 *Manoramā suvyañjanatvāt.*

211 *Çuddhā niruttara-lokottara-pṛṣṭha-labdhatvāt.*

212 *Vimalā sarva-kleça-anuçaya-vāsanā-visaṁyuktatvāt.*

213 *Prabhāsvarā pratīta-pada-vyañjanatvāt.*

214 *Valguḥ sarva-tīrthya-kumati-dṛṣṭi-vighāta-bala-guṇa-yuktatvāt.* Guṇamati (Vyākhyāyuktiṭīkā 172. 4) says: *stobs-kyi-yan-lag- (yon-tan?)-daṅ-ldan-paḥi-phyir ṅes-paḥi-tshig-gi-tshul-gyis sñan-ciṅ-ḥjebs-paḥo.* He evidently regards the word *valgu* (or *balgu*) as consisting of two parts *val* (or *bal* = *bala* = *stobs*) and *gu* (*guṇa* = *yon-tan*) (!!!).

215 *Çravaṇīyā pratipatter nairyāṇikatvāt.* Guṇamati: *thar-ba thob-par-byed-pa-yin.*

216 *Anelā sarva-para-pravādibhir anācchedyatvāt.* With regard to "*anela*" cf. the translation of the Sūtrālaṁkāra by Prof. S. Lévi p. 143, note 2, and M. V. § 20.

217 *Kalā rañjikatvāt.* 218 *Vinītā rāgādi-pratipakṣatvāt.*

219 *Akarkaçā çikṣā-prajñapti-sukha-upāyatvāt.*

220 *Aparuṣā tad-vyatikrama-sampan-niḥsaraṇa-upadeçakatvāt.* Guṇamati (Tg. MDO LX 172 a 7) says: *so-sor-bçags-pa-la-sogs-paḥi thabs-dag-gis ṅes-par-ḥbyuṅ* etc. "shows (a means of) salvation through confession" etc.

221 *Suvinītā yāna-traya-naya-upadeçakatvāt.*

222 *Karṇasukhā vikṣepa-pratipakṣatvāt.*
223 *Kāya-prahlādana-karī samādhy-āvāhakatvāt.*
224 *Citta-audbilya-karī vipaçyanā-āmodya-āvāha-phalakatvāt.*
225 *Hṛdaya-saṁtuṣṭikarī saṁçaya-cchedikatvāt.*
226 *Prīti-sukha-jananī mithyā-aniçcita-apakarṣikatvāt.*
227 *Niḥparidāhā pratipattāv apratisaratvāt.*
228 *Ājñeyā saṁpanna-çrutamaya-jñāna-āçrayatvāt.*
229 *Vijñeyā saṁpanna-cintāmaya-jñāna-āçrayatvāt.*
230 *Viṣpaṣṭā'nācārya-muṣṭi-dharma-vihitatvāt.*

231 *Premaṇīyā'nuprāpta-svakārthānāṁ prema-kāratvāt.* Guṇamati says; *raṅ-gi-don-rjes-su-thob-pa-rnams žes-bya-ba-ni dgra-bcom-pa-rnams-so.*

232 *Abhinandanīyā' nanuprāpta-svakārthānāṁ spṛhaṇīyatvāt.*

233 *Ājñāpanīyā acintya-dharma-samyagdeçikatvāt.* The part. pot. "*ājñāpanīyā*" appears here in the active sense, as shows the Tib. version according to the Tg. (Vyākhyāyukti and ṭīkā) — *kun-çes-par-byed-pa* and Guṇamati's interpretation *ḥdis kun-çes-par-byed-pas-na kun-çes-par-byed-paḥo* (= *ājñāpyate anayā ity ājñāpanīyā*) (Tg. MDO. LX 172. b. 2). Concerning the "matters that belong to the transcendental sphere" (*acintya-dharma*), Guṇamati says (Tg. 172 b. 3—6) — *bsam-gyis-mi-khyab-paḥi-chos de-dag-kyaṅ ji-skad-du bcom-ldan-ḥdas-kyis dge-sloṅ-dag bsam-gyis-mi-khyab-paḥi gnas bži-po ḥdi-dag sems-na myos-par-yaṅ ḥgyur rmoṅs-par-yaṅ ḥgyur-ro. bži gaṅ-dag ce-na bdag-la-sems-pa daṅ sems-can-rnams-kyi las daṅ rnam-par-smin-pa-la sems-pa daṅ ḥjig-rten-las-sems-pa daṅ saṅs-rgyas-rnams-kyi saṅs-rgyas-kyi-yul-yin-no mdo-sdehi-dum-bu gñis-pa-las-bži-po ḥdi-dag çes-bya-ba-las brtsams-nas sems-can-rnams-kyi las daṅ rnam-par-smin-pa daṅ bsam-gtan-pa-rnams-kyi bsam-gtan-gyi-yul daṅ rdzu-ḥphrul-daṅ-ldan-pa-rnams-kyi rdzu-ḥphrul-gyi-yul-lo žes gsuṅs-pa yin-no* —" The matters that belong to the transcendental sphere have been spoken of by the Lord, as follows: — O brethren, if the four topics belonging to the Transcendental Sphere are investigated, mental insanity and(many) errors will be the result. Now, of what kind are these four points? They are as follows: — thoughts, concerning the soul, those with regard to the deeds of living beings and their consequence, consideration, as to what lies beyond the limits of this world and the Sphere of Enlightenment which is that of the Buddhas. In another fragment of a Sūtra (we have), after "those four" etc. and "the deeds of living beings and their consequence ', (the following):— "the sphere of mystic absorbtion (perceived by) such that practise it and the sphere of miraculons agency of those that are endowed with miraculous powers." —

234 *Vijñāpanīyā acintya-dharma-samyagdeçikatvāt.*
235 *Yuktā pramāṇa-aviruddhatvāt.*
236 *Sahitā yathārha-vineya-deçikatvāt.*
237 *Punarukta-doṣa-jahā avandhyatvāt.*
238 *Siṁha-svara-vegā sarva-tīrthya-saṁtrāsakatvāt.*
239 *Nāga-svara-çabdā udāratvāt.*
240 *Megha-svara-ghoṣā gambhīratvāt.*
241 *Nāgendra-rutā ādeyatvāt.*

242 *Kiṁnara-saṁgītighoṣī madhuratvāt.* All the Tibetan translations (that of the Pañcaviṁçatisāhasrikā-ālokā quoted by Bu-ston and that of the

Vyākhyāyukti and of Vasubandhu's Comment have *dri-za* = *gandharva*. Cf. Meghadūta Pūrvamegha 56.

243 *Kalavinka-svara-ruta-ravitā tīkṣṇa-bhangaratvāt.* The reading *tīkṣṇa* is correct (Tib. *rno-ba* — sharp. Cf. translation by Prof. S. Lévi p. 144, n. 5.) The Tib. texts of the Vyākhyāyukti and ṭikā have both *rgyun-mi-chad-pa.* This is evidently a mistake made by the Lotsavas who read "*abhīkṣṇa*" (the letter *bha* in the *lañcā* character being very much like *ta*).

244 *Brahma-svara-ruta-ravitā dūraṁgamatvāt.*

245 *Jīvaṁjīvaka-svara-ruta-ravitā sarva-siddhi-pūrvaṁgama-mangalatvāt.*

246 Tib. *sgra.* 247 Tib. *dbyaṅs.* 248 Tib. *grags-pa.*

249 *Devendra-madhura-nirghoṣā anatikramaṇīyatvāt.*

250 *Dundubhi-svarā sarva-māra-pratyarthika-vijaya-pūrvaṁgamatvāt.*

251 *Anunnatā stuty-asaṁkliṣṭatvāt.*

252 *Anavanatā nindā-asaṁkliṣṭatvāt.*

253 *Sarva-çabda-anupraviṣṭā sarva-vyākaraṇa-sarva-ākāra-lakṣaṇa-anupraviṣṭatvāt.*

254 *Apaçabda-vigatā smṛti-saṁpramoṣe tad-aniçcaraṇatvāt.*

255 *Avikalā vineya-kṛtya-sarva-kāla-pratyupasthitatvāt.*

256 *Alīnā lābha-satkāra-aniçritatvāt.*

257 *Adīnā sāvadya-apagatatvāt.*

258 *Pramuditā akheditvāt.*

259 *Prasṛtā sarva-vidyā-sthāna-kauçalya-anugatatvāt.*

260 *Akhilā sattvānāṁ tat-sakala-artha-saṁpādakatvāt.* Vyākhyāyukti and ṭikā have both *chub-pa* for *tha-ba-med-pa* cf. below.

261 *Saritā prabandha-anupacchinnatvāt.*

262 *Lalitā vicitra-ākāra-pratyupasthānatvāt.* Vyākh. — ṭikā — *ḥbel-ba* for *brjid-pa* cf. below. Xyl. corrupt — *brjod-pa.*

263 *Sarva-svara-pūraṇī eka-svara-naika-çabda-vijñapti-pratyupasthāpanatvāt.*

264 *Sarva-sattva-indrya-saṁtoṣiṇī eka-aneka-artha-vijñapti-pratyupasthānatvāt.*

265 *Aninditā yathā-pratijñatvāt.*

266 *Acañcalā āgamita-kāla-prayuktatvāt.*

267 *Acapalā atvaramāṇa-vihitatvāt.*

268 *Sarva-parṣad-anuravitā dūrāntika-parṣat-tulya-çravaṇatvāt.*

269 *Sarva-ākāravara-upetā sarva-laukika-artha-dṛṣṭānta-dharma-pariṇāmikatvāt.*

270 The work of Vimuktasena. Tib. Ñi-khri-snaṅ-ba. Full title, according to Tg. — Ārya-pañcaviṁçatisāhasrika-prajñāpāramitopadeçaçāstra-Abhisamayālaṁkāra-vṛtti. Tib. — Hphags-pa çes-rab-kyi-pha-rol-tu-phyin-pa Stoṅ-phrag-ñi-çu-lṅa-paḥi man-ṅag-gi bstan-bcos mṅon-par-rtogs-paḥi-rgyan-gyi ḥgrel-pa (Tg. MDO I. 96 a. 4—97 b. 3.)

271 Tib. Sa-sde-lṅa — Tg. MDO. XLIX (The work of Āryāsanga).

272 Tib. Hbum-ṭig, the work of Daṁṣṭrāsena, Tg. MDO XIV.

273 Sūtrālaṁkāra XII 9 b. — *ṣaṣṭyaṅgī sā'cintyā ghoṣo'nantas tu sugatānām.*

274 Cf. above p. 26 note 206. The interpolation occurs Kg, DKON. I 133 b. 5.

275 *ḥchos-kyi-ḥkhor-lo* = *dharma-cakra* "the Wheel of the Doctrine".

276 The Hīnayāna. 277 The Mādhyamika Doctrine.
278 The Yogācāra system.
279 Tib. Dgoṅs-pa-ṅes-ḥgrel. Kangyur MDO V. 24 b. 5—25 a. 4.
280 Tib. *kun-rdzob* = *saṁvṛti.* 281 Tib. *don-dam-pa* = *paramārtha.*
282 Tib. Blo-gros-mi-zad-pa-bstan-pa. Kangyur DKON XVI. Cf. a similar passage of the Akṣayamatisūtra quoted in the Mādhyamika-vṛtti B. B. p. 43. 4 and its translation by Prof. Th. Stcherbatsky in "Conception of Buddhist Nirvāṇa" p. 127.
283 Tib. *yan-lag* = *anga.* These are not separate works, but merely varieties of style.
284 Tib. Sñiṅ-poḥi-mchog. The work of Ratnākaraçānti. Tg. MDO. X.
285 Tib. *mdo-sde.* 286 Tib. *dbyaṅs-kyis-bsñad-pa.*
287 Tib. *luṅ-du-bstan-pa.* 288 Tib. *tshigs-su-bcad-pa.*
289 Tib. *ched-du-brjod-pa.* 290 Tib. *gleṅ-gži.*
291 Tib. *rtogs-pa-brjod-pa.* 292 Tib. *de-lta-bu-byuṅ-ba.*
293 Tib. *skyes-pa-rabs.* 294 Tib. *çin-tu-rgyas-pa.*
295 Tib. *rmad-du-byuṅ-ba(ḥi-chos).* 296 Tib. *gtan-la-phab-par-bstan-pa.*
297 Tib. *smos-paḥi-tshul-gyis.*
298 Tg. MDO. LVI. 120 a. 2—5.
299 Tib. *chos-ñid* = *dharmatā* = *çūnyatā* = Relativity.
300 That of trance (*samādhi*).
301 Tib. *ḥbel-baḥi-gtam-gyis gtan-la-ḥbebs-pa* = *saṁkathya-viniçcaya.*
302 Guṇamati (Tg. LX 123 a 5—6) gives the following example: *dge-sloṅ-dag gsum-po ḥdi-dag-ni tshor-ba-dag-yin-te. gsum-po-dag gaṅ-dag ces-na bde-ba daṅ sdug-bsṅal daṅ bde-ba-yaṅ-ma-yin sdug-bsṅal-yaṅ-ma-yin-paḥo* — "O brethren these three are feelings" (The Sūtra). "What are these three? (may it be asked. The answer will be as follows): — (Feeling) agreeable, disagreeable, and that which is neutral (the "Geya").
303 Chapters VI (Vyākaraṇa-parivarta B. B. p. 144—155) and VIII (Pañca-bhikṣuçata-vyākaraṇa-parivarta p. 199—214).
304 *pada.*
305 Lit. "originated from causes". (*rgyu-las-byuṅ*); from the Mahāyānistic point of view everything originated by causes is by itself unreal, causality being taken in the sense of Relativity cf. Mādhyamika-vṛtti Chapter I, translated by Prof. Th. Stcherbatsky ("Conception of Buddhist Nirvāṇa", appendix).
306 "The Buddhist Creed" —

*Ye dharmā hetu-prabhavā*
*Hetuṁ teṣāṁ tathāgato hy avadat*
*Teṣāṁ ca yo nirodha*
*Evaṁvādī mahā-çramaṇaḥ.*

307 Acc. to Tib. tradition: — *hkhor-ba bden-par-ḥdzin-paḥi-blo ma-skyes-na saṅs-rgyas-yin.*
308 Tg. MDO LVIII. 97 a. 4. 309 Tib. *Nor-can.*
310 Tib. *thams-cad-sgrol*. Cf. Jātakamālā ed. Kern p. 51—67.
311 Lit. "Endowed with the code (*Piṭaka*) of the Bodhisattvas". The Vyākhyāyukti (Tg. MDO. LVIII 97 a. 8) says: *çin-tu-rgyas-paḥi-sde-ni theg-pa-chen-po-yin-te. luṅ-phog gaṅ-gis byaṅ-chub-sems-dpaḥ-rnams pha-rol-tu-*

*phyin-pa-bcu-dag-gis sa-bcu-dag-tu ḥgrub-pa-na stobs-bcuḥi rten saṅs-rgyas-ñid thob-paḥo.* "The Vaipulya class is (to speak otherwise) the Mahāyāna. It is that part of Scripture, by means of which the Bodhisattvas, having attained the (ten) stages of Enlightenment (*bhūmi*) through the ten transcendental virtues (*pāramitā*), attain the state of a Buddha, the substratum of the ten forces."

**312** Cf. Vyākhyāyukti (98 a. 4.) *rnaṁ-par-ḥjoms-pa* "completely vanquishing".

**313** Ibid. **314** Cf. below.

**315** This analysis of the 12 classes is an extract from the Abhidharma-samuccaya Tg. MDO LVI. 120 a. 2—b. 5. It corresponds to that of the Sārottamā (Tg. MDO. X 2 b. 3—3 a. 1).

**316** Tib. *sde-snod = piṭaka.*

**317** Tib. *ñan-thos-kyi-sde-snod = çrāvaka-piṭaka* = Hīnayāna.

**318** Tib. *ḥdul-baḥi-sde-snod = vinaya-pitaka.*

**319** Lit. "the retinue" (*ḥkhor*). **320** Tib. *mṅon-paḥi-sde-snod.*

**321** Tg. MDO. LVI, 121 a. 1—5.

**322** *Saṁgrahataḥ sarva-jñeya-artha-saṁgrahād veditavyam* (Vasubandhu on Sūtrālaṁkāra XI. 1).

**323** *Kāraṇair navabhir iṣṭam* (Ibid. and verse). The following is an extract from the Abhidharma-samuccaya (Tg. MDO. LVI. 121 a. 1—5).

**324** Tib. *ñe-baḥi-ñon-moṅs-pa the-tshom.* Guṇamati (Tg. MDO. LX 18 a, 8) gives a classification of the different kinds of defilement that have their origin in doubt, as follows: — *log-par-lta-ba daṅ mi-rigs-par-chags-pa daṅ brnab-sems* (= *abhidhyā*) *daṅ gnod-sems* (= *vyāpāda*) *daṅ rmugs-pa* (= *styāna*) *daṅ gñid* (= *middha*) *daṅ rgod-pa* (= *auddhatya*) *daṅ hgyod-pa* (= *kaukṛtya*)' false points of view, attachment to that which is wrong, coveteousness, ill-will, depression, drowsiness, and indolence. Vasubandhu's Commentary on Sūtrālaṁkāra XI. 1. has: — *yo yatrā' rthe saṁçayitạs tan-niçcayārthaṁ deçanāt* — "because it has been preached in order to convince such, that have doubt as regards the meaning (of the Doctrine)."

**325** Tib. *ḥdod-pa-bsod-ñams-kyi-mthaḥ = kāma-sukhallika-anuyoga-anta... anta-dvaya-anuyoga-pratipakṣeṇa vinayaḥ. sāvadya-paribhoga-pratiṣedhataḥ kāma-sukhallika-anuyoga-antasya* (Vasubandhu on Sūtrālaṁkāra XI. 1.)

**326** Tib. *ṅal-žiṅ-dub-paḥi-mthaḥ = ātma-klamatha-anuyoga-anta... anavadya-paribhoga-anujñānata ātma-klamatha-anuyoga-antasya* (*pratipakṣeṇa*) (ibid).

**327** *raṅ-gi-lta-ba-mchog-tu-ḥdzin-pa = svayaṁdṛṣṭi-parāmarṣa.* "*svayaṁdṛṣṭi*" is the same as "*satkāya-dṛṣṭi*" (Tib. *ḥjig-tshogs-kyi-lta-ba*) cf. Guṇamati (Tg. MDO. LX 91 a. 6: *raṅ-gi-lta-ba-mchog-tu-ḥdzin-pa žes-bya-ba-ni raṅ-gi-lta-ba ste ḥjig-tshogs-kyi-lta-ba-rnams-las gaṅ-yaṅ-ruṅ-ba-žig.*

**328** *çikṣā-traya-deçanā sūtreṇa* (Vasubandhu on Sūtrālaṁkāra XI. 1.)

**329** *adhiçīla-adhicitta-saṁpādanatā vinayena çīlavato' vipratisārādi-krameṇa samādhi-lābhāt.* (ibid).

**330** *adhiprajñā-saṁpādanatā' bhidharmeṇā' viparīta-artha-pravicayāt* (ibid.)

**331** *dharma-artha-deçanā sūtreṇa.* (ibid).

**332** *dharma-artha-niṣpattir vinayena kleça-vinaya-saṁyuktasya tayoḥ prativedhāt* (Vasubandhu on Sūtrālaṁkara XI. 1.)

**333** *dharma-artha-sāṁkathya-viniçcaya-kauçalyam abhidharmeṇa* (ibid).

**334** *çrutena citta-vāsanataḥ* (ibid).

335 *çintayā bodhanataḥ* (ibid).

336 *bhāvanayā çamathena çamanataḥ* (ibid.).

337 *vipaçyanayā prativedhataḥ* (ibid.).

338 XI. 1. *piṭaka-trayaṁ dvayaṁ vā kāraṇair navabhir iṣṭaṁ vāsana-bodhana-çamana-prativedhais tad vimocayati.*

339 Cf. below p. 38.

340 XI. 2. *Sūtrābhidharmavinayāç caturvidhārthā matāḥ samāsena teṣāṁ jñānād dhīmān sarvākārajñatām eti.*

341 *teṣāṁ jñānād bodhisattvaḥ sarva-jñatāṁ prāpnoti* (Vasubandhu on Sūtrāl. XI. 2.)

342 *Çrāvakas tv ekasyā api gāthāyā artham ājñāya āsrava-kṣayaṁ prāpnoti* (ibid).

343 Tib. *Lam-phran-brtan.*

344 Tib. *mgo-smos-pa.* Corresponds (acc. to Sūtrāl. XII 10, quoted below) — to *udghaṭana.*

345 Tib. *gnas* = *āçraya.* Vasubandhu (on Sūtrāl. XI 3.) says: *tatra āçrayo yatra deçe deçitaṁ yena yasmai ca.*

346 Tib. *rgyal-poḥi-khab.*

347 Vasubandhu (ibid.) gives another interpretation of *lakṣaṇa* and *dharmalaksaṇaṁ saṁvṛti-satya-lakṣaṇaṁ paramārtha-satya-lakṣaṇaṁ ca. dharmāḥ skandha-āyatana-dhātv-āhāra-pratītyasamutpādādayaḥ; artho' nusaṁdhiḥ.*

348 XI. 3. a. *āçrayato lakṣaṇato dharmād arthāc ca sūcanāt sūtram.*

349 Vasubandhu's interpretation is different: *nirvāṇa-abhimukho dharmo' bhidharmaḥ satya-bodhipakṣa-vimokṣamukhādi-deçanāt:* — the Abhidharma is the teaching directed toward (the attainment of) Nirvāṇa, as it demonstrates the truths, tne attributes of Enlightenment, (the eight degrees of) liberation (from materiality) and the other expedients (Comm. on Sūtrāl. XI. 3).

350 Tib. *mtshan-ñid-pa.* 351 *skandha.* 352 *dhātu.*

353 *āyatana.* 354 Tib. *rdzas-yod.* 355 Tib. *btags-yod.*

356 Tib. *gžuṅ-lugs.*

357 *abhibhavati ity abhidharmaḥ para-pravāda-abhibhavanād vivāda-adhikaraṇādibhiḥ* (Vasub. on Sūtrāl. XI. 3).

358 *abhigamyate sūtrārtha etene'ty abhidharmaḥ* (ibid).

359 XI. 3. 6. *Abhimukhato 'thābhīkṣṇyād abhibhava-gatito' bhidharmaç ca.*

360 As shows the following passage, the so-called "etymology" of Vinaya is as follows: — *vipattyādīnāṁ viniçcayādīnāṁ vā naya iti vi* + *naya pṛṣodarāditvāt.* (Paṇini VI. 3. 109.!!)

361 Acc. to Sūtrālaṁkāra XI. 4. and Commentary — *āpatti.*

362 *samutthānam āpattīnāṁ ajñānāt pramādāt kleça-prācuryād anādarāc ca* — the origin of fall — ignorance, negligence, enormity of passions, and disrespect. (Vasubandhu on Sūtrāl. XI. 4.)

363 *pudgalato yam āgamya çikṣā prajñāpyate* (ibid).

364 XI. 4. *Āpatter utthānād vyutthānān niḥsṛteç ca vinayatvaṁ, pudgalataḥ prajñapteḥ pravibhāga-viniçcayāc cai'va.*

365 XI. 1. cf. above.

366 *hīnayāna-agrayāna-bhedena dvayaṁ bhavati çrāvaka-piṭakaṁ bodhisattva-piṭakaṁ ca* (Vasub. on Sūtrāl. XI. 1).

367 Tib. *dman-pa-la-mos-pa* = *hīnādhimukta*. Cf. Conception of Buddhist Nirvāṇa p. 36, note 2.

368 The work of Āryāsanga. (Tib. Theg-bsdus) Tg. MDO. LVI 3 a. 4—5.

369 This and the following is an extract from the Vyākhyāyukti (Tg. MDO. LVIII. 97 b. 6—98 a. 2) in an abridged form.

370 The Çatasāhasrikā-prajñāpāramitā.

371 The Vyākhyāyukti has: *lhag-paḥi-bsam-pa-dag-paḥi-sa-la sems-can thams-cad-la bdag daṅ gžan-du mñam-pa-ñid-kyi bsam-pa thob-paḥi-phyir-ro* — since the equal treatment of oneself and all other living beings is attained in the stage called *Çuddha-adhyāçayika*. Guṇamati (Tg. MDO. LX 125 a. 6) says *lhag-paḥi bsam-pa-dag-paḥi sa ni sa daṅ-po yin no* — the *Çuddha-adhyāçayika* stage is the first stage (of a Bodhisattva = *pramuditā*).

372 XIX 59, 60. **373** Tib. *mtshan-ñid-kyi-theg-pa*.

374 The six transcendental virtues (*pāramitā*).

375 Tib. *sṅags-kyi-theg-pa* = *mantra-yāna* = Tantra.

376 Tib. Mdo. sde-gdams-ṅag-hbogs-pahi-rgyal-po (?).

377 Tib. *rdo-rje-theg-pa* = *vajra-yāna*.

378 Tib. Tshul-gsum-gyi-sgron-me Tg. RGYUD. LXXII 17. b. 5—6.

379 Omniscience. The Tg. has: *don-gcig-ñid-na* for: *don-gcig-na-ḥaṅ*.

380 Tg.: *sṅags-kyi-bstan-bcos* "the Treatises on Mysticism" for *sṅags-kyi-theg-pa*.

381 This and the following is condensed from the Naya-traya-pradīpa Cf. App.

382 Tib. *phyag-rgya* = *mudrā*.

383 Tib. *rig-pa-ḥdzin-paḥi-sde-snod* = *vidyādhāra-piṭaka*.

384 Tib. *byiṅ-gyis-brlabs-pa* = *adhiṣṭhāna*.

385 Tib. *rjes-su-gnaṅ-ba* = *anujñā*.

386 Tib. Ḥphags-pa-sdud-pa.

387 Tib. Ma-skyes-dgraḥi ḥgyod-pa bsal-baḥi mdo. Kg. MDO XVIII.

388 Tib. Kun-tu-bzaṅ-poḥi spyod-pa ston-paḥi mdo. The whole passage is to be found in Haribhadra's Abhisamayālaṁkāra-ālokā (MS. Minaev 22. a. 8—12 = Tg. MDO VI, 21 a. 3—5.) — *Iha kvacit tathāgatānāṁ kāya-vyāpārātmaka-pāṇyādy-adhiṣṭhānena deçanā tad yathā Daçabhūmakādeḥ sūtrasya deçanā. kvacid vacana-adhiṣṭhānena tad yathā Ajātaçatru-çoka-vinodana-sūtradeḥ. Kvacin mano'-dhiṣṭhānena tad yathā Samantabhadra-caryā-nirdeça-sūtrādeḥ.*

389 Tib. Çes-rab-sñiṅ-po. **390** Tib. *gleṅ-gži*.

391 Tib. *mthun-ḥgyur-yi-raṅ*.

392 Tib. Chos-yaṅ-dag-par-sdud-pa Kg. MDO. XXI. Quoted in Haribhadra's Abhisamayālaṁkārālokā (MS. Minaev 6 b. 6—8 = Tg. MDO. VI 6 b. 2) *uktaṁ bhagavatā Dharmasaṁgīti-sūtre. evaṁ mayā çrutaṁ iti kṛtvā bhikṣavo dharmāḥ saṁgātavyā iti. tathā saṁbandhānupūrvā pratipādyā.*

393 Tg. MDO. XLIV. 74 a. 2.

394 Tg. has *rgyal-ba-ston-pa-ḥbaḥ-žig-gi* for *rgyal-baḥi-bstan-pa* etc.

395 Tib. *dug-gsum*. These are: 1. *ḥdod-chags* = *rāga* — lust,
2. *že-sdaṅ* = *dveṣa* — hatred; and
3. *gti-mug* = *moha* — ignorance.

396 Or, as in the verse below "*trāṇa*".

397 The etymology of *çāstra* acc. to the Abhidharmakoça (B. B. 5. 1) and Vyākhyā (8. 18.) is much more natural.

398 Tg. MDO. LVIII 143. 4—6.

399 Cf. Madh. vrtti 3. 3, 4. *yac chāsti vaḥ kleçaripūn açeṣān saṁtrāyate durgatito bhavāc ca, tac chāsanāt trāṇa-guṇāc ca çāstram etad dvayaṁ cā'nyamateṣu nāsti.*

400 Tib. *don-dam-par bstan-bcos-yin.*

401 Nirṇaya-saṁgraha (Cf. below.) Tg. MDO. LII. 205 a. 3—7.

402 Tib. Rnam-par-gtan-la-dbab-par-bsdu-ba. Tg. MDO. LII. 205 a. 4—5 *de-la thos-pa lhur-len-paḥi bstan-bcos ni ḥdi-lta ste bram-zeḥi gsaṅ tshig rnams so. rtsod-pa lhur-len-paḥi bstan-bcos ni ḥdi-lta ste ḥdi-las phyi-rol-pa-rnams-kyi gtan-tshigs-kyi bstan-bcos so.* — The formalistic works are such as (for instance) the Brahmanical charms, and the polemical are the heretical works on Logic.

403 Cf. the following passage of the Jñānavaipulyasūtra, quoted in the Çikṣā-samuccaya (B. B. p. 182. 6.) — *Uktaṁ bhagavatā jñāna-vaipulyasūtre sārthakāni çāstrāṇi çikṣitavyāni apārthakāni parivarjayitavyāni tad yathā lokāyata-çāstrāṇi daṇḍa-nīti-çāstrāṇi kākhorda-çāstrāṇi vāda-vidyā-çāstrāṇi kumāra-krīḍā-çāstrāṇi jambhaka-vidyā-çāstrāṇi'* — it is said by the Lord in the Jñānavaipulyasūtra: Useful works are to be studied and the worthless (and harmful) — rejected. The latter are as follows: — the treatises on materialism, works on politics and criminal law, on magical performances for procuring death, on the science of controversy, on sport & demonology.

404 Tib. Ḥdul-bahi-mdo, otherwise called Mdo-rtsa-ba. Cf. below p. 50.

405 Tib. *ji-sñed-pa = kun-rdzob = saṁvṛti.*

406 Tib. *ji-lta-ba = don-dam-pa = paramārtha.*

407 Tib. *lugs-kyi-bstan-bcos = nīti-çāstra.*

408 Tib. Çes-rab-brgya-ba. Tg. MDO XXXIII and CXXIII No. 26. attributed to Nāgārjuna. The verse quoted below is — in vol. XXIIII—99 b. 8—100 a. 1 and in CXXIII—144 b. 7—8.

409 Tib. Skye-boḥi-gso-thigs. Ibid. No. 28, attributed to Nāgārjuna.

410 Tib. Tshigs-su-bçad-paḥ'-mdzod. Ibid. No. 29, the work of Ravigupta.

411 Tib. Mi-brtag-pa (miḥi-mtshan-ñid-brtag-pa) Ibid. No. 34.

412 XI. 60. — *vidyā-sthāne pañcavidhe yogam akṛtvā sarvajñatvaṁ nai'ti kathaṁcit paramāryaḥ*
*ity anyeṣāṁ nigrahaṇānugrahaṇāya svājñārthaṁ vā tatra karoty eva sa yogam.*

413 Tib. *gtan-tshigs-rig-pa = hetu-vidyā.*
414 Tib. *sgra-rig-pa = çabda-vidyā.*
415 Tib. *gso-ba-rig-pa = cikitsā-vidyā.*
416 Tib. *bzo-rig-pa = çilpa-karmasthāna-vidyā.*

Cf. M. V. § 76 and Vasubandhu's Commentar yon Sūtrālaṁkāra XI. 60.

417 Tib. *naṅ-rig-pa = adhyātma-vidyā.*

418 Tib. *mṅon-sum = pratyakṣa.*

419 Tib. *raṅ-gi-don-gyi-rjes-su-dpag-pa = svārtha-anumāna.*

420 Tib. *gžan-gyi-don-gyi-rjes-su-dpag-pa = parārtha-anumāna.*

421 Tib. *gžan-sel = (anya —) apoha.*

422 Tib. *ltag-(bltag) chod* (or *gcod*) = *jāti.*

423 Tg. MDO. XCV No. 1, the work of Dignāga.

424 These are: —

a) Ālambana-parīkṣā (Dmigs-pa-brtag-pa) of Dignāga Tg. MDO. XCV. No. 4.

b) Trikāla-parīkṣā (Dus-gsum-brtag-pa) of the same author. Ibid. No. 6.

c) Çruti-parīkṣā (Thos-pa-brtag-pa) of Kalyāṇarakṣita CXII. No. 8.

d) Pramāṇa-parīkṣā (Tshad-ma-brtag-pa) of Dharmottara. Ibid. No. 12.

d) Laghu-pramāṇa-parīkṣā (Tshad-ma-brtag-pa-chuṅ-ba) of the same author. Ibid. No. 13.

f) Anya-apoha-vicāra (Gžan-sel-brtag-pa) of Kalyāṇarakṣita. Ibid. No. 10.

g) Karma-phala-saṁbandha-parīkṣā (Las-daṅ-ḥbras-buḥi-ḥbrel-pa-brtag-pa) indicated by Bu-ston as wanting in the Tg.

425 Siddhi: —

a) Sarvajña-siddhi (Thams-cad-mkhyen-pa-grub-pa) of Kalyāṇarakṣita Tg. MDO. CXII No. 7.

b) Bāhya-artha-siddhi (Phyi-rol-don-grub-pa) of the same author. Ibid. No. 8.

c) Anya-apoha-siddhi (Gžan-sel-grub-pa) of Dharmottara. Ibid. No. 14.

d) Paraloka-siddhi (Ḥjig-rten-pha-rol-grub-pa) of the same author. Ibid. No. 15.

e) Kṣaṇabhanga-siddhi (Skad-gcig-ḥjig-pa-grub-pa) of the same author. Ibid. No. 17.

f) Anya-apoha-siddhi (Gžan-sel-grub-pa) of Çaṁkarānanda. Ibid. No. 20.

g) Pratibandha-siddhi (Ḥbrel-pa-grub-pa) of the same author. Ibid. No. 21.

h) Kārya-kāraṇa-bhāva-siddhi (Rgyu-daṅ-ḥbras-buḥi-ṅo-bo-grub-pa) of Jñānaçrīmitra. Ibid. No. 29.

426 Tg. MDO. XCV No. 11.

427 Ibid. No. 10.

428 Tib. *yaṅ-dag-paḥi-çes-pa* = *samyag-jñāna.*

429 The author of the Pramāṇa-viniçcaya-ṭīkā, Tg. MDO. CX. No. 2.

430 The Commentary on the Pramāṇa-viniçcaya by Dharmottara bears the title — Pramāṇa-viniçcaya-ṭīkā ramaṇī nāma (Ibid. CIX and CX No. 1)

431 Tib Gtan-tshigs-thigs-pa. Tg. MDO. XCV. No. 13.

432 *khyab-pa* = *vyāpti* and *phyogs-kyi-chos* = *pakṣa-dharmatā.*

433 Tib. Ḥbrel-pa-brtag-pa. Tg. MDO. XCV. No. 14.

435 Tib. Rtsod-paḥi-rigs-pa. Ibid. No. 16.

436 Tib. *tshar-bcad-kyi-gnas* = *nigraha-sthāna.*

437 Edited by Prof. Th. Stcherbatsky in B. B.

438 Tg. MDO. LVIII 62 b. 4—5, a quotation from an unknown āgama.

439 Correct acc. to Tg. — *deḥi ṅaṅ phyir* for *de ḥaṅ phyi rtag* etc.

440 Corr. *brtag rtog phyir* for *rtag rtog phyir.*

441 Corr. *mṅon-ma-byas-phyir* for *sṅon-ma-byas-phyir* acc. to Vyākhyāyuktiṭīkā (Tg. MDO. LX 53 a. 2—3). The latter says: — *mṅon-sum-du-ma-byas-phyir yaṅ rtog-ge-par rig-par-bya-ste so-soḥi-skye-bo-daṅ-ldan žes-bya-ba-tshig-ḥdis-so. mṅon-sum-du-ma-byas-pa-ñid kyaṅ de-kho-na mṅon-sum-du-mi-byed-pa-ste so-soḥi-skye-bo-yaṅ de-kho-na mṅon-sum-du-mi-byed-pas-so* — a logician is likewise recognised by his having no intuitive perception (the attribute of a Saint = *ārya-pudgala*) since it is said (of him) — "he belongs to the worldlings (*pṛthagjana*)"; the absence of intuitive perception is such with regard to

the Absolute Truth, since worldings have no such perception. Cf. the definition of a worldling acc. to the same work (189 a. 1.) *so-soḥi-skye-bo-šes-bya-ba-ni skye-bo gaṅ bden-pa-mthoṅ-ba-rnams-las so-sor phyi-rol-tu-gyur-pa*, a worldling (*pṛthagjana*) is one, that stands apart from those, that perceive the Absolute Truth.

442 The Vyākhyāyukti has: *yoṅs-su-bzuṅ-phyir šes-bya-ba-ni tshad-maḥi rigs-pa rnam-pa-gsum yoṅs-su-bzuṅ-baḥi-phyir-ro. de-ni so-sohi skye-bo-rnams-kyi sa yin-no* — by complete apprehension means by thorough apprehension of the three modes of proof; such is the position of worldlings. Vasubandhu's mentioning three modes of proof is noteworthy if compared to the standpoint of Dignāga and Dharmakīrti. We have moreover in the same work (102 b. 6—7.) — *mdor-na rigs-pa-ni ḥdir tshad-ma rnam-pa-gsum-po mṅon-sum daṅ rjes-su-dpag-pa daṅ yid-ches-paḥi-gsuṅ-ṅo* — Logic, in short, consists of the three methods of proof, — sense-perception, inference, and authoritative word (= *āpta-vacana, āgama*).

443 Corr. acc. to Guṇamati *yoṅs-su-byaṅ-bar-byas-paḥi-phyir* for *yoṅs-su-bya-ba-byas etc.*

444 I. 12. *niçrito' niyato' vyāpī sāṁvṛtaḥ khedavān api bālāçrayo matas tarkas tasyā' to viṣayo na tat* (= *mahāyānam*).

445 *Adṛṣṭa-satya-āçrayo hi tarkaḥ kaçcid āgama-niçrito bhavati* — Logic is not founded on the direct perception of the (Absolute) Truth; it is, therefore, to a certain degree dependent on Scripture. (Vasubandhu on Sūtrāl. I. 12.)

446 *Avyāpi ca na sarva-jñeya-viṣayaḥ* (Ibid).

447 Tib. *byis pa* = *bāla* = *pṛthagjana.*

448 Tib. *ma-mo.* The A' ' 'arma frequently appears under this appelation. Another "mother" is the Prajñāpāramitā, which is designated by the appelation of *yum.*

449 Tib. *rkyen* = *pratyaya.* 450 Tib. translation Tg. MDO. CXXXV.

451 Tib. *byiṅs* = *dhātu.* 452 Tib. *byed-ldan-gyi-rkyen.*

453 Tib. *de-phan-gyi-rkyen.* 454 Tib. *ñe-bar-bsgyur-ba.*

455 Tib. *mtshams-sbyor* = *saṁdhi.*

456 The work of Çarvavarman. Tg. MDO. CXVI No. 9.

457 The work of Smṛtijñānakīrti, composed in Tibet and translated by the author himself. Ibid. No. 18.

458 *pratisaṁvid.* M. V. § 13.

459 Tib. *sdeb-sbyor* = *chandas.*

460 The work of Ratnākaraçānti Tg. MDO. CXVII No. 4, 5.

461 *prastāra.* The xyl. has *pratāra.*

462 Tib. Ḥchi-med-mdzod. Tib. transl. Tg. MDO. CXVII No. 1.

463 The work of Dandin. Tib. transl. ibid. No. 3.

464 *dhvani.*

465 Poetics (*kāvya*) and the Sāmaveda — which in Tibetan are both designated by the appelation *sñan-dṅags*, — confounded.

466 Tib. *gdon-nad* — diseases ascribed to the influence of evil spirits.

467 The work of Vāgbhaṭṭa Tg. MDO. CXVIII, commented by the author Cimself (Ibid. and vol. CXIX) and by Candranandana (vol. CXX, CXXI and XhXI:. The verse quoted above is an extract from the main work (15 b. 2—3).

468 Tib. gser-ḥgyur-gyi-bstan-bcos = rasāyana-çāstra. Xyl. — gsar-ḥgyur.

469 Tib. sku-gzugs-kyi-tshad = pratimā-māna.

470 The work of Buddhajñānapāda Tg. MDO. XXIX No. 12.

471 The work of Jñānagarbha Tg. MDO. XXIX No. 1.

472 The work of Çāntirakṣita. Ibid. XXVIII No. 4.

473 The work of Āryāsanga Tg. MDO. LI.

474 The work of Āryāsanga Tg. MDO. L.

475 Tib. Chos-kyi-phuṅ-po. 476 Tib. Gdags-paḥi-bstan-bcos.

477 Tib. Khams-kyi-tshogs. 478 Tib. Gaṅ-po.

479 Tib. Rnam-çes-kyi-tshogs. 480 Tib. Lha-skyid.

481 Tib. Ye-çes-la-ḥjug-pa. 482 Tib. Kā-tya-ḥi-bu.

483 Tib. Rab-tu-byed-pa. 484 Tib. Dbyig-bçes.

485 Tib. Yaṅ-dag-ḥgro-baḥi-rnam-graṅs. 486 Tib. Gsus-po-che.

487 These works are mentioned in the Abhidharmakoça-vyākhyā (B. B. p. 12. 3—5).

488 Cf. Abhidharmakoça-bhāṣya B. B. p. 7. 10—13.

489 Tib. Ḥdul-baḥi-mdo or Mdo-rtsa-ba. The work of Guṇaprabha. Tg. MDO. LXXVII.

490 Tib. *rab-byuṅ-gi-gži = pravrajyā-vastu.* Cf. M. V. § 276. 1.

491 Tib. gžuṅ dam-pa Kg. ḤDUL. XIV, XV, XVI.

492 Tib. žu-ba.

493 Tib. Ḥdul-byed.

494 Tib. Phran-tshegs Kg. ḤDUL. XI (2), XII, XIII.

495 Tib. Me-tog-phreṅ-rgyud otherwise called Vinayakārikā. The work of Viçakhadeva Tg. MDO. LXXXIX No. 1.

496 Full title — Ārya-mūla-sarvāstivāda-çramaṇera-kārikā. The work of Çākyaprabha. Ibid. No. 2.

497 Tib. Dbu-ma-baḥi-rigs-tshogs-drug.

498 Tib. Stoṅ-pa-ñid-bdun-cu-ba. Tg. MDO. XVII No. 4.

499 Tib. *rten-ḥbrel = pratītya-samutpāda.*

500 Tib. *spros-pa = prapañca.*

501 Tib. *Rtsa-ba-çes-rab.* Edited by Prof. de la Vallée Poussin with the Commentary of Candrakīrti (Prasannapadā) in B. B.

502 Correct *bdag-daṅ-gžan-las-skye-ba* for *de-las-gžan-skye-ba.*

503 Tib. Rigs-pa drug-cu-ba. Tg. MDO. XVII No. 2.

504 Tib. Rtsod-pa-bzlog-pa. Ibid. No. 5.

505 Tib. Žib-mo-rnam-ḥthag. Ibid No. 3.

506 Tib. Tha-sñad-grub-pa, not translated into Tibetan. The 6th work acc. to the Tg. is the Akutobhaya (tib. Ga-las-ḥjigs-med) ibid No. 6, which appears to be a forgery. Cf. Conception of Buddhist Nirvāṇa p. 66, note 1.

507 Tib. *Mṅon-rtogs-rgyan.*

508 *prajñāpāramitā' ṣṭābhiḥ padārthaiḥ samudīritā*
*sarvākārajñatā mārgajñatā sarvajñatā tataḥ*
*sarvākārābhisaṁbodho mūrdhaprāpto' nupūrvikaḥ*
*ekakṣaṇābhisambodho dharmakāyaç ca te' ṣṭadhā.* Abhisam. I. 3, 4.

509 Tib. *rnam-pa-thams-cad-mkhyen-pa = sarva-ākāra-jñatā.*

510 Tib. *lam-çes* = *mārga-jñatā.* Cf. Vimuktasena's Pañcavimçatisāhasrikā-ālokā. — Appendix.

511 Tib. *gži-çes* = *vastu-jñāna.* Cf. Abhisam. IV. 1. or *kun-çes* = *sarva-jñatā.*

512 Tib. *rnam-pa-kun-rdzogs-sbyor-ba* = *sarva-ākāra-abhisambodha.*

513 Tib. *rtse-moḥi-sbyor-ba* = *mūrdha-abhisamaya.*

514 Tib. *mthar-gyis-sbyor-ba* = *anupūrvābhisamaya.*

515 Tib. *skad-cig-maḥi-sbyor-ba* = *eka-kṣaṇa-abisambodha.*

516 Tib. *Brgyad-stoṅ-don-bsdus.* The work of Dignāga, alias Prajñāpāramitā-saṁgraha-kārikā Tg. MDO XIV. Commented by Triratnadāsa. (Prajñāpāramitā-saṁgraha-vivaraṇa). Ibid.

517 333 a. 8.

518 This and the following is condensed from Triratnadāsa's Commentary.

519 *dṅos-po-med-paḥi-rtog-pa* = *abhāva-vikalpa.* Cf. Vasubandhu on Sūtrāl. XI. 77.

520 *dṅos-poḥi-rtog-pa* = *bhāva-vikalpa.* Cf. Ibid.

521 *sgro-ḥdogs-kyi-rtog-pa* = *adhyāropa-vikalpa.* Cf. Ibid.

522 *skur-ḥdebs-kyi-rtog-pa* = *apavāda-vikalpa.* Cf. Ibid.

523 *gcig-tu-rtog-pa* = *ekatva-vikalpa.* Cf. Ibid.

524 *tha-dad-du-rtog-pa* = *nānātva-vikalpa.* Cf. Ibid.

525 *ṅo-bo-ñid-du-rtog-pa* = *svalakṣaṇa-vikalpa* (sic). Cf. Ibid.

526 *khyad-par-du-rtog-pa* = *viçeṣa-vikalpa.*

527 *miṅ-ji-lta-ba-bžin-du-don-du-rtog-pa* = *yathānāma-artha-abhiniveça-vikalpa.* Ibid.

528 *don-ji-lta-ba-bžin-du-miṅ-du-rtog-pa* = *yathārtha-nāma-abhiniveça-vikalpa.* Ibid.

529 Tib. *naṅ-stoṅ-pa-ñid* = *adhyātma-çūnyatā.*

530 Tib. *dṅos-po-med-paḥi-ṅo-bo-ñid-stoṅ-pa-ñid* = *abhāva-svabhāva-çūnyatā.*

531 Full title: Ārya-çatasāhasrikā-pañcaviṁçatisāhasrikā-aṣṭādaçasāhasrikā-prajñāpāramitā-brhaṭ-ṭīkā. (Tib. ḥbum-tig.) Tg. MDO. XIV.

532 That on Omniscience.

533 Tib. Rab-ḥbyor.

534 Tib. Bslab-btus. Edited by Prof. C. Bendall in B. B.

535 Tib. Mdo-kun-las-btus-pa.

536 Tib. Sgom-rim- rnam-gsum. The works of Kamalaçīla (Pūrva-bhāvanā-krama, Madhyama-bhāvanā-krama and Uttara-bhāvanā-krama). Tg. MDO XXX No. No. 7, 8, 9.

537 Tib. Dbus-mthaḥ-rnam-ḥbyed Tg. MDO. XLIV.

538 Tib. Chos-daṅ-chos-ñid-rnam-ḥbyed. Ibid.

539 Sūtrāl. I. 2. —

*ghaṭitam iva suvarṇaṁ vārijaṁ vā vibuddhaṁ*
*sukṛtam iva subhojyaṁ bhujyamānaṁ kṣudhārtaiḥ*
*vidita iva sulekho ratnapeṭe'va muktā*
*vivṛta iha sa dharmaḥ prītim āgryāṁ dadhāti.*

540 These are:

1. pariniṣpanna-lakṣaṇa (tib. yoṅs-grub) — Absolute Reality.

2. paratantra-lakṣaṇa (tib. gžan-dbaṅ-) — Relative Reality, of the individual ideas.

3. parikalpita-lakṣaṇa (tib. kun-btags) — Imputed Reality, of the external world.

541 The ten forces (M. V. § 7), the four kinds of moral intrepidity (*vaiçāradya*, ibid § 8), the 18 exclusive qualities (*āveṇika-dharma*, ibid. § 9) and the 32 corporeal marks, (ibid § 17).

542 Tib. Sa-sde-lṅa = pañcabhūmi.

543 Tib. Saḥi-dṅos-gži Tg. MDO XLIX.

544 Tib. *rtog-pa* = *vitarka*. 545 Tib. *dpyod-pa* = *vicāra*.

546 Tib. *lhag-bcas-myaṅ-ḥdas* = *sopadhi-çeṣa-nirvāṇa*.

547 Tib. *lhag-med-myaṅ-ḥdas* = *anupadhi-çeṣa-nirvāṇa*.

548 Tib. *rtog-bcas* and *dpyod-bcas* = *savitarka* and *savicāra*.

549 Tib. *rtog-med* and *dpyod-bcas* = *nirvitarka* and *savicāra*.

550 Tib. *rtog-med* and *dpyod-med* = *nirvitarka* and *nirvicāra*.

551 Tib. Rnam-par-gtan-la-dbab-par-bsdu-ba Tg. MDO LII and LIII No. 1.

552 Tib. *mu-bži* = *catuṣkoṭika*.

553 Tib. Gži-bsdu-ba. Tg. MDO. LIII No. 2.

554 Tib. Rnam-graṅs-bsdu-ba. Ibid. LIV No. 2.

555 Tib. *rnam-byaṅ* = *vaiyavadānika*.

556 Tib. *kun-nas-ñon-moṅs-pa* = *sāṁkleçika*. 557 Tib. *gžuñ*.

558 Tib. Rnam-par-bçad-paḥi-sgo-bsdu-ba. Tg. MDO. LIV No. 3.

559 Tg. MDO. LVI. 86 b. 4. (*duḥkha*), 92 b. 8 (*samudaya*), 107 b. 4. (*nirodha*), 109 b. 8. (*mārga*).

560 Ibid. 119 b. 8. 561 Ibid. 125 a. 6. 562 Ibid. 138 a. 8.

563 Cf. above p. 38 note 368. 564 Tg. MDO. LVIII 1—3 b.

565 Ibid. 3 b. 1—4 b. 1. 566 Ibid. 12 b. 6—19 a. 2.

567 Ibid. 156 a. 6—168 b. 6. 568 Edited by Prof. S. Lévi.

570 Pratītyasamutpāda-ādivibhanga-nirdeça Tg. MDO. XXXVI, commented by Guṇamati.

571 Madhyānta-vibhanga-ṭīkā. Ibid. XLV.

572 Tg. MDO. XXXIV. 130—355.

573 Tib. Sdom-pa-ñi-çu-pa. The work of Candragomin. Tg. MDO. LIX No. 12.

574 Tib. So-sor-thar-baḥi-ḥgrel-pa alias Vinaya-samuccaya, ascribed to Vimalamitra Tg. MDO. LXXV, LXXVI and LXXVII.

575 Tib. Ched-du-brjod-paḥi-tshoms-kyi-ḥgrel-pa. The work of Prajñāvarman Tg. MDO. LXXI and LXXII.

576 Tib. Sdud-ḥgrel-gñis. These are: a) the Saṁcaya-Gāthā-pañjikā of Haribhadra (Tg. MDO. VII. I—93.) and the work of Buddhaçrījñāna bearing the same title. (Tg. MDO. VIII 135—223).

577 Tib. Bçes-ḥphrin. The work of Nāgārjuna. Tg. MDO. XXXIII No. 32.

578 Tib. *ḥgrel-pa*. 579 Tib. *bçad-pa*.

580 Tib. *rnam-par-bçad-pa*.

581 Tib. *bçad-sbyar*.

582 Tib. *don-bsdus*. 583 Tib. *dkaḥ-ḥgrel*.

584 Tib. *rgya-cher-ḥgrel-pa*. 585 Tib. *legs-par-sbyar-ba*.

586 Tib. *rnam-par-phye-ba*. Cf. MV. § 66.
587 Cf. p. 42 note 398.
588 Tib. Ḥod-ldan. Full title: Ārya-mūla-sarvāstivāda-çramaṇera-kārikā-vṛtti prabhāvatī nāma. The work of Çākyaprabha Tg. MDO. LXXXIX 183 b. 2—3.
589 Tib. *bdag-med-pa* = *anātma*.
590 Tib. *ḥdus-byas* = *saṁskṛta-(dharma)* = *saṁskāra*.
591 Tib. *zag-bcas* = *sāsrava*.
592 Kg. ḤDUL. 593 Cf. MV. § 63.
594 Tib. *thog-mar-dge-ba* = *ādau kalyāṇa*.
595 Tib. *bar-du-dge-ba* = *madhye kalyāṇa*.
596 Tib. *tha-mar-dge-ba* = *paryavasāne kalyāṇa*.
597 Tib. *don-bzaṅ-po* = *svartha*.
598 Tib. *tshig-ḥbru-bzaṅ-po* = *suvyañjana*.
599 Tib. *ma-ḥdres-pa* = *kevala*.
600 Tib. *yoṅs-su-rdzogs-pa* = *paripūrṇa*.
601 Tib. *yoṅs-su-dag-pa* = *pariçuddha*.
602 Tib. *yoṅs-su-byaṅ-ba* = *paryavadāta*.
603 Cf. Vasubandhu on Sūtrālaṁkāra XII. 4, 5.
604 Tg. MDO LVIII 32 a. 6.
605 Cf. M. V. § 4. 1, 2, 3.
606 Vasubandhu's interpretation (on Sūtrālaṁkāra XII-14) is different: — *svarthaḥ saṁvṛti-paramārtha-satya-yogāt*, — it is of good meaning, since it is connected with both the Empirical and the Absolute Reality.
607 Vasub. on Sūtrāl. XII. 15 — *kevalaṁ parair asādhāraṇatvāt*.
608 Ibid.: — *paripūrṇaṁ tridhātu-kleça-prahāṇa-paripūraṇāt*.
609 Ibid.: — *pariçuddhaṁ svabhāva-viçuddhito' nāsravatvāt*.
610 Ibid.: — *paryavadātaṁ mala-viçuddhitaḥ saṁtāna-viçuddhyā kṣīṇāsravāṇām*.
611 The following is an extract from the Vyākhyāyukti (Tg. MDO LVIII 144 b. 8.)
612 Cf. Guṇamati's Vyākhyāyukti-ṭīkā (Tg. MDO. LX. 153 b. 5, 6. *ñon-moṅs-pa ḥdul-ba-la-snaṅ žes-bya-ba-ni ñon-moṅs-paḥi gñen-po* (= *pratipakṣa*) *gaṅ-yin-paḥo*.
613 Tib. *rten-ḥbrel-gyi-chos-ñid*. Guṇamati (Ibid. 153 b. 6—7) says: *rten-ciṅ-ḥbrel-par-ḥbyuṅ-baḥi-chos-ñid* (= *pratītyasamutpāda-dharmatā*) *daṅ-mi-mthun-pa-ma-yin-pa* (= *aviruddha*) *žes-bya-ba-ni* (= *iti*) *ḥdi yod-pas ḥdi ḥbyuṅ* (= *asmin sati idam bhavati*) *žes-bya-baḥi-chos-ñid-daṅ-mi-mthun-pa* (= *aviruddha*) *ma-yin-no*. 614 Cf. p. 21.
615 XII 14, 15.

*Kalyāṇo dharmo' yaṁ hetutvād bhakti-tuṣṭi-buddhīnāṁ*
*dvividhārthaḥ sugrāhyaç caturguṇa-brahmacarya-vadaḥ*
*parair asādhāraṇa-yoga-kevalaṁ tridhātuka-kleça-vihāni-pūrakam*
*svabhāva-çuddhaṁ mala-çuddhitaṁ ca tac caturguṇa-brahmavicaryam iṣyate*.

616 Cf. above, note 606.
617 Cf. a corresponding passage in Nāgārjuna's Ratnāvalī (Tg. MDO. XCIV 147 b. 3, 4) quoted in the Madhyamakavṛtti (B. B. 360. 2) — *çūnyatā-karuṇā-garbham keṣāṁ cid bodhi-sādhanam*.

618 I. 4. *āghrāyamāṇakaṭukaṁ svādurasaṁ yathau' ṣadhaṁ tadvat dharma-dvaya-vyavasthā vyañjanato' rthena ca jñeyā* (the text edited by Prof. S. Lévi has *vyañjanato' rtho na ca jñeyaḥ*).

619 XII. 8, 9. *uddeçān nirdeçāt tathai'va yānānulomanāt çlākṣṇyāt.*
*prātityād yāthārhān nairyaṇyad ānukulyatvād.*
*vyañjana-saṁpac cai' ṣā vijñeyā sarvathā' grasattvānām.*

620 Tg. MDO. LIV. 56 b. 4—5.

621 The Nyāyabinduṭīkā (B. B. 2 5—6 — Tibetan text and 1. 6—7. Sanscrit text.)

622 Tib. *mkhas-grub.* 623 Tib. *brgyud-pa = paraṁparā.*

624 Tg. MDO. LXXXIX. 79 a. 1—2.

625 Ratnāvalī Tg. MDO. XCIV. 152 a. 2—3.

626 Tib. *dge-baḥi-bçes-gñen = kalyāṇamitra.*

627 Bodhicaryāvatāra V. 102. —
*sadā kalyāṇamitraṁ ca jīvitārthe' pi na tyajet*
*bodhisattva-vrata-dharaṁ mahāyānārtha-kovidam.*

628 Bodhisattva-saṁvara-viṁçaka. Tg. MDO. LXI. 192 a. 3.

629 XVII. 10. — *mitraṁ çrayed dāntaçamopaçāntaṁ guṇādhikaṁ sodyamam āgamāḍhyaṁ*
*prabuddha-tattvaṁ vacasā' bhyupetaṁ kṛpātmakaṁ kheda-vivarjitaṁ ca.*

630 — The *kalyāṇamitra.*

631 Sūtrālaṁkāra XIII. 8. *bahuçruto dṛṣṭa-satyo vāgmī samanukampakaḥ*
*akhinno bodhisattvaç ca jñeyaḥ satpuruṣo mahān.*

632 Tib. *luṅ = āgama.* 633 Tib. *rtogs-pa = adhigamya.*

634 Sūtrālaṁkāra XII. 5. *viṣadā saṁdeha-jahā ādeyā tattva-darçikā dvividhā*
*saṁpanna-deçane' yaṁ vijñeyaṁ bodhisattvānām.*

635 Tib. *kun-nas-ñon-moṅs-pa = sāṁkleçika.*

636 Tib. *rnam-par-byaṅ-ba = vaiyavadānika.*

637 Neither exaggerately verbose nor exaggerately laconic.

638 XII. 10, 11, 12, 13.

639 *vācā padaiḥ suyuktair anudeça-vibhāga-saṁçaya-cchedaiḥ.*
*bahulīkārānugatā hy udghaṭita-vipañcita-jñeṣu.*

640 Tib. *mgo-smos-kyis-go-ba = udghaṭita-jña.*

641 Tib. *rnam-spros-kyis-go-ba = vipañcita-jña.*

642 *çuddhā trimaṇḍalena hite' yaṁ deçanā hi buddhānām*
*doṣair vivarjitā punar aṣṭabhir eṣai'va vijñeyā.*

643 Cf. Vasubandhu's Commentary on this verse: — *yena ca deçayati vācā padaiç ca yathā co' ddeçādi-prakāraiḥ yeṣu co' dghaṭita-vipañcita-jñeṣu*, — the voice and style, by means of which (the Bodhisattva) teaches, the form of teaching, and the persons that receive it, — those that understand a brief indication and those that require details.

644 *kauçīdyam anavabodho hy avakāçasyā' kṛtir hy anītatvaṁ*
*saṁdehasyā' cchedas tadvigamasyā' dṛḍhīkaraṇaṁ.*

645 Correct *brtan-mi-byed* for *bstan-mi-byed.*

646 *khedo' tha matsaritvaṁ doṣā hy ete matā kathāyāṁ hi*
*tadabhāvād buddhānāṁ niruttarā deçanā bhavati.*

647 Tg. MDO. LVIII. 74 a. 2—75 a. 7 (condensed).

648 The author's own words.

649 Tib. *go-rim(s)* = *ānupurvī*.

650 Cf. Guṇamati's Vyākhyāyuktiṭīkā (Tg. MDO. LX. 78 b. 3—4). *yaṅ-dag-phul-can žes-bya-ba-ni ḥphags-paḥi-bden-paḥi gtam-mo* — the communication of high, sublime matters is that of the four Truths of the Saint.

651 Tib. *mgo-gcig-tu-luṅ-bstan-pa* = *ekāṁça-vyākaraṇa*. The other forms of instruction (*vyākaraṇa*) are: —

*rnam-par-phye-ste-luṅ-bstan-pa* = *vibhajya-vyākaraṇa*
*dris-nas-luṅ-bstan-pa* = *paripṛcchā-vyakaraṇa*, and
*gžag-par-luṅ-bstan-pa* = *sthāpanīya-vyākaraṇa*.

Cf. M. V. § 83, Rosenberg, Problems p. 59 and Guṇamati's Vyākhyāyuktiṭīkā (Tg. MDO. LX. 78 b. 7—79 a. 4.)

652 Tib. *tshad-ma* = *pramāṇa*. Guṇamati (ibid. 79 a. 8—b. 1.) says: *mṅon-sum daṅ rjes-su-dpag-pa daṅ yid-ches-paḥi-luṅ-gi-tshad-ma-rnams-daṅ-mi-ḥgal-baḥi-phyir-ro* — by not being in conflict with the modes of cognition which are: — sense-perception, inference, and authoritative Scripture. Cf. above p. 46 note 46.

653 Tib. *bag-chags* = *vāsanā*.

654 Kg. MDO. XXI. 190 b. 5—6 and 191 b. 2.

655 Corr. *le-lo-can* for *le-lo-žan*.

656 Lit "The Wheel" (*ḥkhor-lo*).

657 XII. 1. *prāṇān bhogāṇç ca dhīrāḥ pramudita-manasaḥ kṛcchra-labdhān asārān, sattvebhyo duḥkhitebhyaḥ satatam avasṛjanty ucca-dāna-prakāraiḥ, prāg evo' dāra dharmaṁ hitakaram asakṛt sarvathai' va prajānāṁ, kṛcchre nai' vopalabdhaṁ bhṛçam avasṛjatāṁ vṛddhigaṁ cā' vyayaṁ ca.*

658 The Bodhisattvas. Corr. *brtan-pa* for *bstan-pa*.

659 Corr. *yaṅs* (= *udāra*) for *yaṅ*.

660 Tib. Ḥjam-dpal-rnam-par-ḥphrul-paḥi-mdo. Kg. MDO. II 251 b. 6. and 252 a. 4.

661 Kg. MDO. V. 38 b. 4—5. The version of the Kg. is slightly different from that of Xyl. —

*gaṅ-dag ḥdod-phyir chos-kyi luṅ-ḥbogs-pa rmoṅs-pa de-dag chos-kyi rin-po-che*
*de-dag ḥdod-pa spaṅs-pa phyir-len-te rin-thaṅ-med-pa rñed-kyaṅ-spoṅ-žiṅ-rgyu.*

662 Cf. M. V. § 263, 87 sqq.

663 XII. 24 *iti sumatir akhedavān kṛpāluḥ prathita-yaçāḥ suvidhijñatām upetaḥ bhavati sukathiko hi bodhisattvas tapati jane kathitair yathai' va sūryaḥ.*

664 Tg. MDO. LVI 138 b. 6—139 a. 3.

665 Cf. Abhidharma-samuccaya-bhāṣya of Jinaputra (Tg. MDO. LVII. 129 b. 6.) — *yoṅs-su çes-par-bya-baḥi dṅos-po-ni* (= *parijñeyaṁ vastu*) *phuṅ-po-la-sogs-paḥo* (*skandhādayaḥ*) — the subject that is to be fully apprehended, consists of the five groups of elements etc. Cf. also Vyākhyāyuktiṭīkā (Tg. MDO. LX 9. b. 4—5) *ci-žig yoṅs-su-çes-par-bya že-na gzugs-la-sogs-pa sdug-bsṅal-gyi-bden-pas bsdus-paḥo* (= *rupādayo duḥkha-satyena saṁgṛhītāḥ*).

666 Abhidh. sam. bh. (Tg. MDO. LVII 129 b. 7) *yoṅs-su-çes-par-bya-baḥi-don-ni mi-rtag-pa-ñid* (= *anityatā*) *la-sogs-paḥo*.

667 Ibid. 129 b. 7—8. *yoṅs-su-çes-par-bya-baḥi-rgyu-ni tshul-khrims daṅ*

*dbaṅ-poḥi sgo bsdams-pa-la-sogs-paḥo* — the factors that are conducive to the complete apprehension (of the Truth of Phenomenal Existence) are pure morality and suppression of the senses.

668 Ibid. 129 b. 7—8 *yoṅs-su-çes-pa-ni* (= *parijñānam*) *byaṅ-chub-kyi-chos-rnams-so* (= *bodhipakṣikā dharmāḥ*). Acc. to Guṇamati (Tg. MDO. LX 9 b. 6.) *yaṅ-dag-paḥi lta-ba* (= *samyagdṛṣṭi*).

669 Abhidh. sam. bh. (Tg. MDO. LVII 129 b. 8) — *rnam-par-grol-baḥo* (= *vimukti*).

670 Ibid. 129 b. 8. 671 Ibid. 129. b. 8—130 a. 1.

672 Ibid. 130 a. 6—8.

673 Tib. *chud-za-ba daṅ mi-za-baḥi-sgo*. Abhidh. sam. bh. Tg. MDO. LVII 130 b. 5—131 a. 5.

674 Ibid. 131 b. 8—132 b. 2. The six modes are:

*de-kho-naḥi-don-gyi-tshul* — the mode of the Absolute (underlying the Relativity of phenomenal existence).

*ḥthob-paḥi-tshul* — the mode of attaining (final Enlightenment as a Buddha)

*bçad-paḥi-tshul* — the mode of explaining (the latter).

*mthaḥ-gñis-spaṅs-paḥi-tshul* — the mode of teaching without having recourse to the two extremities.

*bsam-gyis-mi-khyab-paḥi-tshul* — the mode of unthinkable perfection.

*dgoṅs-paḥi-tshul* — the mode of deeper sense.

675 Ibid. 133 b. 2. 676 Ibid. 133 b. 1—133 b. 4.

677 Tg. MDO. LVIII. 33 b. 5—6. The Sanscrit text of this verse is preserved in the Abhisamayālaṁkārālokā (MS. Minaev 16 b. 1—2). It runs as follows: —

*prayojanaṁ sapiṇḍārthaḥ padārthaḥ sānusaṁdhikaḥ, sacodyaparihāraç ca vācyaḥ sūtrārtha-vādibhiḥ.*

678 Ibid. 33 b. 7—34 a. 1. ~~679 Cf~~ below.

680 Tg. MDO LVIII 98 a. 7—8.

681 Cf. Vyākhyāyukti Tg. MDO. LVIII 98 a. 8—6. 1. *rab-tu-dbye-ba-ni brjod-par-bya-ba de gzugs-can daṅ gzugs-can-ma-yin-pa daṅ bstan-du-yod-pa daṅ bstan-du med-pa-la-sogs-paḥi rnam-par rab-tu-dbye-bas-so.*

682 Ibid. 33 b. 8—34 a. 1. 683 *rigs* = *gotra.*

684 Tib. Tiṅ-ṅe-ḥdzin-rgyal-po. Çikṣāsamuccaya BB. 354 6. — 355. 2.

685 *adhyeṣayeyur yadi tvāṁ te dharma-dānasya kāraṇāt*
*prathamaṁ vāca* (sic) *bhāṣeyā nā' haṁ vaipulya-çikṣitaḥ.*

686 *evaṁ tvaṁ vāca bhāṣeyā yuṣme vā vijña-paṇḍitāḥ*
*kathaṁ mahātmanāṁ çakyaṁ purato bhāṣituṁ mayā.*

687 *sahasai' ṣāṁ na jalpeta tulayitvā tu bhājanaṁ*
*yadi bhājanaṁ vijānīyāḥ anadhīṣṭo' pi deçayeḥ.*

688 *yadi duḥçīlān paçyesi* (sic) *pariṣāyāṁ bahūn sthitān,*
*saṁlekhaṁ mā prabhāṣe tvaṁ varṇaṁ dānasya kīrtayeḥ.*

689 Correct *ṅaṅ-tshul* for *ṅan-tshul.*

690 Cf. Çikṣās. page 354 note 8.

691 *bhaveyur yadi cā' lpecchāḥ çuddhāḥ çīle pratiṣṭhitāḥ*
*maitraṁ cittaṁ janitvā tvaṁ kuryāḥ saṁlekhikīṁ kathām.*

692 *parīttā yadi pāpecchāḥ çīlavanto' tra vistarāḥ*
*labdha-pakṣas tadā bhūtvā varṇaṁ çīlasya kīrtayeḥ.*

693 Cf. below.

694 Tib. Dam-paḥi-chos-padma-dkar-po BB. 282. 5, 6 and 283. 6—284. 10, quoted likewise in the Çikṣāsamuccaya BB. 352. 8—354. 2.

695 *kālena co* (sic) *cintayamānu paṇḍitaḥ praviçya layanaṁ tatha ghaṭṭayitvā, vipaçya dharmaṁ imu sarva yoniço utthāya deçeta alīna-cittaḥ.*

696 *sukha-sthito bhoti* (sic) *sadā vicakṣaṇaḥ sukhaṁ niṣannas tatha dharma bhāṣate, udāra-prajñapta karitva āsanaṁ caukṣe manojñe pṛthivī-pradeçe.*

697 *caukṣaṁ ca so cīvara prāvaritvā surakta-raṅgaṁ ca prasanna-raṅgaiḥ āsevakaṁ kṛṣṇa tathā daditvā mahāpramāṇaṁ ca nivāsayitvā.*

698 *sapāda-pīṭhasmi* (sic) *niṣadya āsane vicitraduṣyehi susaṁstṛtasmin* (sic) *sudhauta-pādaç ca upāruhitvā snigdhena çīrṣeṇa mukhena cā'pi.*

699 *dharmāsane cā'tra niṣīdiyāna ekāgra-sattveṣu samāgateṣu upasaṁharec citrakathā bahuç ca bhikṣūṇa ca bhikṣuṇiyāna cai'va.*

700 *upāsakānāṁ ca upāsikānāṁ rajñāṁ tatha rājasutāna cai'va. vicitritārthā madhuraṁ katheyā anabhyasūyantu sadā sa paṇḍitaḥ.*

701 *kilāsitaṁ cā'pi vivarjayeta na ca'pi utpādayi kheda-saṁjñāṁ aratim ca sarvaṁ vijahīta paṇḍito maitrī-balaṁ ca pariṣāya bhāvayet.*

702 *bhāṣec ca rātri-divaṁ agradharmaṁ dṛṣṭānta-koṭī-niyutaiḥ sa paṇḍitaḥ. saṁharṣayet parṣa tathai'va toṣayen na cā'pi kiṁcit tatra jātu prārthayet.*

703 *khadyaṁ ca bhojyaṁ ca tathā' nna-pānaṁ vastraṁ çayyāsanacīvaraṁ ca gilāna-bhaiṣajya na cintayet saḥ na vijñāpet parṣadi kiṁcid anyat.*

704 *anyatra cinteya sadā vicakṣaṇo bhaveya buddho' ham ime ca sattvāḥ etaç ca me sarvasukhopadhānaṁ yaṁ dharma çravemi hitāya loke.*

705 Kg. MDO. XIV 11 b. 1—6, quoted Çikṣāsamuccaya BB. 355. 3—13.

706 *imāni Sāgaramate mantra-padāni dharma-bhāṇakena supravṛttāni kṛtvā dharma-āsanakena supravṛttāni kṛtvā* (wanting in Xyl.) *dharma-āsana-niṣaṇṇena sarvaṁ parṣadaṁ bodhy-ākara-abhinirhṛtayā maitryā spharitvā ātmani vaidya-saṁjñām utpādya dharme bhaiṣajya-saṁjñāṁ dharma-çravaṇikeṣv ātura-samjñāṁ tathāgate satpuruṣa-saṁjñāṁ dharma-netryāṁ cirasthika-saṁjñām utpādya imāni mantra-padāny āmukhīkṛtya dharma-saṁkathā kāraṇīyā tasya samantād yojana-çate* (Çikṣ. *yo janaçate*!!) *na māro na-mārakāyikā vā devatā upasaṁkramayiṣyanti-vicakṣuḥkaraṇe ye'py enaṁ upasaṁkramiṣyanti te'py asya na çakṣyanty antarāyaṁ kartum.*

707 Ibid. 355. 14—15. — *dharma-bhāṇakena caukṣeṇa çuci-samudācāreṇa susnātena çuci-nivasitena bhavitavyam.*

708 *phyin-drug* = *ṣaṭpāramitāḥ.* 709 *sbyin-pa* = *dāna.*

710 *tshul-khrims* = *çīla.* 711 *bzod-pa* = *kṣānti.*

712 *brtson-ḥgrus* = *vīrya.* 713 *bsam-gtan* = *dhyāna.*

714 *çes-rab* = *prajñā.*

715 Tib. Seṅ-ge-bzaṅ-po. The following passage is an extract from the Commentary on the Aṣṭasāhasrikā — Abhisamayālaṁkārālokā in abridged form. The full text is as follows: — (MS. Minaev 64 a. 8—b. 3.) — *bodhisattvasya dharma-dānādi-dānād dāna-pāramitā-saṁnāhaḥ. tasyai'va çrāvakādi-manaskāra-parivarjanāc chīla-pāramitā-saṁnāhaḥ. tasyai'va sarvākāra-jñatā-dharmāṇāṁ kṣamaṇa-rocana-upaparīkṣaṇa-sarvajana-apriya-vāditva-sahanāt kṣānti-pāramitā-saṁnāhaḥ. tasyai'vo' ttarottara-kuçala-mūla-abhivṛddhyarthaṁ chandādi-jananād vīrya-pāramitā-saṁnāhaḥ. tasyai'va yānāntara-avyavakīrṇa-citta-ekāgratayā tatkuçala-mūla-anuttara-samyaksaṁbodhi-pariṇāma-ālambanād dhyā-*

*na-pāramita-saṁnāhaḥ. tasyai'va māyākāra-saṁjñā-ūpasthānena deya-dāyaka-pratigrāhaka-anupalambhāt prajñāpāramitā-saṁnāhaḥ* (= Tg. MDO. VI 63 a. 8—b. 5.)

**716** Egoistic. **717** *mi-dmigs-pa = anupalambha.*

**718** Tg. MDO. LVIII 75 a. 8—b. 8.

**719** Tg. MDO. LVIII 77 a. 3—4.

**720** Lit. — the stains (*dri-ma*). **721** Ibid. 76 a. 2—8.

**722** Tib. *Lus-skyes-dus-pa (?).*

**723** Tib. Bźi-brgya-pa. The work of Āryadeva. Tg. MDO. XVIII. 14 b 1—2.

**724** Vyākhyāyukti. Tg. MDO. LVIII 146 a. 1—5.

**725** The Abhisamayālaṁkārālokā MS. Minaev. 152 b. 3—5 — *Prajñā-pāramitā satkṛtyā adhyāçayena çrotavye'ty apanīta-avaguṇṭhanikādinā nīcāsana-sthena vikṣepa-doṣaṁ parihṛtya mokṣa-kāma-āçayena saddharmaḥ çrotavyaḥ.* (= Tg. MDO. VI. 162 a. 1—2).

**726** *lhag-paḥi-bsam-pa = adhyāçaya.* For definition cf. Çiksāsamuccaya p. 285. 14—286. 5.

**727** Tg. MDO. LVIII 143 b. 2—4. **728** Ibid. 140 b. 7—141 a. 1.

**729** Tib. *rtogs-pa-brjod-pa = avadāna.* **730** Tib. *dgaḥ-bo.*

**731** Vyākhyāyukti Tg. MDO. LVIII 143 b. 8—144 a. 1.

**732** Tib. *chos-dgaḥ.*

**733** Kg. DKON. III. 25 a. 3.

**734** *dge-baḥi-bçes-gñen = kalyāṇamitra.* Cf. Çikṣāsamuccaya. Kār. VI.

**735** Tg. MDO. LVIII 142 b. 6—143 a. 4.

**736** *bag-la-ñal = anuçaya.*

**737** Cf. above p. 5 *çrutānusāra-pratipatti-sāräḥ* (Jātakamālā Ed. Kern, Harvard Series p. 215. 2.)

**738** Ibid. 220. 9—12. *nīcaistarāsana-sthānād vibodhya vinaya-çriyaṁ.*
*prītyārpitābhyāṁ cakṣurbhyāṁ vāṅ-madhv āsvādayann iva*
*gauravāvarjitaikagra-prasannāmala-mānasaḥ*
*satkṛtya dharmaṁ çṛṇuyād bhiṣag-vākyam ivā'turaḥ.*

**739** Kg. DKON. I 119 a. 7—119 b. 1. Cf. below.

**740** Tib. Rgya-cher- rol-pa. Ed. Lefmann. 412. 13—18. (Dharma-cakra-pravartana-parivarta)

*duravāpyaṁ mānuṣyaṁ buddhotpādaḥ sudullabhā* (sic) *çraddhā*
*çreṣṭhaṁ ca dharma-çravaṇaṁ aṣṭākṣaṇa-vivarjana durāpaḥ*
*prāptaç ca te'dya sarve buddhotpādaḥ kṣaṇas tathā çraddhā*
*dharma-çravaṇaç ca varaḥ pramādam akhilaṁ vivarjayataḥ*
*bhavati kadācid avasthā yat kalpa-nayutair na çrūyate dharmaḥ*
*saṁprāptaḥ sa tavā'dya pramādam akhilaṁ vivarjayataḥ.*

**741** M. V. § 120. **742** Tg. MDO. LVIII 147 a. 3—4.

**743** Ibid. 149 b. 3—4.

**744** Ibid. 139 a. 2—3. Cf. Saddharma-puṇḍarīka BB. 57. 3.
*sudurlabhā īdṛçakāç ca sattvāḥ çrutvāna ye çraddadhi agradharmaṁ*
*audambaraṁ puṣpa yathai'va durlabhaṁ kadāci kahiṁci kathaṁci dṛçyate.*

**745** *srid-pa = bhava.*

**746** Çikṣāsamuccaya 189. 5—6.
*kiyad bahū dharma-paryāyu-neyya çīlaṁ na rakṣeta çrutena mattaḥ*

*na bāhuçrutyena sa çakyu* (sic) *trāyitum duḥçīlayena* (sic) *vrajamāna durgatim.*

747 Tib. Btsun-pa-chos-la-gnas-paḥi-dge-sloṅ žes-bya-baḥi-mdo. A Sūtra bearing such a name is not to be found in the Indices of the Kangyur.

748 XII. 3. *tasmān nai'va nirarthikā bhavati sā yā bhāvanā yogināṁ*
*tasmān nai'va nirarthikā bhavati sā yā deçanā saugatī,*
*dṛṣṭo'rthaḥ çruta-mātrakād yadi bhavet syād bhāvanā'pārthikā*
*açrutvā yadi bhāvanām anuviçet syād deçanā' pārthikā.*

749 Çikṣāsamuccaya. Kārikā XX.
*kṣameta çrutam eṣeta saṁçrayeta vanaṁ tadā*
*samādhanāya yujyeta bhāvayed açubhādikam.*

750 Ibid. 194. 7, 8.—
*sahadharmikeṇo* (sic) *vacanena uktāḥ krodhaṁ ca dveṣaṁ* (Çiks. — *doṣam*) *ca apratyayaṁ ca.*
*prāviṣkaronti* (sic) *imi bāladharmā imam artha vijñāya na viçvasanti.*

751 VIII. 26.

752 Sic according to Tib. The editions of the Sanscrit text by Professors Minaev and de la Vallée Poussin have both: —
*nā'vadhyāyanti taravo na cā'rādhyāḥ prayatnataḥ*
*kadā taiḥ sukha-saṁvāsaiḥ saha vāso bhaven mama.* —
The Tib. seems to be a translation from another reading of the text, which must have been: —
*nā'vadhyāyanti taravo vane ca mṛgapakṣiṇaḥ*
*kadā taiḥ* etc.

753 Çikṣāsamuccaya 196. 9—10. — *yadi punaḥ çrutavān imāṁ kṣaṇa-saṁpadam āsādya lābhādāv āsaktaḥ cittaṁ na çodhayet sa evai'kaḥ sadevake loke vañcakaḥ* (*Çikṣ.* — *vañcitaḥ*) *syāt.*

754 Ibid. 196. 11—14. — *tad yathā Kāçyapa kaçcid eva puruṣo mahatā udaka-ārṇaveno' hyamāna udaka-tṛṣṇayā kālaṁ kuryād evam eva Kāçyapa ihai' ke çramaṇa-brāhmaṇā bahūn dharmān udgṛhya paryāvāpya na rāga-tṛṣṇāṁ vinodayanti na dveṣa-tṛṣṇāṁ na moha-tṛṣṇāṁ vinodayanti te mahatā dharma-ārṇaveno' hyamānāḥ kleça-tṛṣṇayā kālagatā durgati-vinipāta-gāmino bhavanti.*

755 The author's own words.

756 Çikṣāsamuccaya 108. 5—111. 4.

757 *Agauravo bhoti çrutena matto vivāda-mantreṣu niviṣṭa bhoti*
*muṣita-çrutiç cā' pyasaṁprajanyo bhāṣye ramantasya* (sic) *ime hi doṣāḥ.*

758 *adhyātma-cintāt tu sudūra bhotī cittaṁ na kāyaç ca prasanna bhoti*
*unnāma-nāmāni bahūni gacchatī* (sic) *bhāṣye....*

759 Corr. *ḥhud* for *mdud.*

760 *saddharma-cittāt tu praṇaṣṭu bālaḥ sukarkaço bhoti asnigdha-cittaḥ*
*vipaçyanāyāḥ çamathāc ca dūre bhāṣye....*

761 *agauravo bhoti sadā gurūṇāṁ paligodha-mantreṣu ratiṁ janitvā*
*asāra-sthāyī parihīna-prajño bhāṣye....*

762 *amānito deva-gaṇaiḥ* (Çikṣ. — *guṇaiḥ*) *sa bhoti nā'py asya tasmin spṛha saṁjananti*
*pratisaṁvidāto* (sic) *bhavatī* (sic) *vihīno bhāṣye....*

763 *paribhāṣyate cā'pi sa paṇḍitebhir ye kacid* (sic) *astī* (sic) *pṛtha-kāya-sākṣī*
*nirarthakaṁ jīvitu* (sic) *tasya bhoti bhāṣye....*

764 *sa çocate kālu* (sic) *karotu* (sic) *bālaḥ pratipatti-hīno' smi kim adya kuryāṁ*
*suduṣkhito* (sic) *bhoti alabdha-gāḍho bhāṣye....*
765 *calācalo bhoti tṛṇaṁ yathe' ritaṁ vicikitsate evaṁ asau na saṁçayaḥ na tasya jātu dṛḍha buddhi bhoti bhāṣye....*
766 *naṭā yathā tiṣṭhati ranga-madhye anyāṇa* (sic) *çurāṇa* (sic) *guṇān prabhāṣate*
*svayaṁ ca bhoti pratipatti-hīno bhāṣye....*
767 *çaṭhaç ca so bhoti laghur nirāçaḥ punaḥ punaç cā' rabhate vivādaṁ so dūrato ārya-dharmasya bhoti bhāṣye....*
768 Corr. *re-chad* for *re-ḥchad.*
769 *saṁhṛṣyate satkṛta alpa-sthāmaḥ prakampate viprakṛto ajānī kapir yathā cañcala-citta bhoti bhāṣye....*
770 This and the following two verses are omitted in Çikṣ.
771 *ramitvā bhāṣyasmi* (sic) *ciraṁ pi kālaṁ na vindate prītiṁ ihā' gra-saukhyaṁ.*
*varaṁ hi ekasya padasya cintanā prītiṁ pade yatra lābhed anantām.*
772 *ne' kṣu-tvace sāram ihā' sti kiṁcin madhye' sti tat sāra supremaṇīyaḥ.*
*bhuktvā tvacaṁ ne' ha punaḥ saçakyaṁ labdhuṁ nareṇe' kṣu-rasaṁ pradhānam.*
773 *yathā tvacaṁ tatvad avai' hi bhāṣyaṁ yathā rasas tadvad ihā' rtha-cintā tasmād dhi bhāṣye tū ratiṁ vihāya cintetha arthaṁ sada apramattāḥ.*
774 Tib. *saṅs-rgyas-kyi-žiṅ = buddha-kṣetra.*
775 Tib. *bskal-pa-bzaṅ-po = bhadra-kalpa.*
776 Tib. *mi-mjed-pahi-ḥjig-rten-kyi-khams = sahā-loka-dhātu.*
777 Cf. below.
778 Tib. Sñan-pa-chen-po.
779 Tib. Yon-tan-bkod-pa.
780 Tib. Bskal-bzaṅ
781 Tib. Sñiṅ-rje-pad-ma-dkar-po. Ed. by Çarat Candra Das, Buddh. Text. Soc.
782 Tib. De-bžin-gçegs-paḥi-gsaṅ-ba-bsam-gyis-mi-khyab-paḥi-bstan-pa. Kg. DKON. I.
783 Tib. Ḥdzin-pa. Kar.-puṇḍ. BTS. 17. 5—10. sqq.
784 Tib. Rtsibs-kyi-mu-khyud.
785 Tib. *ḥkhor-los-bsgyur-ba = cakravartin.*
786 Tib. Mig-mi-ḥdzum-pa.
787 Tib. *mdun-na-ḥdon-(pa) = purohita.*
788 Tib. Rgya-mtshoḥi-rdul.
789 Tib. Rgya-mtshoḥi-sñiṅ-po
790 Tib. Rin-chen-sñiṅ-po.
791 KP. BTS. 21. 16.
792 Ibid. 21. 25—27.
793 Ibid. 22. 1. — *kupathena dakṣiṇābhimukhaṁ gacchataḥ.*
794 Ibid. 24. 12—14.
795 Ibid. 24. 30.
796 Ibid. 24. 31. — *saṁsāra-abhirataḥ.*
797 Ibid. 25. 24—26.
798 Tib. me-loṅ-bkod-pa. Ibid. 25. 28.
799 Ibid. 26. 7.
800 Kar. Puṇḍ. BTS. 26. 30—31.
801 Tib. Tshe-dpag-med.
802 Tib. Bde-ba-can. Ibid. 36. 24—25.

803 Tib. Mig-mi-ḥdzum-pa.
804 Tib. Ḥod-zer-kun-nas-ḥphags-pa-dpal-brtsegs-kyi-rgyal-po. Ibid. 38. 14—16.
805 Tib. Mthu-chen-thob. M. V. § 23. 9.
806 Tib. Rab-tu-brtan-pa-yon-tan-nor-bu-brtsegs-paḥi-rgyal-po. Kar. Puṇḍ. 39. 11.
807 Tib. Kun-tu-gzigs.
808 Tib. Dag-pa-rdul-bral-yaṅ-dag-brtsegs. Ibid. 42. 17—21.
809 Tib. Kun-tu-bzaṅ-po. Ibid. 43. 17.
810 Tib. Pad-ma-dam-pa. Ibid. 44. 23.
811 Tib. (Chos-kyi)-dbaṅ-bsgyur-dbaṅ-phyug. Ibid. 45. 19.
812 Tib. Snaṅ-ba-rdul-bral-spos-mtho-dbaṅ-phyug-rgyal-po. Ibid. 48. 25.
813 Tib. Ye-çes-rdo-rje-rnam-par-bsgyiṅs-paḥi-dbaṅ-phyug-(kyi-tog). Ibid. 50. 16.
814 Tib. Mi-ḥkhrugs-pa. Ibid. 53. 14.
815 Tib. Gser-gyi-me-tog. Ibid. 56. 28.
816 Tib. Rgyal-baḥi-zla-ba. Ibid. 57. 4. Sic acc. to Tib., but Sūtra: — *tad buddhakṣetraṁ Jayasomaṁ nāma bhaviṣyati. tatra tvam anuttarāṁ samyaksaṁbodhim abhisaṁbhotsyase Nāgavimarditeçvaraghoṣo nāma bhaviṣyasi yāvad buddho bhagavān.*
817 Tib. Rnam-par-gzigs. M. V. § 2. 6.
818 Tib. Gtsug-tor-can. Ibid. § 2. 7
819 Tib. Thams-cad-skyob. Ibid. § 2. 8
} Kar. Puṇḍ. BTS. 62. 11—12.
820 Tib. Skar-ma-skyoṅ.
821 Tib. Ḥkhor-ba-ḥjig. Kar. Puṇḍ. BTS. 63. 13.
822 Tib. Gser-thub. Ibid. 63.20.
823 Tib. Ḥod-sruṅs. Ibid. 64. 17. 824 Tib. Dri-med-ḥod.
825 Tib. Byams-pa. Ibid. 66. 16.
826 Tib. *bsñen-bkur-ba* = *upasthāyaka*. Ibid. 67. 15—68. 3.
827 *kiyad bahavo bhagavann anāgate' dhvani muni-bhaskarā' smin bhadrakalpe udayanti.*
828 Ibid. 68. 7—9. 829 Ibid. 68. 31 sqq.
830 Tib. Gsal-mdzad. Ibid. 69. 29.
831 Tib. *mtshams-med-pa* = *anantarya*. Cf. M.V. § 122.
832 Ibid. 97. 23.
833 Tib. Mdzes-par-snaṅ-ba = Çubhāloka (?)
834 Tib. Rnam-par-brgyan pa.
835 Tib. Yon-tan-mthaḥ-yas-rin-chen-sna-tshogs-bkod-paḥi-rgyal-po. Kg. DKON. 117 b. 7—118 a. 2.
836 Tib. Rnam-par-dag-pa-can.
837 Tib. Yul-ḥkhor-bsruṅ. Ibid. 118 b. 1—2.
838 Kg. DKON. I. 118 b. 6—119 a. 1.
839 Ibid. 119 a. 2—5. 840 Ibid. 119 a. 7—119 b. 1.
841 *tsan-dan sbrul-gyi sñiṅ-po* = *goçirṣa-uragasāra-candana.*
842 Kg. DKON. I. 120 a. 7. sqq. 843 Ibid. 120 b. 2.
844 Tib. Ma-smad-pa. 845 Tib. Dpe-med-pa.
846 Tib. Chos-sems.
847 Tib. Chos-kyi-blo-gros. Kg. DKON. I. 121 b. 5.—122 a. 3.

848 Ibid. 123 a. 2—6. 849 Tib. Rnam-par-dag-paḥi-blo-gros.
850 Tib. Ḥkhor-ba-ḥjig. Ibid. 123 a. 6—123 b. 1.
851 Tib. Rnam-par-rgyal-baḥi-sde.
852 Tib. Gser-thub. Kg. DKON. I. 123 b. 2.
853 Tib. Dbaṅ-po-ži-ba. 854 Kg. DKON I. 123 b. 3.
855 Tib. Don-thams-cad-grub-pa.
856 Ibid. *de-ni-ṅa-yin-te* ...this was myself. 857 Tib. Ska-rags-can.
858 Kg. DKON. I. 123 b. 4. 859 Tib. Mchog-gi-blo-gros.
860 Tib. Seṅ-ge. Ibid. Cf. Fr. Weller: Tausend Buddhanamen des Bhadrakalpa. — 6.
861 Tib. Glog-gi-lha (Xyl. Klog-gi-lha).
862 Tib. Tog. Kg. DKON. I. 123 b. 5. Weller, — 410.
863 Tib. Bzaṅ-po(ḥi rgyal-po).
864 Tib. Me-tog-dam-pa. Kg. DKON. I. 123 b. 5. Weller, — 941.
865 Tib. Ḥod-kyi-dpal.
866 Tib. Me-tog. Kg. DKON. I. 123 b. 6. Weller, — 759.
867 Tib. Rnam-par-snaṅ-baḥi-padma.
868 Tib. Skar-rgyal Kg. DKON. I. 123 b. 6. Weller, — 15.
869 Tib. Dri-ma-med-paḥi-ḥod.
870 Tib. Spyan-legs. Kg. DKON. I. 123. b. 7. Weller, — 645.
871 Tib. Rdul-med.
872 Tib. Lag-bzaṅs. Kg. DKON. I. 123. b. 7. Weller, — 470.
873 Tib. Blo-gros-rgyal-po.
874 Tib. Ḥod Kg. DKON. I. 124 a. 1.
875 Tib. Dge-baḥi-bkod-paḥi-rgyal-po.
876 Tib. Skar-ma-la-dgaḥ-ba. Kg. DKON. I. 124 a. 1. Weller, — 754.
877 Tib. Phyogs-ḥbyor.
878 Tib. Mṅon-par-ḥphags-pa-gçegs-pa. Kg. DKON. I. 124 a. 2. Weller, — 497. (?)
879 Tib. Rnam-par-dag-pa-bkod-paḥi-rgyal-po.
880 Tib. Yon-tan-(mchog-gi)-mṅaḥ-ba. Kg. DKON. I 124 a. 2. Weller, — 550 (?).
881 Tib. Dpal-sbas.
882 Tib. Nor-dpal. Kg. DKON. I. 124 a. 3.
883 Tib. Lus-çin-tu-rnam-par-ḥbyed-pa.
884 Tib. Ye-çes-ḥbyuṅ-gnas. Kg. DKON. I. 124 a. 3. Weller, — 99.
885 Tib. Drag-çul-can.
886 Tib. Rin-po-cheḥi-ḥbyuṅ-gnas. Kg. DKON. I. 124 a. 4. Weller, — 102.
887 Tib. Rin-chen-grags. 888 Tib. Kun-tu-snaṅ-ba.
889 Tib. Cod-pan-brgyan-pa.
890 Tib. Yon-tan-mthaḥ-yas-grags-pa.
891 Tib. Blo-mthaḥ-yas-grags-pa.
892 Tib. Blo-(gros)-mthaḥ-yas. Kg. DKON. I. 124 a. 6—7.
893 Ibid. 124 a. 7—124 b. 2.
894 Tib. Mos-pa. Ibid. 124 b. 3.
895 Ibid. 124 b. 6—7. 896 Tib. Rdo-rjes-rnam-par-gnon-pa.
897 Tib. Tshaṅs-pa-gtsug-phud-can. Kg. DKON. I. 125 a. 5.
898 Tib. Mar-me-mdzad. Ibid. 125 a. 3.

899 Kg. MDO. VI. 91a7—b4. 900 Kg. MDO. II. 31b.

901 *gnas-bskal.*

902 *pañca-kaṣāya* Cf. M. V. § 124.

903 BTS. 95. 27—32. *tatra Anguṣṭhā nāma lokadhātuḥ. tatra Anguṣṭhāyāṁ lokadhātau daçavarṣāyuṣkā manuṣyā durvarṇā drohoḍimakā akuçalamūle samavadhānagatā anguṣṭhāmātram uccatvena. tatra Jyotīrāmo-nāma tathāgato' rhan samyaksaṁbuddhaḥ* etc.

904 Tib. Skar-ma-la-dgaḥ-ba.

905 Karuṇā-puṇḍarīka B.T.S. 63. 12.

906 Ibid. 63. 20. 907 Ibid. 64. 17. 908 Ibid. 66. 9.

909 Kg. MDO. I. 102 a. 4, 5. sqq. On Buddha Çākyamuni — 102 b. 7—103 a. 2.

910 Tib. Mchog-tu-dgaḥ-baḥi-rgyal-po.

911 Tib. Ser-skya. 912 Tg. MDO. I.

913 Kg. RGYUD. I. 914 Tib. *mi-mjed-pa.*

915 BTS. 63. 8—12. *kena kāraṇena sahe' ty ucyate. sahās te sattvā rāgasya sahās te dveṣasya sahās te mohasya sahās te kleça-bandhanānāṁ tena kāraṇena sahe' ty ucyate. tatra sahāyāṁ lokadhātau bhadrako nāma bhaviṣyati mahākalpaḥ kena kāraṇena ucyate bhadraka iti. bhadrake mahākalpe raga-dveṣa-moha-caritānāṁ sattvānāṁ sahasraṁ mahākāruṇikāṇāṁ buddhānāṁ bhagavatām utpatsyate.*

916 Kg. DKON. III. 262a5—7.

917 Gnas-chen-po-brgyad-kyi-mchod-rten-la-bstod-pa = Aṣṭa-mahāsthāna-caitya-stotra. Tg. BSTOD I.

918 Tib. *grańs-med = asaṁkhya.* This is not an indefinite number, but, as we shall see (Cf. below-) —

1.000.000.000.000.000.000.000.000.000.000.000.000.000.000.000.000.000.

919 These are: *ñon-mońs-paḥi-bdud, ḥchi-bdag-gi-bdud, phuń-poḥi-bdud,* and *lhaḥi-buḥi-bdud.*

920 Tib. Gsal-grags. 921 Tib. Yul-ḥkhor-skyoń.

922 This Buddha Çākyamuni is of course not the Buddha of our age, but an extinct Buddha of former times to whom the Teacher addressed his first Initial Vow.

923 Tib. Legs-mdzad. 924 Tib. Dbań-po-rgyal-mtshan.

925 Tg. MDO. LXIII. 15 b. 7—8.

926 Tib. *bse-ru-lta-bu = khaḍga-viṣāṇa-kalpa.* This passage is a quotation from the Abhidharma-Koça Tg. MDO. LXIII.

927 Tib. *sbyor-lam = prayoga-mārga.*

928 Tib. *chos-sku = dharma-kāya.*

929 Tib. *gzugs-sku = rūpa-kāya.*

930 IV. 1. *mahotsahā mahārambhā mahārthā 'tha mahodayā*
*cetanā bodhisattvānāṁ dvayārthā citta-sambhavaḥ.*

931 I. 18. *cittotpādaḥ parārthāya samyaksaṁbodhi-kāmatā*
*samāsavyāsataḥ sā ca yathāsūtraṁ sa co' cyate.*

932 Tg. MDO. IX. 91 a. 8—b 3 cf. Haribhadra, Abhisamayālaṁkārālokā, MS. Minaev. 23 b. 14.

933 IV. 7. *mitra-balād dhetu-balān mūla-balāc chruta-balāc chubhābhyāsāt adṛḍhadṛḍhodaya uktaç cittotpādaḥ parākhyānāt.*

934 Cf. Vasubandhu's Commentary to this verse: *hetu-balād vā gotra-sāmarthyāt.*

935 Ibid.: — *kuçala-mūlād vā' tīta-puṣṭitaḥ.*

936 Sūtrālaṁkāra IV. 8. *sūpāsitasaṁbuddhe susaṁbhṛta-jñāna-puṇya-saṁbhāre*
*dharmeṣu nirvikalpa-jñāna-prasavāt paramatā'sya.*

937 The following verse is quoted in Haribhadra's Abhisamayālaṁkārālokā, MS. Minaev 24 a. 10, 11. *tatrā' dau gotra-sāmarthyāt kṛpā-bīja-prabodhataḥ*
*prayogāçaya-saṁpattyā bodhi-citta-parigrahaḥ.*

938 Kg. DKON. V. 203 b.

939 *bodhi-praṇidhi-citta.* Cf. Bodhicaryāvatāra I. 15.

940 *bodhi-prasthāna.* Ibid.

941 *samādāna-saṁketika.* Cf. Vasubandhu on Sūtrālaṁkāra IV. 7.

942 IV. 2. *cittotpado' dhimokṣo' sau çuddhādhyāçayiko' paraḥ*
*vaipakyo bhūmiṣu matas tathā' varaṇa-varjitaḥ.*

943 I. 20. *bhū-hema-candra-jvalanair* etc. Cf. below.

944 IV. 15. *pṛthivīsama utpādaḥ* etc.

945 Tg. MDO. LII. 300 a. 7—300 b. 3.

946 *mos-pas-spyod-paḥi-sa* = *adhimukti-caryā-bhūmi.* Is a synonym of the Path of Training (*prayoga-mārga*).

947 *chos-kyi-sprin* = *dharma-meghā.*

948 *dkaḥ-ba-spyod-pa* = *duṣkara-caryā.*

949 Cf. above p. 94. 950 Kg. MDO. I.

951 Tib. Drin-lan-bsab-pa Kg. MDO. XXXII.

952 Tib. Phuṅ-po-gsum-pa. Kg. MDO. XXIV.

953 Tib. Mṅon-dgaḥ. 954 Tib. Mdzes-chen.

955 Tib. Snaṅ-byed.

956 XVIII. 38 — *saṁbhāro bodhisattvānāṁ puṇya-jñāna-mayo' samaḥ*
*saṁsāre' bhyudayāyai' kaḥ anyo' saṁkliṣṭa-saṁsṛtau.*

957 *zag-bcas* = *sāsrava.* 958 *zag-med* = *anāsrava.*

959 *mṅon-mtho* = *abhyudaya.* Is defined acc. to the Lamaist tradition as: — *ṅan-soṅ-gsum-las mṅon-mtho* — an existence higher than the three Evil Births.

960 *ṅes-legs* = *niḥçreyasa.* Is a synonym of Nirvāṇa. Cf. M. V. § 95. 5.

961 Sūtrālaṁkāra, XVIII. 39.
*dānaṁ çīlaṁ ca puṇyasya prajñā jñānasya saṁbhṛtiḥ.*
*trayaṁ cā' nyad dvayasyā' pi pañcā' pi jñāna-saṁbhṛtiḥ.*

962 XVIII. 40. *saṁtatyā bhāvanām etya bhūyo bhūyaḥ çubhasya hi āhāro...*

963 Sic acc. to Vasubandhu's Commentary. The Xyl. has *rati* (?).

964 Ibid.... *sa saṁbhāro dhīre sarvārtha-sādhakaḥ.*

965 Sūtrālaṁkāra XVIII. 41.
*praveçāyā' nimittāyā' nābhogāya saṁbhṛtiḥ*
*abhiṣekāya niṣṭhāyai dhīrāṇām upacīyate.*

966 Tib. *mtshan-ma-med-pa* = *animitta.* Haribhadra's Abhisamayālaṁkārālokā (MS. Minaev 43 b. 7—11. = Tg. MDO. VI 43 a. 6—8) has: — *nimittam asādhāraṇaṁ rūpaṁ tattvena anyonyam eka-rūpatvān nāsty ato' grahaṇam iti yāvat. etad uktam. dharma-dhātu-rūpatayā anityatādi-sarvākārajñatā-*

*çūnyatānāṁ sva-svabhāvena niḥsvabhāvatvāt parasparam eṣām aikātmyena animittatva-niviṣṭaṁ rūpādy-ālambanam iti.*

967 Tib. *lhun-gyis-grub-pa* = *anābhoga.*

968 Tib. *dbaṅ-bskur-ba* = *abhiṣeka.*

970 Tib. *mos-pas-spyod-paḥi-sa* = *adhimukti-caryā-bhūmi.*

971 Tib. *riṅ-du-soṅ-ba* = *dūraṁgamā.*

972 Tib. *mi-gyo-ba* = *acalā.*

973 Tib. *legs-paḥi-blo-gros* = *sādhu-matī.*

974 Tg. MDO. XCIV. 139 a. 3.

975 Tib. *gzugs-kyi-sku* = *rūpa-kāya.*

976 Tib. *chos-sku* = *dharma-kāya.*

977 The king for whom Nāgārjuna wrote the Ratnāvalī. Cf. below.

978 Tg. MDO. XVII.

978a Tib. *mtshan-mar-ḥdzin-pa* = *nimitta-grahaṇa.* Cf. *animitta* above.

978b Kg. MDO. V. 289a 1 sqq.

979 *çes-rab* = *prajñā.*

980 Ratnāvalī. Tg. MDO. XCIV. 147 b. 3—4, quoted in the Mādhyamika-vṛtti BB. 360. 2. — *çūnyatā-karuṇā-garbhaṁ keṣāṁ cid bodhi-sādhanam.* Cf. also Abhisamayālaṁkārālokā MS. Minaev 24 a. (Tg. MDO. VI) — *çūnyatā-karuṇā-garbha-bodhi-cittam utpādya* — having made the Creative Effort founded upon (the conception) of Relativity, endowed with the essence of Great Commiseration.

981 XVI. 29. *sarve çuklā dharmā vikṣipta-samahitobhayā jñeyāḥ dvābhyāṁ dvābhyāṁ dvābhyāṁ pāramitābhyāṁ parigṛhītāḥ.*

982 Cf. Vasubandhu's Commentary on this verse.

983 Ibid. XVI. 5. *bhogeṣu cā' nabhiratis tīvrā gurutā dvaye akhedaç ca yogaç ca nirvikalpaḥ samastam idam uttamaṁ yānam.*

984 Vasubandhu says: — *kṣāntyā vīryeṇa cā 'khedo dvaye yathākramaṁ duḥkhe ca sattva-asattva-kṛte kuçala-prayoge ca.*

985 Mahāyāna-saṁgraha-upanibandhana, the work of Asvabhāva. Tg. MDO. LVI. 308 a. 2—3.

986 Tib. *bse-ru-lta-bu* = *khaḍga-viṣāṇa-kalpa.*

987 Cf. Haribhadra's Abhisamayālaṁkārālokā (MS. Minaev 39 a. 11—16. = Tg. MDO. VI. 39 a. 2) *nanu çrāvaka-yāne'pi bodhisattva-dharmā dānādayo nirdiṣṭā eve' ty āçankyā' ha.... evaṁ manyate: çrāvakādi-dharmās tat-piṭake vistareṇa abhihitā bodhisattva-dharmās tu prasangataḥ.*

988 Tg. MDO XCIV. 147 a. 7.

989 I. 9. *vaikalyato virodhād anupāyatvāt tathā' py anupadeçāt na çrāvaka-yānam idaṁ bhavati mahāyāna-dharmākhyam.*

990 Tg. MDO XCIV. 149 b. 2—3.

991 Tib. Skyabs-gsum-bdun-cu-ba. The work of Candrakīrti. Tg. MDO XXXII. 294 a. 2—3.

992 Tib. *dgra-bcom-pa* = *arhat.* 993 M. V. § 50.

994 Tib. *dkar-po-rnam-par-mthoṅ-baḥi-sa* = *çukla-vidarçana-bhūmi.*

995 Tib. *rigs-kyi-sa* = *gotra-bhūmi.*

996 Tib. *brgyad-paḥi-sa* = *aṣṭamaka-bhūmi.*

997 Tib. *mthoṅ-baḥi-sa* = *darçana-bhūmi.*

998 Tib. *bsrabs-paḥi-sa* = *tanū-bhūmi.*

999 Tib. *ḥdod-chags-daṅ-bral-baḥi-sa* = *vītarāga-bhūmi.*
1000 Tib. *byas-pa-rtogs-paḥi-sa* = *kṛtāvi-bhūmi.*
1001 Tib. *raṅ-saṅs-rgyas-kyi-sa* = *pratyekabuddha-bhūmi.* Is not mentioned in the M. V.
1002 Tib. *rab-tu-dgaḥ-ba* = *pramuditā.* The others are: —
*dri-ma-med-pa* = *vimalā.*
*ḥod-byed-pa* = *prabhākarī.*
*ḥod-ḥphro-ba-can* = *arciṣmatī.*
*çin-tu-sbyaṅs-dkaḥ-ba* = *sudurjayā.*
*mṅon-du-gyur-pa* = *abhimukhī.*
*riṅ-du-soṅ-ba* = *dūraṁgamā.*
*mi-gyo-ba* = *acalā.*
*legs-paḥi-blo-gros* = *sādhu-matī.*
*chos-kyi-sprin* = *dharma-meghā.* Cf. M. V. § 31.
1003 This is detailed in the Abhisamayālaṁkārālokā. Cf. Appendix.
1004 Tib. *dad-paḥi-sa* = *çraddhābhūmi.*
1005 Tib. *tshogs-lam* = *saṁbhāra-mārga.*
1006 Tib. *mos-pas-spyod-paḥi-sa* = *adhimukti-caryā-bhūmi.*
1007 Tib. *sbyor-lam* = *prayoga-mārga.*
1008 Ed. Rahder p. 26. Tg. MDO LI 218 a. 6—7.
1009 Tib. *rigs-kyi-sa* = *gotra-bhūmi.*
1100 Tib. *mos-pas-spyod-paḥi-sa* = *adhimukti-caryā-bhūmi.*
1011 Tib. *lhag-paḥi-bsam-pa-dag-paḥi-sa* = *çuddha-adhyāçayikā-bh.*
1012 Tib. *ṅes-paḥi-sa* = *niyatā-bhūmi.*
1013 Tib. *spyod-paḥi-sa* = *caryā-pratipatti-bhūmi.*
1014 Tib. *spyod-pa-ṅes-pahi-sa* = *niyata-caryā-bh.*
1015 Tib. *mthar-thug-par-ḥgro-baḥi-sa* = *niṣṭhā-gamana-bhūmi.*
1016 Tib. *bsdu-ba-bźi* = *catvāri saṁgraha-vastūni.*
1017 XVI. 72. *dānaṁ samaṁ priyākhyānam artha-caryā samārthatā*
*taddeçanā samādāya svānuvṛttibhir iṣyate.*
1018 Tib. *sbyin-pa* = *dāna.*
1019 *sñan-par-smra-ba* = *priya-vāditā.*
1020 Tib. *don-spyod-pa* = *artha-caryā.*
1021 Tib. *don-mthun-pa* = *samāna-arthatā.*
1022 XX—XXI. 42. *mahāyāne' dhimuktānāṁ hīnayāne ca dehināṁ*
*dvayor āvarjanārthāya vinayāya ca deçitāḥ*
*caryāç catasro dhīrāṇāṁ yathā-sūtrānusārataḥ.*
1023 Tib. *pha-rol-tu-phyin-paḥi-spyod-pa* = *pāramitā-caryā.*
1024 Tib. *byaṅ-chub-kyi-phyogs-daṅ-mthun-paḥi-spyod-pa* = *bodhipakṣa-caryā.*
1025 *mṅon-çes-kyi-spyod-pa-* = *abhijñā-caryā.*
1026 Tib. Gtsug-na-rin-chen-gyi-mdo. Kg. DKON. IV.
1027 Tg. MDO. LI. 220 b. 7.
1028 Tib *mi-zad-pa* = *akṣaya* 1029 Tg. MDO. IX. 92 b. 3—4.
1030 Tib. *bsam-pa* = *āçaya.* 1031 Tib. *sbyor-ba* = *prayoga.*
1032 Tib. *lhag-pahi-bsam-pa* = *adhyāçaya.*
1033 Tib. *tshad-med-pa* = *apramāṇa.*
1034 Tib. *mṅon-par-çes-pa* = *abhijñā.*

1035 Tib. *so-sor-yaṅ-dag-par-rig-pa = pratisaṁvid.*

1036 *dharma-pratisaranena bhavitavyaṁ na pudgala-pratisaraṇena.* M. V. § 74.

1037 *artha-pratisaraṇena bhavitavyaṁ na vyañjana-pratisaraṇena.* M. V. § 74.

1038 *nītārtha-sūtra-pratisaraṇena bhavitavyaṁ na neyārtha-sūtra-pratisaraṇena.* Ibid.

1039 *jñāna-pratisaraṇena bhavitavyaṁ na vijñāna-pratisaraṇena.* Ibid.

1040 Tib. *byaṅ-chub-kyi phyogs-daṅ-mthun-paḥi-chos = bodhipakṣikā dharmāḥ.*

1041 Tib. *ži-gnas = çamatha.* 1042 Tib. *lhag-mthoṅ = vipaçyanā.*

1043 Tib. *gzuṅs = dhāraṇī.* 1044 Tib. *spobs-pa = pratibhāna.*

1045 Tib. *ḥdus-byas = saṁskṛta.* 1046 Tib. *zag-bcas = sāsrava.*

1047 Tib. *bdag-med-pa = anātmaka.*

1048 Tib. *bgrod-gcig-pa = ekāyana.*

1049 Tib. *thabs-la-mkhas-pa = upāya-kauçalya.* 1050 Kg. DKON XVI.

1051 Tib. Thub-pa dgoṅs-paḥi rgyan. The work of Abhayākaragupta. Tg. MDO. XXIX.

1052 I. 19, 20. *bhū-hema-candra-jvalanair nidhi-ratnākarārṇavaiḥ*
*vajrācalauṣadhī-mitraiç cintāmaṇy-arka-gītibhiḥ*
*nṛpa-gañja-mahāmārga-yāna-prasravaṇodakaiḥ*
*ānandokti-nadī-meghair dvāviṁçati-vidhaḥ sa ca.*

1053 Abhisamayālaṁkārālokā MS. Minaev 25 b 4—2 7a. 1 (= Tg. MDO VI. 24 b. 1.—25 b. 8).

1054 Tib. *ḥdun-pa = chanda.*

1055 Tib. *chos-kyi-dgaḥ-ston = dharmoddāna.*

1056 IV. 15—20. 1057 Cf. Abhisamayālaṁkārālokā — Appendix.

1058 Tib. *rnam-kun-rdzogs-sbyor-ba = sarva-ākāra-abhisaṁbodha.* Cf. above p. 51.

1059 Tib. *rtse-mo-ḥi-sbyor-ba = mūrdha-abhisamaya.*

1060 Tib. *mthar-gyis-sbyor-ba = anupūrva-abhisamaya.*

1061 Tib. *skad-cig-maḥi-sbyor-ba = ekakṣaṇa-abhisaṁbodha.*

1063 Tib. *sgrub-pa = pratipatti.* The definition of *pratipatti* acc. to the Abhisamayālaṁkārālokā (MS. Minaev. 63 b. 1. sqq.) is as follows: — *sā ca trisarvajñatā-viṣaye sāmānyena çukladharma-adhiṣṭhānā sa vākārābhisaṁbodhādau caturvidhe' bhisamaye pratyabhisamayaṁ ṣaṭpāramitā-adhiṣṭhānā ca kriyā pratipattiḥ* — *pratipatti* is the action which, in regard of the three forms of omniscience (*sarvākāra-jñatā, mārga-jñatā* and *sarva-jñatā*), is, in general, founded upon all the virtuous qualities, and, as concerns the four methods of intuition, each of them taken respectively, — is based upon the six Transcendental Virtues.

1063 Tib. *go-chaḥi-sgrub-pa = saṁnāha-pratipatti.*

1064 Tib. *ḥjug-paḥi-sgrub-pa = prasthāna-pratipatti.*

1065 Tib. *tshogs-kyi-sgrub-pa = sambhāra-pratipatti.*

1066 Tib. *ṅes-par-ḥbyuṅ-baḥi-sgrub-pa = niryāṇa-pratipatti.* These four Actions are enlarged upon in the Abhisamayālaṁkārālokā. Cf. Appendix.

1067 Tib. *tshogs-lam = saṁbhāra-mārga.*

1068 Tib. *sbyor-lam = prayoga-mārga.*

1069 Tib. *mthoṅ-lam = darçana-mārga.*

1070 Tib. *sgom-lam* = *bhāvanā-mārga.*

1071 Tib. *mthar-phyin-paḥi-lam.* Is the same as *mi-slob-lam* = *açaikṣa-mārga.*

1072 Tib. *zag-bcas* = *sāsrava.*

1073 Tib. *kun-rdzob* = *saṁvṛti.*

1074 Tg. MDO. LII. 199 a. 6.

1075 Ibid. 199 b. 1. — *rnam-par-dag-paḥi-lam* (= *viçuddhi-mārga*) *ni mthoṅ-ba daṅ bsgom-pa daṅ mthar-thug-paḥi-lam-gyis bsdus-pa* — the Path of Complete Purification is contained in the Paths of Illumination, Concentration, and that of the Final Result.

1076 Tg. MDO. LVI. 110 a. 1.

1077 Tg. MDO LVII. 68b. 4, 5.

1078 Tg. MDO. LII.

1079 Tib. *kun-hbyuṅ* = *samudaya.*

1080 Tib. *zag-med* = *anāsrava.*

1081 Tg. MDO LII. 270 a. 7—270 b. 3.

1082 Tib. *dran-pa-ñe-bar-gžag-pa* = *smṛty-upasthāna.*

1083 Tib. *ṅes-par-ḥbyed-paḥi-cha-daṅ-mthun-pa* = *nirvedha-bhāgīya.* These are: —

*dro-bar-gyur-pa* or *drod* = *ūṣmagata.* Heat
*rtse-mo* = *mūrdhāna* — Climax.
*bzod-pa* = *kṣānti* — Steadfastness.
*ḥjig-rten-paḥi-chos-kyi-mchog* = *laukika-agra-dharma* — Highest Mundane Virtues.

1084 Tib. *ḥjig-rten-paḥi-chos-mchog* = *laukika-agra-dharma.*

1085 Tib. *bar-chad-med-lam.*

1086 Tib. *tshul-khrims-kyi-bslab-pa* = *adhiçīla-çikṣā.*

1087 Tib. *sems-kyi-bslab-pa* = *adhicitta-çikṣā.*

1088 Tib. *çes-rab-kyi-bslab-pa* = *adhiprajñā-çikṣā.*

1089 XVI. 7. — *Çikṣātrayam adhikṛtya ca ṣaṭ pāramitā jinaiḥ samākhyātāḥ. ādyā tisro dvedhā antya-dvayatas tisṛṣv ekā.*

1090 Moral Discipline.

1091 Charity (*dāna*), Morality (*çīla*), and Patience (*kṣānti*). Cf. Vasubandhu on verse quoted.

1092 Concentration (*dhyāna*) and the Climax of Wisdom (*prajñā-pāramitā*).

1093 Mental Discipline and the Training in Highest Wisdom. Vasubandhu says: — *dvidhe'ty adhicittaṁ adhiprajñaṁ ca çikṣā sā antena dvayena saṁgṛhītā yathākramaṁ dhyānena prajñayā ca.*

1094 That of Energy (*vīrya*).

1095 *tisṛṣv api çikṣāsv ekā vīrya-pāramitā veditavyā, sarvāsāṁ vīrya-sahāyatvāt.* Ibid.

1096 Tib. *bsod-nams-bya-baḥi-dṅos-po* = *puṇya-kriyā-vastu.* Cf. above p. 16.

1097 M. V. § 43.

1098 Tib. *graṅs-med-pa* = *asaṁkhya.*

1099 Tg. MDO. LXIII.

1100 Tg. MDO. XXIX.

1101 Tib. *graṅs-kyi-gnas.*

1102 M. V. § 249. 1—52.

1103 Tib. *khri* = *prabheda.*

1104 Tib. *ḥbum* = *lakṣa.*

1105 Tib. *sa-ya* = *atilakṣa.*

1106 Tib. *bye-ba* = *koṭi.*

1107 Tib. *duṅ-phyur* = *madhya.*

1108 Tib. *ther-ḥbum* = *ayuta.*

1109 Tib. *ther-ḥbum-chen-po* = *mahāyuta.*

1110 Tib. *khrag-khrig* = *nayuta.*

1111 Tib. *khrag-khrig-chen-po* = *mahānayuta.*

1112 Tib. *rab-bkram* = *prasuta.*
1113 Tib. *rab-bkram-chen-po* = *mahāprasuta.*
1114 Tib. *gtams* = *kaṁkara.*
1115 Tib. *gtams-chen-po* = *mahākaṁkara.*
1116 Tib. *dkrigs* = *bimbara.*
1117 Tib. *dkrigs-chen-po* = *mahābimbara.*
1118 Tib. *mi-ḥkhrugs-pa* = *akṣobhya.*
1119 Tib. *mi-ḥkrugs-pa-chen-po* = *mahākṣobhya.*
1120 Tib. *khyad-phyin* = *vivāha.*
1121 Tib. *khyad-phyin-chen-po* = *mahāvivāha.*
1122 Tib. *paṅ-steṅ* = *utsanga.*
1123 Tib. *paṅ-steṅ-chen-po* = *mahotsanga.*
1124 Tib. *ded-ḥdren* = *vāhana.*
1125 Tib. *ded-ḥdren-chen-po* = *mahāvāhana.*
1126 Tib. *mthaḥ-snaṅ* = *tiṭibha.*
1127 Tib. *mthaḥ-snaṅ-chen-po* = *mahātiṭibha.*
1128 Tib. *rgyu-rig* = *hetu.*
1129 Tib. *rgyu-rig-chen-po* = *mahāhetu.*
1130 Tib. *ḥod-mdzes* = *karabha.*
1131 Tib. *ḥod-mdzes-chen-po* = *mahākarabha.*
1132 Tib. *dbaṅ-po* = *indra.* 1133 Tib. *dbaṅ-chen* = *mahendra.*
1134 Tib. *legs-phyin* = *samāpta.*
1135 Tib. *legs-phyin-chen-po* = *mahāsamāpta.*
1136 Tib. *rtog-ḥgro* = *gati.* 1137 Tib. *rtog-ḥgro-chen-po* = *mahāgati.*
1138 Tib. *ḥbyiṅ-rdul* = *bimbarajaḥ.*
1139 Tib. *ḥbyiṅ-rdul-chen-po* = *mahābimbarajaḥ.*
1140 Tib. *rgya-rtags* = *mudrā.*
1141 Tib. *rgya-rtags-chen-po* = *mahāmudrā.*
1142 Tib. *stobs-ḥkhor* = *bala.*
1143 Tib. *stobs-ḥkhor-chen-po* = *mahābala.*
1144 Tib. *brda-ças* = *saṁjñā.*
1145 Tib. *brda-ças-chen-po* = *mahāsaṁjñā.*
1146 Tib. *rnam-ḥbyuṅ* = *vibhūta.*
1147 Tib. *rnam-ḥbyuṅ-chen-po* = *mahāvibhūta.*
1148 Tib. *stobs-mig* = *balākṣa.*
1149 Tib. *stobs-mig-chen-po* = *mahābalākṣa.*
1150 Tib. *graṅs-med* = *asaṁkhya.*

1152 Their names are: — *apramāṇa, aprameya, aparimita, aparimāṇa, atulya, amāpya, acintya, anabhilāpya.*

1153 Tg. MDO. LI. 212 b. 2—4 sqq. 1154 The Abhisam. ālokā.

1155 *dgoṅs-pa-can* = *draṅ-don* = *neyārtha.*

1156 *ṅes-don* = *nītārtha.* 1157 *rab-tu-dgaḥ-pa* = *pramuditā.*

1158 *dri-ma-med-pa* = *vimalā.* 1159 *riṅ-du-soṅ-ba* = *dūraṁgamā.*

1160 *mi-gyo-ba* = *acalā.*

1161 *sgra-ji-bžin-pa* = *yathāruta.* Is the same as *ṅes-don* = *nītārtha.*

1162 *chos-kyi-sprin* = *dharma-meghā.* Cf. Ratnāvalī Tg. MDO. XCIV. 150 a. 8—b. 1. *bcu-pa-chos-kyi-sprin-yin-te, dam-pa chos-kyi char ḥbebs-phyir. byaṅ-chub-sems-dpaḥ saṅs-rgyas-kyi ḥod-zer-dag-gis dbaṅ-bskur phyir.* — The tenth stage is that of the Clouds of the Truth. It is (called so), because the rain of the Highest Truth descends upon the Saints and the Bodhisattvas are consecrated with the Light of the Buddha.

**1163** Ed. Lefmann 10. 4, 5. **1164** Tg. MDO. XC.

**1165** Sūtrālaṁkāra XIV. 29.

*sā' syā' çraya-parāvṛttiḥ prathamā bhūmir iṣyate.*
*ameyaiç cā' sya sā kalpaiḥ suviçuddhiṁ nigacchati.*

**1166** That is one immeasurable period.

**1167** Ibid. XIV. 44. *bhāvanāyāç ca niryāṇaṁ dvyasaṁkhya-samāptitaḥ.*

**1168** Kg. MDO. XX.

**1169** Tib. Sgrib-pa-thams-caa-rnam-par-sel-ba. Cf. M. V. § 23. 7.

**1170** Tg. MDO. LVI. 36 b. 1—2.

**1171** Tib. Theg-pa-chen-po-bsdus-paḥi-bçad-sbyar. The work of Asvabhāva. Tg. MDO. LVI. 316 b. 4—8.

**1172** *kalyāṇamitra.* **1173** Tib. *mthoṅ-paḥi chos = dṛṣṭa-dharma.*

**1174** Tg. MDO. LI.. 212 a. 6—7.

**1175** Tib. *mos-pas-spyod-paḥi-sa = adhimukti-caryā-bhūmi.*

**1176** Tg. MDO. LV. **1177** Tg. MDO. LI. 189 a. 1—2.

**1178** Tg. MDO. LVII. 110 a. 1—2.

**1179** Munimatālaṁkāra Tg. MDO. XXIX.

**1180** Tg. MDO. LII.

**1181** Tib. Dbu-ma-pa Chos-kyi-bçes-gñen. The author of the Commentary on the Abhisamayālaṁkāra called Praṣphuṭa-padā. Tg. MDO. VIII. The passage quoted is f. 70 a. 3—4.

**1182** Kg. DKON. II. **1183** Tib. Mdzes-par-snaṅ-ba.

**1184** Tib. Ḥdzam-bu-chu-boḥi-gser. **1185** Tib. Dgra-thul.

**1186** Tib. Bzaṅ-len-ldan.

**1187** Tib. *mi-skye-baḥi-chos-la-bzod-pa = anutpattika-dharma-kṣānti.* Cf. Mādh. vṛtti 362. note 3.

**1188** Cf. Çikṣāsamuccaya BB. 17. 1 sqq.

**1189** Tib. Bya-rgod-phuṅ-po = Ghṛdhrakūṭa. **1190** Cf. above p. 30.

**1191** The two latter points are enlarged upon in the Uttaratantra Tg. MDO. XLIV.

**1192** Kg. MDO. XXIV. 37a 5 sqq.

**1193** Tib. *chos-kyi-dbyiṅs-rnam-par-dag-pa = dharma-dhātu-viçuddhi.* M. V. § 4. 6.

**1194** Tib. *me-loṅ-lta-buḥi-ye-çes = ādarça-jñāna.*

**1195** Tib. *mñam-pa-ñid-ye-çes = samatā-jñāna.*

**1196** Tib. *so-sor-rtog-paḥi-ye-çes = pratyavekṣaṇa-jñāna.*

**1197** Tib. *bya-ba-sgrub-paḥi-ye-çes = kṛtya-anuṣṭhāna-jñāna.* M. V. § 5 and Sūtrālaṃkāra IX 67.

**1198** Cf. Abhisamayālaṁkāra I. 17.

*svābhāvikaḥ sasaṁbhogo nairmāṇiko' paras tathā*
*dharma-kāyaḥ sakāritraç caturdhā samudīritaḥ.*

**1199** IX. 59, 60. *svabhāva-dharma-saṁbhoga-nirmāṇair bhinna-vṛttikaḥ*
*dharma-dhātur viçuddho' yaṁ buddhānāṁ samudāhṛtaḥ*
*svābhāviko' tha sāṁbhogyaḥ kāyo nairmāṇiko' paraḥ*
*kāyabhedā hi buddhānāṁ prathamas tu dvayāçrayaḥ.*

1200 Tib. *mi-gnas-paḥi-mya-ṅan-las-ḥdas-pa = apratiṣṭhita-nirvāṇa.* Is defined as: *srid-žir-mi-gnas-pa = bhave çame ca na pratiṣṭhitaḥ.*

1201 IX. 63. *ameyaṁ buddha-nirmāṇaṁ kāyo nairmāṇiko mataḥ*
*dvayor dvayārtha-saṁpattiḥ sarvākārā pratiṣṭhitā.*

1202 The Apparitional Body and the Body of Bliss. Vasubandhu comments this verse as follows: — *sāṁbhogikaḥ (kāyaḥ) svārtha-saṁpatti-lakṣaṇaḥ, nairmāṇikaḥ parārtha-saṁpatti-lakṣaṇaḥ. evāṁ dvayārtha-saṁpattir yathākramāṁ dvayoḥ pratiṣṭhitā sāṁbhogike ca kāye nairmāṇike ca.*

1203 Cf. Abhisamayālaṁkāra VIII. 1.
*sarvākāra-viçuddhiṁ ye dharmāḥ prāptā nirāsravāḥ*
*svābhāviko muneḥ kāyas teṣāṁ prakṛti-lakṣaṇaḥ* —
and Haribhadra thereon (MS. Minaev 379 b. 13—380 a. 2) — *yathārutatve tokottarān evā' nāsrava-dharmān abhyupagamya teṣāṁ yā prakṛtir anutpādatā lallakṣaṇaḥ sa svābhāvikaḥ kāyaḥ sa eva dharmatā-kāyo dharmakāya iti bhāva-pratyaya-lopo vyapadiçyate.*

1204 Transbaikalian (Aga Monastery) Edition 4 a. 4. This work is wanting in the Peking Tangyur.

1205 Cf. the following very characteristic verse of the Uttaratantra (Tg. MDO. XLIV. 56 a 5—6) —
*rdzogs-saṅs (rdzogs-paḥi-saṅs-rgyas) sku-ni ḥphro-phyir daṅ*
*de-bžin-ñid dbyer-med-phyir daṅ*
*rigs-yod-phyir-na lus-can kun*
*rtag-tu saṅs-rgyas sñiṅ-po-can.* "As the Body of the Supreme Buddha manifests itself (in everything), as it does not differ from the Absolute, and as there exists the Germ (of Enlightenment), every living being is for ever and anon possessed of the Essence of Buddhahood".

1206 Cf. below.

1207 IX. 75 b. *citrāprameyācintyaç ca sarvasattvārtha-kārakaṁ (kṛtyanuṣṭhāna jñānaṁ).*

1208 IX. 65. *tribhiḥ kāyais tu vijñeyo buddhānāṁ kāya-saṁgrahaḥ*
*sāçrayaḥ svaparārtho yas tribhiḥ kāyair nidarçitaḥ.*

1209 Cf. Uttaratantra, Tg. MDO. XLIV. 55 a. — *gžan-gyi-rkyen-gyis (= para-pratyayena) rtogs-nin-pa (anavagamyaḥ)* not cognisable by other factors, — and Āryāsanga thereon (Uttaratantrabhāṣya, Ibid. 78 b. 4—5.) *raṅ-byuṅ-gi-ye-çes-kyis rtogs-par-bya-baḥi-phyir rtogs-par-bya-ba-ma-yin-no.* (The Buddha is not to be cognised by other factors, since he may be perceived exclusively by the Divine Wisdom, originated from Himself.

1210 Tg. MDO. XCIV. 150 a. 8—b. 2.

1211 Tib. *dbaṅ-phyug-chen-po = maheçvara.* Is here a synonym of the Body of Bliss.

1212 Prasphuṭapadā, Tg. MDO. VIII. 62 b. 3.

1213 Tg. MDO XXXII. 291 b. 6—7.

1214 Tib. *rgyal-sras = jinātmaja.* An epithet of the Bodhisattvas.

1215 Tib. *dro-bar-gyur-ba* or *drod = ūṣmagata.* Is the first of the four degrees conducive to Illumination (*nirvedha-bhāgiya*). Cf. Haribhadra (MS. Minaev 41 a. 16—41 b. 1) — *nirvikalpa-jñāna-agni-pūrvarūpatvād ūṣmagatam vo'ṣmagatam.* — It is (called) the Degree of Heat being like the Heat that precedes the fire of undifferentiated knowledge.

1216 XIV. 47.

1217 VIII. 9. *paripākaṁ gate hetau yasya yasya yadā yadā*
*hitaṁ bhavati kartavyaṁ prathate tasya tasya saḥ.*

The Xyl. has for *rgyu-ni yoṅs-su-smin-gyur-nas* (*paripākaṁ gate hetau*) — *gaṅ-la gaṅ-ḥdul-la snaṅ-ste*(?). Haribhadra explains this verse as follows: — (MS. Minaev 381 a. 11—14) — *yasya sattvasya yasmin kāle dharma-deçanādi kriyamānaṁ yatra pathyaṁ bhavati tadā asya artha-karaṇāya pūrva-praṇidhāna-samṛddhyā tattatpratibhāsa-ānurūpyeṇa artha-kriyākaro bhagavān.* — When some living being requires the explanation of the Doctrine, or some other kind of help, — then the Lord, by the force of his previous vows, fulfills the projects of this living being, manifesting Himself in this or that form.

1218 Corr. *gdul-bya-min-paḥam skal-pa med-paḥi* (= *abhavya*) *gdul-bya-rnams-la mi-snaṅ-ste* for *gdul-bya-min-paḥam mi-snaṅ-bas gdul-bya-rnams-la* etc. Cf. Abhisamayālaṁkāra VIII. 10: —

*varṣaty api hi parjanye nai'vā 'bījaṁ prarohati*
*samutpāde' pi buddhānāṁ nā' bhavyo bhadram açnute.*

1219 IX. 16. *yatho' dabhājane bhinne candra-bimbaṁ na dṛçyate.*
*tathā duṣṭeṣu sattveṣu buddha-bimbaṁ na dṛçyate.*

1220 Tib. *ḥdus-byas* = *saṁskṛta.*

1221 Tib. *ḥdus-ma-byas* = *asaṁskṛta.*

1222 Prasphuṭapadā. Tg. MDO. VIII. 112 a. 3.

1223 Tib. *ḥog-min.* 1224 Tib. Bkaṣ-bcad-bar-ba (?).

1225 Tib. *gnas-gtsaṅ-ma.*

1226 Ed Bunyiu Nanjio 269. 4—7: *Akaniṣṭha-bhavane divye sarva-pāpa-vivarjite tatra budhyanti saṁbuddhā nirmitas tv iha budhyate.* Acc. to Tib. . . . *divye nānā-ratna-virājite.*

1227 Tib. *dbaṅ-phyug-chen-poḥi-gnas* = *Mahā-maheçvara-āyatana.* M. V. § 131. 7.

1228 Prasphuṭapadā, Tg. MDO. VIII. 97 a. 6—8.

1229 Tib. *gži-daṅ-sñiṅ-po-me-tog-gis-brgyan-paḥi-žiṅ.*

1230 Tib. *gliṅ-bži-pa* = *caturdvīpaka* (*lokadhātu*).

1231 Tib. *stoṅ-gsum* = *trisāhasra.*

1232 Tib. *rab-ḥbyam-gyi-mtshams-sbyor-ba.*

1233 Tib. *rab-ḥbyam-gyi-rgyud.*

1233a Tib. *rab ḥbyam-gyi-rgyud-bar-pa.*

1234 Tib. *rnam-par-snaṅ-mdzad* or *rnam-snaṅ.*

1235 *mahā-puruṣa-lakṣaṇa* M. V. § 17.

1236 *anuvyañjana.* Ibid. § 18.

1237 For all these passages cf. Abhisamayālaṁkārālokā (MS. Minaev 381 b. 15—382 a. 3.) — *daça-bhūmi-praviṣṭa-mahābodhisattvaiḥ saha parama-anavadya-mahāyāna-dharma-saṁbhoga-prīti-sukha-upabhogāt sāṁbhogiko' yaṁ kāyo dvatriṁçal-lakṣaṇa-açīty-anuvyañjana-virājita-gātro rūpa-kāya-svabhāvo... buddhasya bhagavato grāhyaḥ.*

1238 IX. 64. *çilpa-janma-mahābodhi-sadā-nirvāṇa-darçanaiḥ*
*buddha-nirmāṇa-kāyo' yaṁ mahopāyo vimocane.*

(The text edited by Prof. S. Lévi has: *mahāmāyo vimocane*?)

1239 Tib. *las-thams-cad-pa.*

1240 IX. 26. *buddhānām amale dhātau nai'katā bahutā na ca ākāçavad adehatvāt purva-dehānusāratah.*
1241 Ibid. IX. 77. *gotrabhedād avaiyārthyāt sākalyād apy anāditaḥ abhedāṅ nai' ka-buddhatvaṁ bahutvaṁ cā' malāçraye.*
1242 Prasphuṭapadā, Tg. MDO. VIII 121 a. 2—3.
1243 Tib. dgaḥ-ldan. 1244 Tg. MDO. XCIV.
1245 Tib. skra-can.
1246 A passage, similar to that quoted, occurs in Dharmamitra's Prasphuṭapadā Tg. MDO. VIII. 121 a. 8 sqq. *ḥdir-chos-nub-par ston-pa yaṅ gdul-bya rab-tu-ma-gus-pa-dag-gi chos daṅ chos-smra-ba-la rten-paḥi sdig-pa mi-ḥbyuṅ-bar-bya-baḥi-phyir saṅs-rgyas-kyi mdzad-pa-chen-po-ste.*
1247 The two last stanzas are omitted in the Xyl. Their Tibetan text is as follows:

*sems-can-rnams-ni gdul-baḥi-phyir*
*mya-ṅan-ḥdas-la-sogs-par ston.*

The Sanscrit text is: — (Abhisam. ālokā MS. Minaev 103a 11—12)

*na Buddho parinirvāti na ca dharmo' ntardhīyate*
*sattvānāṁ paripākāya nirvāṇaṁ tū' padarçayet.*

1248 IV. 20. *tuṣita-bhavana-vāsādi-saṁdarçanataḥ.*
1249 Haribhadra on Abhisamayālaṁkāra I. 20. MS. Minaev. 27 a. 1.
1250 Cf. below. 1251 Tg. MDO. XXXIX, XL, XLI.
1252 Kg. DKON. IV. 33a 5 sqq.
1253 B. B. 323. 7, 8 (Tathāgata-āyuṣ-pramāṇa-parivarta).
1254 Ed. Bunyiu Nanjio 361. 5, 6 (v. 774): *Kāmadhātau tathā 'rūpye na vai Buddho vibudhyate, rūpadhātv-akaniṣṭheṣu vītarāgeṣu budhyate.*
1255 Kg. MDO. VI. 17a 6 sqq. 1256 Tg. MDO. XLIV. 65 a. 5—8.
1257 Tg. MDO. LVIII. 129 b. 4—5.
1258 Tg. MDO. LX 160 b. 8—161 a. 4 (condensed).
1259 Tib. Riṅ-ḥphur.
1260 Tg. MDO. LVI 130 a. 6—8.
1261 Tg. MDO. LVII. 109 b. 8—110 a. 1.
1262 Lalita-Vistara. Ed. Lefmann, 10. 10, 11.
1263 Ibid. 12. 6. 7.

---

## Das Uttaratantram.

Über das für die Kenntnis des späteren Buddhismus hervorragend wichtige Uttaratantra (vgl. Jewelry of Scripture p. 21 u. Anm. 166) schreibt unterm 15. IV. 1930 Herr Dr. Obermiller an Herrn Prof. H. Jacobi:

Im Winter 28—29 beschäftigte ich mich hauptsächlich mit der Ergründung des Abhisamayālaṃkāra; zu diesem Zweck benutzte ich den Kommentar von Haribhadra (Abhisamayālaṃkāra-ālokā) und die großen tibetischen Kompendien von Bu-ton, Tsoṅ-kha-pa und Jam-yaṅ-žad-pa. Der ganze Inhalt des Abhisamayālaṃkāra wird von den genannten Werken in 8 Hauptteile und 70 kleinere eingeteilt. Eins von den letzteren ist der Gotra-dhātu-tathāgata-garbha, welches als die Stütze oder das Fundament der ganzen Tätigkeit des Bodhisattva (pratipatter ādhāraḥ) bezeichnet wird. Aus den Kommentaren erweist sich, daß dieses gotra oder dhātu als ein besonderes Element anzusehen ist, welches die Verwandlung (parāvṛtti) der Eigenschaften des gewöhnlichen Wesens in die des Buddha bewirkt. Dieses wird von den beiden Mahāyānistischen Schulen, den Yogācāra und Mādhyamika anerkannt. Ich gewann für dieses Thema ein besonderes Interesse und widmete mich während meines Aufenthalts in Transbaikalien im Sommer 1929 dem speziellen Studium entsprechender Teile der Kommentare des Tsoṅ-kha-pa und Jam-yaṅ-žad-pa. Dabei erwies sich, daß die Hauptquelle zur Erforschung der Lehre vom gotra oder dhātu in dem Uttaratantra, dem letzten der sogenannten 5 Werke Maitreyas, zu suchen ist. Ich unternahm daher das Studium dieses Werkes mit dem Abt (Schiretü) des buddh. Klosters Dgah-ldan-dar-rgyas-gliṅ, welcher circa 15 Jahre in Tibet studiert hat und in Transbaikalien für einen gründlichen Kenner dieses Zweiges der buddh. Literatur gilt. Dieses Studium hatte zur Folge eine englische Übersetzung des Uttaratantra, die ich in diesem Winter zum Druck vorbereitet habe. Das Werk scheint mir von größter Wichtigkeit zu sein, als eine gründliche Darlegung der Theorie vom gotra-dhātu-tathāgata-garbha. Leider steht uns das Sanskrit-Original nicht zur Verfügung; ich mußte mich daher mit der tibetischen Übersetzung des mūla und Āryāsaṅga's Vyākhyā sowie mit dem ausführlichen Kommentar von Tsoṅ-kha-pa's Schüler Dar-ma-rin-chen (Gyal-tshabh) begnügen. Nichtsdestoweniger ermöglichte der überaus klare Text der tibetischen Übersetzung eine ziemlich getreue Übertragung derselben ins Englische, welche nun vollständig fertig ist und auf eine Gelegenheit gedruckt zu werden wartet.

# Index

Part I - The Jewelry of Scripture by Bu-Ston
(Bibliotheca Indo-Buddhica no.42)

Part II - The History of Buddhism in India and Tibet by Bu-Ston
(Bibliotheca Indo-Buddhica No.26)